D0758354

Roads to Freedom

FRIEDRICH A. VON HAYEK

Roads to Freedom

Essays in Honour of Friedrich A. von Hayek

Edited by

Erich Streissler
Managing Editor

Gottfried Haberler

Friedrich A. Lutz

Fritz Machlup

REPRINTS OF ECONOMIC CLASSICS

AUGUSTUS M. KELLEY · PUBLISHERS
NEW YORK 1971

First published 1969
By Routledge & Kegan Paul Limited
Broadway House, 68-74 Carter Lane
London, E.C.4
Reprinted 1970
Printed in Great Britain
By W & J Mackay & Co. Ltd
London and Chatham
© Routledge & Kegan Paul Ltd
No part of this book may be reproduced
in any form without permission from
the Publisher, except for the quotation
of brief passages in criticism.
ISBN 0 7100 6616 3

Published in the U. S. A. by
AUGUSTUS M. KELLEY, PUBLISHERS
Clifton, New Jersey

Notes on Contributors

ERICH STREISSLER is Professor of Economic Theory and Econometrics at the University of Vienna, and a consultant of the Austrian Institute of Economic Research. He is co-editor (with Monika Streissler) of *Konsum und Nachfrage*, and is author or co-author of various articles in encyclopaedias and numerous papers in scientific periodicals, especially on growth theory, demand theory, decision theory and econometrics.

JACQUES RUEFF is a member of the Académie Française and Chancellor of the Institut de France. He joined the French Finance Inspectorate in 1923 and has followed a career in administration which has brought him to high state office, and a career in science which is reflected in numerous publications: *Théories du Phénomène Monétaire, L'Ordre Social, Epitre aux Dirigistes, L'Age de l'Inflation, Le Lancinant Problème des Balances de Paiement* and *Les Dieux et les Rois*.

PETER T. BAUER is Professor of Economics (with special reference to Economic Development and Underdeveloped Countries) in the University of London at the London School of Economics, and is a Fellow of Gonville and Caius College, Cambridge. His publications are: *The Rubber Industry*, 1948; *West African Trade*, 1954; *The Economics of Underdeveloped Countries* (with B. S. Yamey), 1957; *Markets, Market Controls and Marketing Reform* (with B. S. Yamey), 1968; articles on economic subjects.

JAMES M. BUCHANAN is Professor of Economics at the Virginia Polytechnic Institute. His research interests are political economy, collective decision making, public finance. His main publications are: *Fiscal Theory and Political Economy*, 1960; *The Calculus of*

Consent (with G. Tullock), 1962; *Public Finance in Democratic Process*, 1967; *Demand and Supply of Public Goods*, 1968; *Cost and Choice*, 1969.

GOTTFRIED HABERLER is Professor of Economics at Harvard University; became associated with the Board of Governors of the Federal Reserve System, Washington, 1943; member of the American Economic Association and the Royal Economic Society (Vice President, American Economic Association, 1948); Charter Member of Econometric Society; President of International Economic Association, 1950–1, Honorary President since 1953; President of National Bureau of Economic Research, 1955; President, American Economic Association, 1963.

GEORGE N. HALM is Professor of Economics at the Fletcher School of Law and Diplomacy, Tufts University, Medford, Massachusetts. His main publications are: *Die Konkurrenz*, 1929; *Ist der Sozialismus wirtschaftlich möglich?*, 1929; *Monetary Theory*, 1942; *Economic Systems*, 1951; *Geld, Aussenhandel und Beschäftigung*, 1951; *International Monetary Co-operation*, 1945; *Economics of Money and Banking*, 1956; *The 'Band' Proposal*, 1965.

LUDWIG M. LACHMANN is Professor of Economics and Economic History, University of Witwatersrand, Johannesburg. His fields of research are capital theory, the methodology of the social sciences. He has published: *Capital and its Structure*, 1956.

FRIEDRICH A. LUTZ is Professor of Economics at Zurich University. His main fields of research are monetary theory, theory of interest, international economics. His main publications are: *The Theory of the Investment of the Firm* (with Vera C. Lutz), 1951; *Geld und Währung* (a collection of articles), 1962; *The Theory of Interest*, 1967.

FRITZ MACHLUP is Walker Professor of Economics and International Finance at Princeton University. Among his sixteen books published in English are: *The Economics of Sellers' Competition* 1952; *Essays on Economic Semantics* (with M. H. Miller), 1963; *The Production and Distribution of Knowledge in the United States*.

FRANK W. PAISH is Professor of Economics with special reference to Business Finance at the London School of Economics. His publications are: *Insurance Funds and their Investment* (with G. L. Schwartz), 1934; *The Post-war Financial Problem and Other Essays*, 1950; *Business Finance*, 1953; *Studies in an Inflationary Economy*, 1962; *Long-term and Short-term Interest Rates in the United Kingdom*, 1966; articles in *Economic Journal, Economica*, etc.

MICHAEL POLANYI was Professor of Physical Chemistry at the University of Manchester from 1933 to 1948, Professor of Social Studies at the University of Manchester from 1948 to 1958 and Senior Research Fellow, Merton College, Oxford, from 1958 to 1961.

KARL R. POPPER is Professor of Logic and Scientific Method at the University of London. His fields of research are epistemology, probability. His main publications are: *Logik der Forschung*, 1934; *The Open Society*, 1945; *The Poverty of Historicism*, 1957; *The Logic of Scientific Discovery*, 1959; *Conjectures and Refutations*, 1963.

GÜNTER SCHMÖLDERS is Professor of Political Economy at the University of Cologne. In 1957 he founded the Centre for Empirical Economics, to conduct socio-economic behaviour research. In 1968 he was elected President of the Mont Pélèrin Society.

GORDON TULLOCK is Professor of Economics and Public Choice, Virginia Polytechnic Institute. His main field of research is the application of essentially economic reasoning to areas outside the sphere of classical economics.

Contents

ix

CONTENTS

x

Introduction

'History is pluralistic. It deals not only with man but with men', Sir Karl Popper says in this volume. Presenting essays in honour of a great scholar is in a certain sense a 'round-about' attempt to write history. And in writing it, most of us have further deepened our prior convictions that the outcome could be no less than pluralist; that Friedrich August von Hayek's life was so full of content that it could easily have filled the lives of many men; that he has, in fact, been many men at once to many different people.

F. A. von Hayek was born in Vienna on May 8, 1899, the son of a university professor. He was just old enough to serve as an officer in the old Austrian *K.u.K.* Army during the First World War (of which he is even now capable of telling close acquaintances tragic or comic stories, e.g., the one of being in charge of a transport of live eels and having to hunt for them in a bedewed meadow where they somehow got loose). After the war, he studied at the University of Vienna and became a Doctor of Law in 1921 and a Doctor of Political (or Social) Science in 1925. His teachers in economics were the old Friedrich von Wieser and Ludwig von Mises (who, although a very dominating influence, never held a chair in Vienna). After a few years in the civil service, he became the first director of the Austrian Institute of Economic Research in 1927. He was – apart from Alexander Mahr – the eldest of a group of distinguished young Austrian economists, among them Martha Stefanie Braun, Gottfried von Haberler, Fritz Machlup, Oskar Morgenstern and Gerhard Tintner, most of whom were strongly influenced by him. He made his first major impression among economists at the *Verein für Socialpolitik* (the economic society for all German-speaking scholars) in 1928 with the first presentation of his Monetary Theory of the Trade Cycle. (It was the same meeting in which Werner

Sombart, one of the Privy Councillors dominating the society, predicted there would never be another depression, because governments now had at their finger tips all the necessary instruments of policy to prevent them.) After having become a part-time lecturer in economics ('Habilitation' Vienna 1929), he gave a lecture tour at the London School of Economics and Political Science in early 1931, which was so successful (it was the foundation of *Prices and Production*) that he was appointed to a chair there in late 1931 (he was later awarded a degree of D.Sc. in Economics). In 1950, he went to the University of Chicago as Professor of Social and Moral Sciences – a title well suited to describe Hayek's wide interests. He again changed his field of activity in 1962 when he became Professor of Economic Policy at the Albert-Ludwigs-Universität of Freiburg in Germany, where he became Professor Emeritus in 1967. He is also Professor Emeritus of the University of Chicago, a Fellow of the British Academy and an Honorary Doctor of Ryukyu University, Tokyo.

Hayek as a teacher has left his mark on no less than five countries: on Austria, England, the United States, Germany and on Japan, which he has come to visit regularly in recent years. Few scholars can claim to have had so wide a variety of pupils and disciples in so many intellectual and social climates. But it is, of course, on Liberalism on which he has left his most enduring mark. He is the Founder and Honorary President of the Mont Pélèrin Society, its institutionalized gathering. And it is in this capacity that our volume is intended to honour him. It would have been easy to have increased the number of scholars contributing to a volume in his honour tenfold. This volume, however, was confined to certain members of this society and to a very few outside old friends. It is to be presented at the Meeting of the Mont Pélèrin Society following his seventieth birthday.

Professor Hayek became world famous with his *Road to Serfdom*, translated into twelve other languages. As the public knows him best by that book, a variation on its title was suggested by Sir Karl Popper as the title of this volume. We have called our volume *Roads to Freedom* in honour of Hayek's life-long fight in the cause of Liberty. We have chosen the plural 'Roads' to denote that, while Serfdom is by its compulsive nature conformist, Liberals must always allow a plurality of approaches; and that such a plurality is demonstrated in an exemplary fashion in Hayek's own work.

A good test of the impression which a scholar has made is how closely essays in his honour mirror his work. How is Hayek's achievement mirrored in this volume?

It starts out with the French flourish of Jacques Rueff's laudation, appropriately linking up with *The Road to Serfdom*. That volume is one of the most decisive in the literature of Comparative Economic Systems. It has questioned categorically that Planning and the Market System can successfully be mixed and has, thereby, doomed to failure the now so fashionable theory of convergence of the two. This challenge is taken up by George Halm, in the light of a further quarter century of history. After a thorough empirical study, he comes to the Hayekian conclusion: 'Economic systems do not converge – unless we mean by convergence merely that superficial similarities are on the increase'. There is convergence only in the sense that, with higher income levels, the government sector tends to increase (also in the West) and there is greater desire for freedom of consumption (also in the East). There is, however, so far nowhere a symbiosis in the sense of a collection of the advantages of all systems. With the same starting point in Hayek's work, Michael Polanyi's essay is in many ways complementary to Halm's. While Halm contrasts the Market Mechanism and Planning, Polanyi, by trying 'to purify the concept of state ownership from the illusions of central direction usually attached to it', in fact contrasts private and public ownership of the means of production within the context of a market system. After all, there can be a fully working price mechanism if enterprises owned by the public compete with each other or with privately held firms. Even for such a system, by its very (probably unrealistic) assumptions the one most favourable to socialism, he comes to the conclusion: 'Public ownership of industry creates no new powers to eliminate the various imperfections of private capitalism: the administrative task . . . (of) trying to control managers . . . is exactly the same'. The complexity of the problems to be solved makes control by public authority an illusion. Nationalization within a market system then is useless. But will not, in fact, the selection of managers function better under private ownership?

This is the question examined most lucidly by Gordon Tullock. Against both Adam Smith and Berle and Means, he tries to re-establish a 'democratic' theory of corporate enterprises, generously attributing many of the ideas developed in the essay to Professor

H. Manne: through the working of the market system as a whole, stock holders can be shown to have much more control over a corporation's policy and managers have to stick much closer to profit maximization than is currently assumed. 'Management is confronted with a risk schedule. In general, the higher the profit it can make, the less likely it will suddenly find itself displaced . . . Management risk is proportional to the percentage of total income diverted.' Performance of management has thus to be good – and there are more and more institutions, like investment trusts or conglomerates to enforce this; it can, however, by the very nature of the real world never be ideal. As so often in the study of Comparative Systems, investigators have not been able to distinguish ideal and reality and have thereby come to the wrong conclusion.

Thus, the three essays by Halm, Polanyi, and Tullock form a closely linked whole. While all three of them depend heavily upon *The Road to Serfdom*, the last two are also intimately concerned with another strand in Hayek's thought: the problems of complexity, especially the resultant informational problems, presented by the economic process. Hayek first touched upon these problems in his seminal article 'Economics and Knowledge'. Of late, he has become particularly fond of defining the market system as an 'optimal discovery procedure', thereby changing altogether Mises' argument against planning: instead of stressing its impossibility, planning is presented as a poor machine for gathering, transmitting and evaluating information. It is exactly in this vein that Tullock argues whereas Polanyi shows that mere nationalization does not change the informational problem.

Already in that paper, Hayek had stressed that it is quite wrong to argue that man is moved by objective data in a kind of push-button mechanism. What matters is man's subjective perception, an idea to which he has devoted a whole book, *The Sensory Order*, at the same time proving to be an amateur psychologist of great power. It is therefore highly appropriate that Günter Schmölders, one of the best known Psychological Economists, has taken up this idea with great consequence in exactly that field in which Hayek himself has developed it least: in monetary economics. Professor Hayek started out to fame as a monetary economist, as the writer of *Geldtheorie und Konjunkturtheorie* and *Prices and Production*; but in these works he examined the indirect consequences of the creation of money rather than the direct impact of money itself.

There are no less than four essays inspired by Hayek's monetary writings: those of Schmölders, Lutz, Haberler, and Paish. Schmölders demonstrates convincingly that 'the dispositions *towards* money shape the disposition *of* money' and draws important conclusions from his copious material on such important problems of Hayekian concern as inflation, money illusion, saving, and the influence of interest rates. He finds that 'the actual experience with inflation does not influence the overall monetary scene in Germany', a fact which astonishes Haberler in the case of the United States. He proves the interesting point that 'money illusion acts as a vital safety mechanism for any market system', demonstrating thereby how right Hayek was in embodying a certain measure of it in his disequilibrium process. Finally, he shows that 'interest rates simply are not perceived by bank customers until they have a certain amount in their account', thereby shooting off a nasty arrow out of Hayek's own quiver of perceptions against the Wicksellian concept of a natural rate of interest.

The question of non-neutrality of money, stressed in theory by Hayek before anybody else, is thus convincingly demonstrated. Its theoretical implications and ramifications are taken up in his lucid manner by Friedrich Lutz. He distinguishes two groups of writers on neutral money: those who have seen in it a policy recommendation and those who have used it as a theoretical benchmark. He shows that the essential aspect of non-neutrality of money is its effect on income distribution, the effect that Hayek has belaboured most of all.

Hayek's Monetary Theory of the Trade Cycle was, to a large extent, a theory of the causes and effects of a relatively mild inflation. Haberler and Paish deal with this problem in a modern context. Gottfried von Haberler examines especially Hayek's point that labour unions are a threat to price stability and full employment, presented, e.g., in 'Unions, Inflation, and Profits'. He examines whether, on the one hand, there can be said to be a wage-push inflation and, on the other, whether – if it exists – it is just one aspect of a general monopolistic cost-push. He answers the first question in the affirmative and the second in the negative: There is a decisive difference in behaviour between industrial monopolies and trade unions. While the former try to maximize a *profit level*, the latter try to maximize a *rate of wage increase*. There is then no symmetry between the inflationary effects of the two. (One might also say that monopolies can try to increase their profits in manners favouring as well as fighting inflation, e.g. by lowering costs, while trade unions practically have only the first course of rational action.) Haberler thus presents convincing grounds for one of Hayek's typical stances: he was always harder on trade unions than on industrial monopolies – in sharp contrast to many German Neoliberals. Frank Paish in his empirical study for Great Britain is concerned with a similar problem. While Hayek was concerned with finding the benchmark of neutral money, Paish tries to determine, so to speak, neutral employment (and neutral wage increases resulting from it). Incidentally, he presents interesting evidence showing that Britain is experiencing *increasing* productivity increases (which should really make her policy problems easier); he demonstrates in a very Hayekian vein – that the direct restrictions on wages in England in 1966 had a mere temporary postponement effect.

Hayek's monetary theory was, at the time of its conception, however, much more than monetary: it was, above all, a theory of production, a theory of capital. This close integration of monetary and production analysis is shown in Paish's contribution, whereas I attempt to take up primarily its real aspect. Following a suggestion by Sir John Hicks, I argue that Hayek, more than being an analyst of the trade cycle, was a precursor of modern growth theory. I try to prove this claim by embodying his scheme in a von Neumann growth model, encompassing both real production and the production of 'credit', and argue that Hayek's peculiarity was in building a multi-sectoral growth model with fluctuating production coefficients. He thereby achieved a strategically disaggregated and a medium-term growth analysis from which we have much to learn.

After his monetary and capital-theoretic phase, Hayek turned to deep-seated problems of methodology in which *The Counter-Revolution of Science* became a memorial of both the width and depth of his thought. The articles by Bauer, Buchanan, Lachmann, and Popper bear witness to its strong influence and are again, in a sense, complementary. Ludwig Lachmann starts from Hayek's central idea in the thirties: 'The market economy . . . (is a) process in continuous motion . . . (due to) the occurrence of unexpected change as well as the inconsistency of human plans', but elevates it to a plane of wider methodological applicability: 'We shall not be satisfied with any type of explanation of social phenomena which does not lead us ultimately to a human plan'. As a result of his

xvi

enquiry, he points to two frequent fallacies of thought: the attempt to construct a hypothetical distribution of wealth, considered socially more just, as a starting point in the examination of a more desirable price system (thereby forgetting that actual distribution is part and parcel of the actual price system) and the neglect of the importance of the stock market in the examination of the workings of the market. His last point brings to mind the devastating remark which Hayek once made in Freiburg on the lecture delivered by the candidate for a chair. The young scholar demonstrated how simple it would be to find the present value of a firm: one calculates all its future expected profits and discounts them to the present. To which Hayek only added he had always thought that, for this purpose, the stock market had developed.

Lachmann examines the danger of a scientistic analysis mainly for a developed economy. P. T. Bauer takes up this problem for the discipline of development economics. He criticizes effectively the allegedly scientific reasoning of much contemporary development economics; and he also disposes of the claims to political realism often advanced by influential writers in this field. Bauer also examines in the context of development economics the interaction of the variables of economic analysis with the factors usually treated parametrically, as well as the effects on academic discussion of the climate of opinion, and of some of the factors influencing it. These subjects are close to Professor Hayek's interests.

In the above-mentioned essay and many others that followed, Hayek has given a strong stimulus to the philosophy of science. This is attested by James Buchanan's article. He contrasts a *logic* of choice which is free of behavioural assumptions and, in a sense, alone subjective with a behavioural theory, introducing objective 'pay offs' (objective in the sense of Buchanan and probably Popper, though subjective in the sense of Lachmann, as it still starts out from human plans). In the light of the amount of behavioural postulates 'plugged in', Buchanan analyses the typically Hayekian problem of the limits of prediction. Furthermore, he shows, again in the vein of Hayek, especially of the Hayek of *The Sensory Order*, that many policy confusions result from confusing logic and behavioural theory of choice: Pigovian policy of imposing equalization taxes assumes, e.g., that the subjective pay-offs of the recipients of the objective tax are known and equal to the objective stimuli.

One of the most touching tributes to Hayek is the article by Sir

Karl Popper. Popper wanted to write another article but found it impossible. But he could produce an essay concerned in many respects intimately with Hayek in spite of the fact that it had originally not been written for this purpose: one of those phenomena 'of human action but not of human design' which have much interested Hayek lately.

Hayek's last great book, *The Constitution of Liberty*, has finally found its reflection in the tribute by Fritz Machlup. Machlup, in his enlightening semantic discourse, is concerned with the many conceptual confusions which 'fuzzy liberalism' has produced, confusions against which Hayek fought all his life. He supplements Hayek in many ways, e.g., when he starts an interesting argument with him on the question of the indivisibility of freedom.

Thus, the articles in this volume cover a wide field of thought. It is still, however, by far not wide enough to do justice to Hayek. After all, our contributors are mainly economists or, at least, social scientists. We have not reflected, e.g., Hayek's growing legal interest; his psychological and philosophical, even biological, ideas are under-represented here. It was therefore agreed that this volume would be followed soon by a Festschrift originating with his many Japanese friends, who have given particular attention to these ideas of Hayek, a Festschrift to be edited by Professor Nishiyama. Needless to say, that Festschrift will not stop at the borders of Japanese erudition and will, of course, also include many distinguished economists as contributors, Milton Friedman among others.

This volume of honorary essays has mainly sprung from the pen of his oldest friends. Its editors, whom I herewith thank for their generous help and advice, were the intimate friends of his youth in Vienna, Gottfried von Haberler and Fritz Machlup, and the President of the Mont Pélèrin Society at the time of the conception of the volume, Friedrich Lutz. Of the contributors, I am one of the youngest, but I may claim to have been close to Hayek during the last years at the University of Freiburg. To me, Hayek has been a fatherly friend, with whom I was joined in curious ways: by pure chance he was present at my 'trial lecture' as university lecturer in Vienna; by pure chance we were, independently, called to occupy chairs in Freiburg at the same time; and by pure chance we have again both withdrawn from our professorships there at the same time – he to retire, I to occupy the chair of economic theory at the University of Vienna, at one time held by one of Hayek's teachers, Friedrich von Wieser (and by Carl Menger before him).

While I assume the responsibilities of a managing editor, I cannot claim to have performed many of the duties attached to this position. The heavy load of correspondence and the details of editing have been in the hands of my wife.

It is our hope and that of all the contributors that we have achieved a worthy tribute to Friedrich August von Hayek.

ERICH STREISSLER

Laudatio:
Un Message pour le Siècle

'C'est la nuit qu'il est beau de croire à la lumière'
('Chantecler', acte II-scène III)

Toute l'oeuvre de Frédérick von Hayek est importante. Elle apporte une contribution capitale à la théorie économique et à la philosophie sociale de notre époque. Mais au-dessus d'elle se dresse un livre magistral: *La Route de la servitude*, qui, tel un puissant phare, balaie de ses rayons le dernier demi-siècle et jette de sombres lueurs sur notre proche avenir.

L'ouvrage fut publié en décembre 1943: assez tard pour qu'on pût trouver dans les faits la confirmation du diagnostic qu'il formulait, assez tôt pour que le message qu'il apportait pût affecter la reconstruction des pays qui sauraient le recevoir.

Qui peut douter aujourd'hui, alors que le désordre sévit dans de nombreux pays de l'Occident, alors que le contrôle des changes répand ses semences totalitaires en Angleterre et en France, ainsi qu'à quelque degré aux Etats-Unis, que la liberté soit en grand danger dans l'Occident?

Le grand, l'immense mérite du livre de Hayek est d'avoir tracé la route que suit imperturbablement la civilisation occidentale, marqué son point de départ, fixé son orientation et permis de prévoir, si rien n'est fait pour en modifier le cours, son point d'aboutissement.

Grâce à Hayek, j'ai compris la terrible fatalité qui a fait sortir du désordre de Weimar le nazisme hitlérien. Ecoutez-le lorsqu'il nous dit:

J'ai maintenant une vérité désagréable à dire: à savoir que nous sommes en danger de connaître le sort de l'Allemagne. Le danger n'est pas immédiat, certes, et la situation dans ce pays [Hayek veut dire l'Angleterre de 1940] ressemble si peu à celle que l'on

1

a vue en Allemagne ces dernières années qu'il est difficile de croire que nous allions dans la même direction. Mais pour longue que soit la route, elle est de celles où l'on ne peut plus rebrousser chemin une fois qu'on est allé trop loin . . . Nous ne pourrons éviter le danger qu'à la condition de le reconnaître à temps.[1]

C'est à nous le faire reconnaître que Hayek s'est appliqué avec une puissance d'analyse et une rigueur peu communes.

Il a marqué d'abord la mutation intervenue dans l'appétit de liberté. Pour les grands apôtres de la liberté politique, être libre 'c'était être dégagé de toute coercition, de tout arbitraire exercé par autrui', c'était pouvoir se réaliser pleinement en tant que personne humaine. Pour les théoriciens modernes, au contraire, la nouvelle liberté c'est celle qui libère de tout besoin physique, qui écarte toutes limitations et toutes contraintes émanant des exigences de l'ordre économique.

A l'abri de cette mutation 'la plupart des intellectuels embrassent le socialisme comme l'héritier présomptif de la tradition libérale; aussi n'est-il pas surprenant qu'ils n'aient pas reconnu que le socialisme mène à l'opposé de la liberté'.

C'est à la démonstration de cette thèse qu'est consacré tout l'ouvrage. Aucune des conséquences du nouveau concept de liberté n'est laissée dans l'ombre. Celui du planisme pseudo-libéral est étudié avec une particulière rigueur. Aux termes de l'analyse qui en est présentée, il apparaît comme incompatible avec la règle de la loi et exclusif de toute liberté de pensée.

Qui a lu *La Route de la Servitude* ne peut douter que c'est, en définitive, le statut de la personne humaine que la nouvelle liberté met en cause.

Désormais le monde est coupé en deux. D'un côté, les civilisations de marché où l'homme peut être laissé libre de ses choix, de ses actes et de ses pensées. De l'autre, celui des civilisations totalitaires, où l'homme est commandé, non seulement dans son comportement économique, mais aussi dans ses attitudes personnelles et familiales. Entre les deux, une large bande de civilisations mixtes, où le socialisme embrasse des secteurs de plus en plus étendus de la vie nationale, mais sans oser appliquer les contraintes qui sont la condition de son efficacité. Dans ces pays règne le désordre. Par un étrange paradoxe, l'opinion y appelle comme remède non pas la

1 *La Route de la Servitude* – Librairie Médicis, p. 10.

2

suppression des causes qui l'ont fait naître, mais des interventions toujours plus étendues dans la vie économique et dans le régime social. C'est de ces régimes troublés que sont sortis nazisme et fascisme.

Puissions-nous, en méditant à temps les enseignements de Hayek, épargner à nos pays le sort de la République de Weimar.

JACQUES RUEFF
de l'Académie française
Chancelier de l'Institut de
France

3

Development Economics: The Spurious Consensus and its Background
Peter T. Bauer

I

1. In Sections I and II of this paper I argue that the much publicized consensus in contemporary development economics is spurious, both in that its main components are invalid, and also in that, contrary to the claim of its principal exponents, they are not universally accepted.[1] Subsequently, I consider some of the influences behind the emergence of the invalid ideas of the consensus, as well as some results and implications of their acceptance.

There is widely-canvassed agreement among the most prominent and influential development economists on the main relevant characteristics of underdeveloped countries, on the causes of their material backwardness, and on the policies appropriate to their development. Such a large measure of agreement on description, analysis and policy in a major branch of applied economics is unexpected, because a failure (both alleged and real) to agree even on analysis, let alone on policy, has for long been a common charge against economists. And paradoxically the consensus is on ideas and suggestions which are inconsistent with simple empirical observation, established elementary propositions of economics, and also with widely accepted and well documented ideas of cognate disciplines, notably economic history and social anthropology. This situation and its background and implications are the main concern of this paper. My principal purpose is to examine the most influential ideas in a major branch of economics, and of certain contemporary intellectual influences, rather than to take issue with specific writers

1 Following current academic and professional practice, I shall use the terms development economics and the economics of underdeveloped countries interchangeably, although one or other of these terms is more appropriate in a particular context.

5

or even schools of writers. I shall not, therefore, refer critically to specific authors or publications, with one or two exceptions required for clarity of exposition, or the need to show that certain arguments have in fact been advanced. I adopt this course to focus on major pervasive influences from which attention would be diverted by specific controversy.[2]

There are, of course, differences of emphasis and to some extent even of argument among subscribers to the consensus; and there are academic economists often in senior positions who reject the consensus. But neither differences among supporters of the consensus, nor the presence of dissenters, has affected the substance or tenor of the main stream of the discussion. Indeed, prominent exponents of the consensus have argued that failure to subscribe to its major elements reflects lack of competence.

II

2. The following are the principal components of the consensus. The primary common characteristic of underdeveloped countries is their extreme poverty which distinguishes them sharply from the developed world, and also establishes a basic similarity within the underdeveloped world for purposes of description, analysis and policy. Moreover, the underdeveloped world is not only poor, but also stagnant because poverty is self-perpetuating. It reflects past poverty and causes future misery through the operation of the vicious circle of poverty because poverty itself sets up practically insurmountable obstacles to its own conquest, chiefly by inhibiting the capital formation required for raising income. The past poverty which set up the vicious circle is in turn the result of historical accident and colonial exploitation. The rich countries of the West have in various ways contributed to the plight of the underdeveloped world, chiefly through colonial exploitation; the operation of the international demonstration effect (that is stimulating consumption expenditure in poor countries thereby obstructing what little saving and investment might otherwise take place there); and by restrictive trade policies which curtail the markets for the exports of

2 The main elements of the consensus can be illustrated with countless specific examples from easily accessible publications of academic writers, development centres and institutes, international agencies and government departments.

6

underdeveloped countries which damages their economies in various ways especially by retarding the development of viable manufacturing industry, and also by depressing further the unfavourable and deteriorating terms of trade of underdeveloped countries.

Other features of the backwardness of the underdeveloped world emphasized by the consensus include the rapid population growth; the restricted domestic markets; the responsibility of landlordism and high rents for agricultural stagnation; the quantitative insignificance of manufacturing industry; the tendency of well-to-do people to dissipate their surpluses in luxury consumption, to hoard their savings, to export their funds abroad, or otherwise to direct them into socially unproductive uses.

The consensus is surprisingly even more pronounced on issues of policy than on matters which are ostensibly descriptive or analytical. The salient aspects of the consensus on policy are insistence on comprehensive central planning in the sense of a large measure of state control of economic activity outside subsistence farming; on compulsory saving, that is special taxation for government financed development expenditure, beyond the investment required by the traditional and necessary government functions; and on large scale foreign aid in the sense of inter-governmental grants or subsidized loans. These domestic and international policies are regarded by the consensus as indispensable for the material progress of poor countries. Other policies widely advocated in the development literature include close control of external economic relations, large scale state sponsored or operated development of manufacturing, and also partial or total expropriation of landowners.

3. Detailed critical discussion of the consensus is not possible here. The major elements are manifestly invalid in the sense of being inconsistent with obvious empirical evidence, elementary logic or well established propositions of economics. And the most obviously invalid ideas are those most insistently and widely publicized. Here are some examples. The vicious circle of poverty, the notion that poverty is self-perpetuating and that individuals, groups and societies are debarred by their poverty from improving their position, is plainly inconsistent both with everyday experience and the evidence of economic history. The suggestion that the mere presence of rich countries inhibits the progress of the underdeveloped world is refuted by the fact that the idea of material progress is of Western origin; by the fact that throughout the underdeveloped

7

world the most prosperous areas are those with which the West has established closest contact, and by the extreme backwardness of societies and regions without external contacts; and by the material backwardness of most underdeveloped countries at the time when the West first established contact with them.

According to the consensus, comprehensive central planning and foreign aid are indispensable for economic advance although in fact they were not used in the development of any of the now highly developed countries, nor in the course of the progress of the many poor countries which have advanced substantially since the late nineteenth century. Nor do the exponents of the consensus explain why the replacement of the decisions of individual consumers and producers by those of the state should in any way augment resources and promote a rise in incomes or in living standards. Again, state sponsored development or operation of manufacturing industry, including capital goods industries, is deemed indispensable for material advance in this literature, without examination of cost, or of the demand for the output, and without noting that the industrialized countries were already highly prosperous while still agricultural, and had much higher incomes than those foreseen for poor countries for decades ahead.

Nor is the underdeveloped world a homogeneous stagnant mass sharply distinct from the developed countries. Different underdeveloped countries differ greatly in levels of income and rates of material progress achieved over recent decades; many areas, especially in the Far East, in West Africa and Latin America have progressed rapidly since the second half of the nineteenth century. Moreover, the line of division between underdeveloped and developed (that is poor and rich) countries is arbitrary and shifting, not clear or permanent. Its shifting nature is clear from the promotion in recent years of some countries from the underdeveloped to the developed group, as for instance Japan, Hong Kong and parts of Southern Europe.

The list of the defects of the major components of the consensus could be readily extended. And the validity of the criticism is independent of a political position, and even of the results of the policies proposed by the consensus.

4. There are certain readily recognizable characteristic features, arguments and approaches in the exposition of the consensus which are in part themselves components of the consensus and in part

characteristics of other components.[3] In much of development economics the relevance of prices and costs is ignored and supply and demand are treated as fixed magnitudes and not as variables related to prices, costs and incomes; demand is often described or discussed as requirement, and supply as capacity or as output. The relevance and effects of prices are either disregarded altogether or occasionally dismissed as inapplicable in underdeveloped countries, for such reasons as the alleged rigidity of market conditions, or the alleged commercial ignorance or unresponsiveness of the local population. An important instance is the treatment of an activity, or the output of a commodity, as a net increment of total output, income or welfare, regardless of cost, i.e. of the alternative uses of the human, financial or physical resources used – general practice in development literature on state sponsored trade and commercial corporations.

This approach is inadmissible. Over a wide range of conditions the relationship between demand, supply and prices derives from the limitation of incomes and the presence of costs both of which reflect the universal limitation of resources. The specific response of demand and supply to prices and costs in poor countries is supported by a vast amount of empirical evidence, and is recognized in the practice of governments in subsidizing activities which they wish to encourage and taxing those which they wish to discourage, a practice which recognizes the functional relationship between supply and demand and prices and costs.

The allegedly unavoidable externally caused balance of payments difficulties of underdeveloped countries are another major theme of the consensus, in the face of countless examples of rapid and sustained development without such problems. These difficulties are usually discussed without reference to the effects of monetary and fiscal policy on domestic incomes and prices, or on the volume of imports or exports and thus on the balance of payments. Again, in these discussions, which usually allege that the export prospects of underdeveloped countries are inherently poor, a decline in the volume of exports of a commodity from a country or group of countries is often instanced as an indicator of a low level of demand or of a decline of demand. Such a treatment confuses the supply of a product from one source with the aggregate demand for it. These

3 Many of the characteristics discussed in this section are present also elsewhere in contemporary economics, though usually in a less pronounced form and in a less inappropriate context than in development economics.

transgressions, the list of which could be greatly extended, are frequent in ostensibly technical writings, and reflect a disregard of the simplest elements of economic analysis, as well as of obvious empirical evidence.

5. An exceedingly imprecise use of abstract concepts characterizes much of the consensus literature whose acceptance it has served to promote.

The vague nature of many of the concepts of the social sciences, including development economics, has rendered these concepts susceptible of widely differing and indeed even incompatible interpretations; familiar instances include equality, discrimination, stabilization and economic independence. Moreover, some of the principal concepts of development economics which appear to be more clearly defined are often used in widely different senses in the technical literature, at times even in the same publication. The uses and interpretation of the term 'planning' range from phasing of government expenditure to detailed state control over all major forms of economic activity. Those of the term 'investment' range from specified expenditure designed to increase productive capacity (in order to augment the net flow of desired goods and services) to all expenditure favoured by the advocate of investment, or even to all change supported by him. The concept of economic progress itself is often used in a number of widely different senses even within the same publication: the criteria adopted implicitly or explicitly often include such diverse concepts as income per head, general living standards, industrial output, political independence, and others as well.

References to underdeveloped countries or poor countries (underdeveloped is only a euphemism for poor, or rather for materially backward countries) also implies substantial abstraction. These apparently innocuous terms have to be handled carefully. The term underdeveloped is apt to suggest that the position of such countries is abnormal, reprehensible, and at the same time readily rectifiable which is by no means generally true. More important and less obvious are the perils of the practice of referring to countries. The habitual reference to countries is apt to obscure the fact that our concern is appropriately with groups of people not with geographical entities. There are various implications of this simple consideration.

First, the practice of referring to countries conduces to a neglect of the significance of human faculties and motivations as determinants of development. Second, such references promote and reinforce misleading uses or interpretations of the concepts of the average, which are widely prevalent in the economics of poor countries. The economies of countries and regions comprise groups of persons with differing incomes. If the relative numbers of these groups change, the average income per head (whether arithmetic mean, median or mode) can, and often does, move in a direction opposite to that of the incomes of the groups and persons. For instance the *per capita* income of each group or indeed every person can increase and yet the average for the collectivity, i.e. the country or region, can fall, if the groups with *per capita* income below average increased numerically, compared to the rest. Such an outcome is a familiar result of a change in the relative importance of the component elements of an aggregate. This consideration bears on many contemporary discussions of the alleged stagnation of the underdeveloped world, and of the international inequality of income. Major elements of the position of the underdeveloped world are obscured by habitual references to countries and to average incomes, which divert attention from the position of persons and groups.

Again, references to countries rather than to people, suggest a homogeneous interest within a country and one which is opposed to that of the outside world. This approach obscures various problems of the relationships between groups within a country, such as a divergence of interest between the rulers and the ruled, or the question of the complementary or competitive nature of the activities of different groups. It also promotes an unwarranted identification, or rather confusion, of the government with the population at large. The usage also obscures fundamental distinctions between different types of decision-making units and between radically dissimilar situations. For instance, references to capital exports of a country obscure the differences between situations where the decision is that of the government, that is a single decision-making unit (as in the case of government-to-government aid) and those situations where decisions are taken by a multiplicity of agents or units acting independently. These considerations are particularly significant in underdeveloped countries, where the interests of the rulers or ruled often diverge widely, and where the ethnic composition of the population is often exceedingly heterogeneous.

Thus there are good reasons for insisting on the recognition that

11

the appropriate concern is with groups and persons, not with countries.[4]

The use of abstract concepts is indispensable for systematic reasoning. Moreover, a combination of abstraction and the employment of technical language can lend precision to a discussion. But to be valuable for such purposes abstract concepts must be used with consistency. When they are used with shifting or inconsistent interpretations, the concepts become useless either as instruments for systematic reasoning, or as guides to policy. They can, however, become effective instruments for those who appreciate the political possibilities set up by shifting the interpretation of the abstract notions to select the particular interpretation in each instance which promotes or justifies the policies they favour.

6. Neglect of major determinants of material progress and a disregard of the historical background are other and related characteristics of the literature of the consensus.

The most influential publications of the consensus literature either disregard altogether or at best greatly underrate the significance of people's capacities, attitudes, values and motivations, and of the social institutions and mores which reflect these.[5]

There are far-reaching and deep-seated differences between people in these matters and these differences largely explain differences in economic performance and in levels and rates of material progress. The principal differences between persons and groups emphasized in the development literature are differences in incomes and property rights. If these were the only material differences they would be accidental in origin, superficial in extent, impermanent in duration and easy of removal. However, the relevant differences are pervasive and tenacious. The neglected determinants are patently important in the development process, usually much more significant than such widely emphasized factors as the volume of investment expenditure, savings ratios, the size of the market or foreign

4 The misleading habit of thinking in terms of countries rather than of people is reflected also in the frequent but inaccurate and inappropriate references to the achievement of freedom to denote the attainment of independence, i.e. national sovereignty, a concept which has nothing to do with the personal freedom of the inhabitants.

5 The literature of the consensus often discusses such matters as landlordism, the relations between landlords and tenants and the attitudes of vested interests. Quite apart from the analytical and empirical defects of many of these discussions, these particular factors are generally far less important as factors in development than personal faculties and attitudes and cultural traditions.

12

exchange availability; these are factors which even in conditions when they are quantitatively significant are more appropriately treated as effects and dependent variables of the development process than causes or independent variables.

Much of the consensus literature neglects the historical background of the societies it discusses, and *a fortiori* differences in these backgrounds. An appreciation of this background is indispensable for an understanding of the economic landscape of most of the underdeveloped world. For instance the economic development of major parts of Africa since the 1880s and the economic and social problems and development prospects of these regions cannot be properly assessed without recognition of the materially extremely primitive indeed barbarous conditions of the sub-Saharan Africa of the nineteenth century. Nor can the economic position and prospects of India be understood without recognition of the depth, intensity, antiquity and pervasiveness of attitudes and values uncongenial to material advance going back thousands of years.

7. Thus the reasoning behind the principal elements of the consensus is insubstantial. The consensus of the currently most influential development literature is quite unlike the agreement reached by scholars and scientists after examination and interpretation of evidence and the testing of conclusions. The consensus is akin to the so-called unanimous agreement of the mass meeting, the political gathering, or the international conference: uniform in expression and meaningless in content. In the rest of this paper I consider the influences behind the acceptance of the spurious consensus and also some of the implications of its acceptance.

III

8. The validity of an argument is not affected by the factors and motives behind it. Discussion of the background of the consensus is irrelevant to the validity of its arguments and conclusions. However, examination of the reasons behind its emergence is nevertheless worthwhile. Critical discussion of widely-held and canvassed opinions is likely to be more convincing if it succeeds in tracing their emergence and acceptance. Moreover in an area of study in which major issues of method are unresolved, criticism of widely held opinions may gain not only in credibility and thus effectiveness, but

13

also in firmness by an examination of the reasons behind these opinions and of the methods by which they have been reached.

The consensus is spurious both in that its main components are invalid, and also in that they are not universally accepted. In examining the influences behind the consensus my primary concern will be those responsible for the intellectual shortcomings of the consensus, rather than with those behind the claim that it is generally accepted. However, the various influences are closely related and mutually reinforce each other; and none of the subsequent argument is affected by questions of the relative significance of the various factors in these two contexts.

I shall deal mainly with the following related factors and influences behind the consensus: the dominance of political purpose in ostensible academic reasoning, and the failure to distinguish between the advancement of knowledge and the promotion of political aims; certain characteristics of the contemporary cultural scene especially in the West, including the operation of ideological forces; the problems created by the sudden rapid expansion of interest in development economics; the influence of political and psychological motives and of commercial and administrative interests which reinforce these motives; and certain methodological problems in development economics. I shall examine at greater length the factors and phenomena which seem relatively less familiar and which are less verifiable in easily accessible sources.

9. The contemporary insistence on the paramountcy of politics has greatly affected the discussions in development economics since the Second World War. The significance of political factors, and of psychological influences related to these factors, underlies the great increase in interest in underdeveloped countries in recent decades. Recognition of this factor is common ground between those who accept and those who reject the consensus, though the two groups would differ in their assessment of the significance and of the validity of the different forces at work. The relevant factors seem to include the following: the emergence of numerous politically independent poor countries; the rise of the international agencies with large staffs and resources; the increase in the political and military power of communist countries; the loss of poise and self-assurance of the major Western countries of which the emergence of a guilt feeling, especially in America and Britain, towards the underdeveloped world is one manifestation. The loss of poise,

notably the emergence of a guilt feeling, in turn reflects various other influences including disappointment and dissatisfaction with the results of material progress; uncertainty in the face of rapid collapse of traditional beliefs; the activities of various groups, including professional humanitarians, anxious to promote the power and influence of the international agencies and of underdeveloped countries, and possibly of the Soviet-bloc countries, compared to the West. These influences have engendered massive financial support for work in development economics, which in these conditions has come to be largely directed into activities likely to be politically popular, and to yield politically acceptable results.

In these conditions the pursuit of knowledge has been largely subordinated to the pursuit of political ends, even in ostensibly objective or technical discussion. While this phenomenon is present also elsewhere in economics, it is particularly pronounced in development economics because the subject has become so popular at a time when the paramountcy of politics, the principle of *politique d'abord*,[6] has become so widely accepted. It is in development economics that Professor Myrdal and others have argued with special emphasis that objective reasoning in economics is impossible, that the distinction between the pursuit of knowledge and the promotion of policy is fanciful, because both the concepts of the subject and the reasoning employed are value-loaded and politically oriented. On this argument, neither objective reasoning nor agreed conclusions are possible in economics, except in terms of the so-called unanimous resolutions of political meetings. Even the basis of disagreement cannot be defined as between matters of logic and fact on one hand, and of political objectives on the other hand.

This unwarranted position has become exceedingly influential in development economics, where its acceptance has greatly enhanced the difficulties of establishing and maintaining even minimum standards of competence and integrity. Political acceptability and effectiveness become the criteria of intellectual achievement and assessment. Criticisms of a statement, however defective in logic or inaccurate in fact, can always be dismissed as reflecting political differences, and the statement rationalized or justified by reference

6 In the words of Julien Benda, *La Trahison des Clercs*: 'Politique d'abord, veut un apôtre de l'âme moderne; politique partout, peut-il constater, politique toujours, politique uniquement.' Quoted by N. C. Chaudhuri, *The Autobiography of an Unknown Indian*, London 1951, p. 304.

15

to real or alleged political aims. And the political effectiveness of a view is enhanced by the suggestion that it commands universal support.

Examples abound in development economics of corollaries of this position. The frequent reply to criticisms of the thesis of the vicious circle of poverty is that insistence on it has served to promote the flow of aid. International civil servants often readily admit privately that their presentation of economic argument and statistical material is designed to advance what they regard as the interests of under-developed countries, the promotion of which they consider is the proper objective of economic and statistical exercise. And senior professors of economics find it proper to recommend that the United States government should supply all the capital which any under-developed country can use productively (in the sense that it will increase the national income) thereby equating a scarce resource with a free good.

In academic or intellectual life the adoption of political effective-ness and acceptability as criteria of merit implies a reversion to barbarism. The acceptance of the spurious consensus has done more damage to economics as a form of disciplined search for truth than the much publicized disagreements of the past. The implications of the acceptance of political effectiveness as a criterion of intellectual merit and the corresponding absence of intellectual standards, were clearly recognized a generation ago by Ortega y Gasset:

> There is no culture where there is no acceptance of certain final intellectual positions to which a dispute may be referred. . . .
> The traveller who arrives in a barbarous country knows that in that territory there are no ruling principles to which it is possible to appeal. Properly speaking there are no barbarian standards. Barbarism is the absence of standards to which appeal can be made. . . .
> It is not the fact of judging rightly or wrongly – truth is not within our reach – but the lack of scruple which makes them omit the elementary requirements for right judgment. . . .[7]

These remarks epitomize the situation in much of development economics.

10. The dominant political influence in development economics has

7 *The Revolt of the Masses*, London 1932, p. 79.

16

been almost exclusively meliorist in character. Although meliorism is a dictionary term and a useful one, it is rarely employed. Dr Kenneth Minogue has examined at length in *The Liberal Mind*[8] the concept of meliorism and the attitudes it denotes.

Meliorism describes the belief or attitude that everyone has a duty to work for the improvement of human conditions.[9] Dr Minogue writes:

> The effects of this harmless-looking doctrine have been so striking that it has acquired a name which, for want of a better, we shall adopt: meliorism. Meliorism is the assertion that political and social thinkers ought to concern themselves more with 'practical affairs'. It is a special development of the utilitarian view that everything gains its value from its usefulness. The value of intellectual activities will therefore be determined by their conduciveness to reform or improvement. Intellectual criticism of politics can only be justified as a preparation for 'doing something about it'.[10]

Meliorism is in turn related to the doctrine of needs, the idea that man everywhere has certain clearly definable similar needs; and that if anywhere there are unsatisfied needs there is a corresponding universal obligation to provide for their satisfaction. The need is defined by the advocate of action with no, or only nominal, examination of the social context.[11]

8 London, 1963.

9 Dr Minogue rightly observes that *prima facie* this duty would not be particularly onerous because through the ordinary activities of our daily lives we normally appreciably contribute to the improvement of the conditions of others without espousing meliorist notions.

10 *The Liberal Mind*, p. 112 f.

11 Dr Minogue points out that these attitudes encourage the politically effective but intellectually damaging practice of negative definition, a practice prominent in development economics.

> The proletariat was defined (even by Marx, who in some moods was perfectly aware of this trap) as the poor, the deprived, the suffering class – defined in other words in terms of non-possession. The bourgeois insistence on personal possession is so powerful as to create entire definitions which leave the subject a complete mystery. Who are the poor? They are those who do not possess what others have. This is rather like defining a horse and cart as a thing that lacks an engine. It is equally a matter of ideology to talk about the 'underdeveloped countries'. He is simply concerned with the fact that in the 'underdeveloped countries' people do not live as he does. And they ought to.

Op. cit. p. 106.

The widespread contemporary presence of this attitude has much enhanced the appeal of the consensus. For instance the meliorist attitude has promoted the belief that the material backwardness of underdeveloped countries establishes a fundamental similarity between underdeveloped countries; and that the primary or only differences between people are differences in incomes which are clearly ascertainable, and which determine the degree of need. By the same token this attitude has discouraged the examination of people's capacities, attitudes, beliefs and conditions, as such an examination would distract from the political thrust of the doctrine of needs. The investigation of conditions is subordinate to the moral duty of satisfying the need; the task of enquiry is subordinate to political purpose.

Meliorists usually reject critical examination of their ideas and proposals. They term criticism as unconstructive or negative, especially when no so-called constructive alternative is proposed. Such objections are obviously irrelevant; our inability to cure cancer does not mean that we are not entitled to expose a quack. Recognition of the obvious defects of this attitude unfortunately does not enhance the effectiveness or acceptability of criticism.[12]

The unpopularity of so-called negative or unconstructive criticism has inevitably assisted in the acceptance of the development consensus, the appeal of which has benefited from the suggestion that the principal obstacles to the material advance of the underdeveloped world are easy to understand and not too difficult to remove with some good will and practical sense. Such an approach has special appeal in America and in a political and intellectual climate much influenced by American ideas.

The meliorist influence in development economics accords with expectations since the public and political interest in this field is obviously of meliorist origin. Meliorist policies include government-to-government aid; the extension of the activities of the international agencies; and less obviously and directly, but none the less substantially, the enlargement of state control over the economies in underdeveloped countries; and also the extension of economic controls and of redistributive (progressive) taxation from the national to the international or supranational level in order to promote greater standardization of conditions internationally. These

12 Dr. Minogue has aptly summarized the meliorist attitude to criticism, *cf. op. cit.* p. 114.

18

policies appeal to substantial and effective groups and interests in the West.

The suggestions that the peoples of underdeveloped countries are helpless victims of environmental or external forces has special psychological appeal in the West. Social reformers are often emotionally dependent on the groups whose condition they ostensibly seek to ameliorate. The humanitarians and social reformers particularly need people who can be plausibly classified as helpless victims of causes and conditions beyond their control. And the classification of groups as helpless then actually promotes their helplessness, thus serving the psychological, and political aims and possibly also the financial aims of the classifiers.

11. The influence of meliorism in development economics has been reinforced by that of Marxism which is in itself an especially powerful species of meliorism.

Many writers, including Marxist sympathizers, have noted the dominant influence of Marxist ideas in the development literature. This influence is obvious in the allegations of the responsibility of Western countries for the poverty of underdeveloped countries, in the allegations of the exploitative nature of private capital, and in the proposals for substantial expropriation of propertied classes. It is reflected also in the proposals for state trading and state supported and organized co-operative movements and in the insistence on monetary investment as the crucial factor in development.

Although the writings of Marx and Engels abound in logical inconsistencies and in spectacularly unsuccessful prophecies, these founding fathers of Marxism revealed considerable insights into major phenomena relevant to development economics. Examples include their recognition of the long period of material progress in Europe before the industrial revolution, as well as their consistent treatment of phenomena as part of a historical process, and their assessment of developments and of policies in terms of their overall effects. However, the extensive influence of Marxist-Leninist ideas in development economics owes little to these insights. The appeal derives mainly from influences largely unrelated to these insights. These influences include among others the prestige conferred on these ideas by the political and military successes of the Soviet Union; the attraction of an all-embracing secular messianic faith; the appeal of the emphasis on the responsibility of environmental, and especially of external, factors for material backwardness, an

19

appeal which is obvious in the case of the leaders of underdeveloped countries, but which affects also those influential groups in the West who in various ways stand to gain from the emergence and spread of a guilt feeling there; the quasi-scientific appeal of a system working with a few apparently clearly defined variables, sharp distinctions and grand functional relationships; the promise in a communist society of the integration of intellectuals with the rest of the community; the confident promise of the ultimate victory of the revolution; the appeal of social engineering and of apparently conscious control over social forces and human destiny. A specific major example or component of this last influence has been the attraction of a political and social system which envisages and apparently justifies the compulsory elimination of all distinctions between persons and groups except those between the political rulers and their subjects, and which also justifies the pulverization of existing institutions. Such a system appeals to those who resent differences between persons and groups and who foresee themselves as the rulers in the systems and societies envisaged by these ideas.

The paramountcy of political objectives is carried to its logical conclusion in Marxist theory and practice according to which objective truth depends on the promotion of the cause of the communist revolution. The influence of this philosophy has inevitably enhanced further the difficulties of establishing standards of reasoning and evidence in development economics.

12. The difficulties of effective critical examination of prevailing views on underdeveloped countries and their development have been aggravated by the problem of quality control brought about by the rapid expansion of activity and output. This problem of quality control at times of rapid expansion of activity is familiar in any field of study where invalid inference or unsuccessful hypotheses cannot be readily exposed by means of contrived experiment. It is specially acute in development economics, where the rapid expansion of output reflects a sudden increase in demand motivated by political and popular concerns and supported by vast financial resources.

The political and popular interest in underdeveloped countries has generated an enormous volume of publicity and publications, a phenomenon which has both enhanced the difficulty of maintaining standards of competence, and has also enhanced the plausibility of the unfounded suggestion of universal agreement on the ideas of the consensus. The principle of the paramountcy of politics implies that even intellectually plainly insubstantial material has to be taken seriously if it is politically acceptable. The sheer volume of material then serves to drown dissenting voices. Effective censorship can be established by persistent noise, as well as by enforced silence, and the former method is especially insidious because its operation is unrecognized.

These various influences have aroused the interest of the mass media in development economics, a development which has further increased the volume of comment in this area, thereby reinforcing the effects of the other influences inhibiting effective exposure even of manifestly untenable ideas.

13. The various descriptive terms which have been proposed as appropriate for the twentieth century include among others the age of violence, of resentment, of messages and of credulity, all of which are appropriate in different contexts. The appropriateness of the last two terms bears on the acceptance of the development consensus.

In many ways our age is more uncritical and credulous than perhaps any other age in recorded history. People in antiquity and the Middle Ages were indeed credulous in certain distinct spheres. But most of their concerns were with events and phenomena of which they had first-hand knowledge. In the twentieth century people concern themselves with a wide range of events and phenomena about which they only have second- or third-hand information whose meaning and reliability they cannot assess. The public is flooded with information and messages whose purveyors insist on the urgency, relevance and truth of the information they supply, and also explicitly or implicitly on the ability and qualifications of their audience to assess the information conveyed. This latter influence imposes presentation in over-simplified form (often, however, combined with pretentious jargon) which is evident from the selling of toothpaste to the selling of foreign aid. These procedures reinforce various other political and intellectual influences which have undermined the people's critical faculty including recognition of their limitations for the assessment of information conveyed to them.[13]

There is a close connection between the age of messages and the

13 Among others, Ortega y Gasset has noted the operation of this factor: 'This is one particular case of the disproportion which I indicate later on as existing between the complexity of present day problems and the capacity of present day minds.' *Op. cit.* p. 91.

21

age of credulity. Over-simplified presentation in the interests of accessibility and political palatability has often obscured primary relevant aspects of phenomena and of processes. The adoption of such procedures amounts to intellectual pampering. And these procedures and their results have seeped into ostensibly technical or scholarly discussion in those branches of the social sciences which are close to the political arena.

The emission of a sufficient volume of information, whether on a particular topic or a range of subjects, can saturate the recipients who are left with no time, opportunity or intellectual strength to consider alternative views. The emergence of effective dissent can be obstructed by such means.

The processes and effects of a large expansion of the supply of misleading and over-simplified information resemble the operation and results of the debasement of the currency through an inflationary expansion of its volume. The debasement of language undermines effective communication on which the reasonably smooth functioning of civilized society largely depends. Rapid inflation of the currency disintegrates an advanced economy pervaded by the use of money. Words are to discussion what units of currency are to a monetary system; and communication is to social life as use of money is to the operation of an advanced economy. The processes of the debasement of language and money thus promote social and economic disintegration. The persons and groups who can issue additional supplies of the media of communication and of transactions (words and money) gain, as long as the rest of society accepts the additional supplies generated by them. They can appropriate for themselves additional shares of the volume of discussion and of economic resources. They gain until the point is reached when discussion becomes impossible and is replaced by orders, and the exchange economy breaks down and is replaced by a command economy or barter economy.

For various discernible reasons the operation of the factors which debase the intellectual currency, i.e. language, has considerably affected the substance and tenor of discussions in development economics. The reasons include the rapid increase in the volume of development literature; the close connection between development economics and current politics; the physical and cultural distances separating the public in the West from the underdeveloped countries and their populations; the multiplicity of complex factors behind material progress, and the unfamiliarity of the public in the West with the operation of some of the principal determinants of material advance in poor countries and with their imperviousness to quantification; and a failure to appreciate the importance of a time perspective and of some historical knowledge for an understanding of the position and development prospects of underdeveloped countries. These influences and considerations explain the exceptionally uncritical approach (exceptional even by contemporary standards both of the public and of academic economists) to the methods and conclusions of the development literature; and this uncritical approach in turn helps to explain the measure of acceptance of the consensus.[14]

IV

14. Even these powerful political and near-political influences might not have sufficed to bring about the emergence and the widespread acceptance of the spurious consensus. Their operation has been reinforced by certain mental habits, intellectual predispositions and methods of approach which again are interrelated among themselves, and also with the political factors already discussed. These factors and influences include some characteristics of the contemporary intellectual climate, as well as certain problems of approach and method in social studies.

Disregard of the time dimension of historical processes, and equation of quantifiability with relevance and significance, are notable characteristics of the contemporary climate; these two characteristics together with their corollaries, and with other closely related influences, have much affected the contemporary development literature.

15. Some years ago, Professor Gombrich commented on what he appositely termed the amputation of the time dimension from our culture.[15] There are many manifestations of this significant phenomenon on the contemporary scene including widespread ignorance of both the recent and the most distant past; the

14 The influences listed in this section operate also in other branches of the social sciences, but their operation can be seen particularly clearly in development economics, in much the same way as according to Toqueville the merits and defects of the Bourbon monarchy were most clearly visible in French Canada.

15 *The Tradition of General Knowledge*, London 1962.

consciously ephemeral nature of contemporary art; and the loss of collective memory reflected in public and political discussion. The rapid rate of social and technical change, the growth of specialization, and the multiplicity of events, phenomena and items of information impinging on the public, and the large and diverse supply of frequently changing information, have contributed to the loss of memory and to the disregard of the time dimension in discussion of social and economic processes.

The relevance of the historical background is plain for a worthwhile discussion of economic development, which is part of the historical progress of society. Yet much of contemporary development economics ignores the historical background and the time element or dimension of change, or reveals only the most superficial knowledge of the relevant information. Such a time-less approach to development economics empties the subject of its basic constituents, in much the same way as price-less and cost-less economics empties static economic theory of some of its primary elements.

Many of the most widely publicized writings of the development consensus effectively disregard the historical background and the nature of development as a process. The discussions of the vicious circle of poverty, which regard a low level of income as evidence of stagnation, and thus of a zero rate of change, are a familiar instance. Other examples are the frequent comparisons in the literature between present day Africa and Asia on one hand and nineteenth-century Europe and North America on the other hand, or the comparisons of the process of industrialization of nineteenth-century Britain and Western Europe with government-sponsored industrialization of contemporary Africa and Asia.[16] Such comparisons ignore the highly-advanced state of the economies of Western Europe, Britain and North America in the nineteenth century, regions with centuries or even millennia of material development behind them and largely pervaded by the institutions and attitudes of the exchange economy. Some writers even go as far as contrasting the cocoa industry of West Africa with the export industries of nineteenth-century North America to the detriment of the former for not having transformed the society of West Africa sufficiently to reach the material standards of present day North America.

16 In the 1950s India and Indonesia were freely compared with Britain and the United States of the early nineteenth century as countries on the verge of the so-called 'take off'.

This disregard of historical background and of the time dimension of change is reflected in the frequent demands for immediate and thoroughgoing social reform in underdeveloped countries. As an American colleague has said, the advocates of reform demand instant social change in much the same way as they demand instant coffee.[17] If the reform or change demanded is not quick or thoroughgoing enough, the national and international society is said to stand condemned.

Once such emotions and activities are aroused, whether from idealism or calculated political motives, failure to achieve the postulated results is often adduced for further and more intensified action in the same direction. This outcome is probable when substantial sacrifices have already been made on behalf of a principle widely regarded as desirable and by means of policies axiomatically deemed effective. Once a policy is axiomatically regarded as effective, then even its failure can be adduced as an argument for its reinforcement. And the greater the sacrifices, the more difficult it becomes to question the principles for which they have been incurred. The advocates of policies seem often to appreciate these implications of their demands which are at times advanced in the confident belief that the expectations aroused cannot be satisfied. The failure to satisfy the demands and to achieve the stipulated aims is expected to serve as justification for large scale compulsion. However, quite often the discussion surrounding these demands reflects genuine ignorance of the relevance of the time dimension of change.

16. In the consensus literature the effects of the disregard of the historical background and of the time-dimension of development have been reinforced by a related intellectual attitude, namely, over-emphasis on quantification and a corresponding neglect of non-quantifiable factors.

The contemporary appeal of quantifiability is familiar. It is widely believed that only those phenomena or aspects of phenomena are significant which lend themselves to quantification, whether genuine or spurious. Of course, quantifiability is unrelated both to significance and to causality. The most important aspects of a situation are not necessarily those which can be readily quantified. Moreover, quantification cannot generally explain influences and processes behind a situation, including the factors behind the genuinely quantifiable aspects.

17 However, they are sometimes prepared to pay for the coffee themselves.

The appeal of quantifiability is partly political and partly intellectual in origin. Emphasis on the quantifiable aspect of a situation often obscures the complexities and problems of policy proposals, such as those of meliorism. Again, emphasis on quantification promotes the case of social engineering, especially the treatment of human beings as standardized interchangeable units; it diverts attention from those differences between human beings and their conditions which cannot be readily quantified. There are also intellectual attractions to quantification, some genuine, some spurious. The attraction is genuine when the concepts quantified are firm and the quantifiable aspects of the situation are significant. In such conditions quantification can greatly and often decisively enhance the significance and meaning of a discussion. Familiar examples include major parts of demography, monetary economics, public finance and international trade. However, quite often the appeal of quantification derives from the unwarranted belief that the process of quantification can itself promise or ensure precision, intelligibility, reliability and concreteness. Of course, it does nothing of the sort; in particular, quantification often involves a large measure of abstraction.

In much of development economics the appeal of quantification derives from political purpose, intellectual naïveté, or both. The uncritical use of national income statistics for the measurement of international differences in living standards and welfare presents a familiar example both of the political basis and of the intellectual naïveté behind the appeal of quantification.[18] The treatment of underdeveloped countries as being substantially similar among themselves and differing from developed countries only in levels of incomes, is an instance of the belief that the only relevant and significant differences are those which can be quantified with at least superficial plausibility.

17. People's faculties, attitudes, motivations, and mores are not

---

18 In the 1950s some prominent academic economists seriously suggested that an increase of 1 per cent in *per capita* incomes in underdeveloped countries over several consecutive years was evidence that the country had reached the stage of the so-called take-off; and that this criterion in turn should serve as basis for important proposals for the granting of foreign aid. Quite apart from the question of the meaning of the concept of the take-off, and of the meaning and interpretation of the national income statistics of underdeveloped countries, the errors in estimates of *per capita* incomes in these countries, let alone in changes in these incomes, exceed 1 per cent by orders of magnitude (i.e. tenfold or a hundredfold).

26

generally amenable to useful quantification; and the same applies to many major institutions of society. Yet these matters and factors are major determinants of economic performance and thus of material progress. These personal and cultural factors have until recently been very largely ignored in the development literature. As I have already noted, much of this literature, especially the consensus literature, ignores the fact that an economy consists of people. More recently these factors have somewhat gained in recognition but they are still greatly underrated in the literature. Yet they are plainly much more important and relevant to development than such influences as the terms of trade, foreign-exchange reserves, capital output ratios or external economies, which fill the pages of the consensus literature.

Two preliminary points are necessary before a discussion of these factors. It still seems necessary to insist that references to human capacities, faculties and attitudes refer solely to those behind material success, which do not always or even usually confer either happiness or dignity on those who possess them. Second, the presence of influences adverse to material advance does not validate the thesis of the vicious circle of poverty, which alleges that poverty by itself prevents material progress, even in the absence of unfavourable faculties and attitudes.

Here are a few examples of widely prevalent faculties and attitudes adverse to material advance. Whatever their origins and the likelihood of their persistence, their relevance to economic performance is plain.

Outside the consensus literature, the adverse effect on material progress has often been noted of two widely prevailing attitudes in Asia – the prestige of a contemplative compared to an active life, and the belief in the inviolability of sentient animal life. It is less often noted that these attitudes are related to the belief in the unity of nature, with the implied absence of a clear distinction between man and the rest of creation. There is a profound difference between the attitudes which affirm the unity of man and nature and those that differentiate between them. This difference, the origins of which extend into the pre-Christian era, has far reaching implications for the determinants of material progress.

The whole emphasis of this mental attitude or attitudes is on permanence and is against change, let alone deliberate control or change of the environment. The emphasis is also on underlying

27

36366

unity and continuity and against distinctions, even such distinctions as between good and evil, or duties and rights. These attitudes, beliefs and modes of conduct are both widespread and deep-rooted over large areas of Asia. Assessment of their persistence is conjectural, though I believe that over much of South Asia they will persist for many generations.[19]

The insistence on the unity of man and nature thus plainly encourages attitudes and responses which lead to material backwardness, but which also often conduce to serenity and spiritual harmony. The corollaries of the western tradition of the subordination of nature to the purposes of man conduce to material advance, but also to spiritual tension and restlessness. The same is true of the much more pronounced spirit of competitiveness and emulation in the West.

While the belief or systems of belief in the unity of man with the universe may have arisen in response to the disruption of the universal dominance of magic, its acceptance has tended to preserve magical beliefs by discouraging the quest for change and the emergence of an experimental outlook. In Africa the disintegration of the pervasive hold of magic has begun only very recently and has made only limited progress.

18. The list of personal and cultural factors adverse to material progress in underdeveloped countries could be extended almost in-

19 The elements of South Asian, especially Hindu, philosophical beliefs and some of their principal implications for personal conduct and social institutions are major themes of Mr. Nirad C. Chaudhuri's writings, especially *The Autobiography of an Unknown Indian* and *The Continent of Circe*. For instance, he writes in *The Autobiography of an Unknown Indian*:

> The more I read and learned, the more I came to prize differentiation and complexity. I implicitly believe that culture is indeed the faculty of making distinctions.
>
> I think there is even in the highest and most characteristic teaching of Hinduism (apart from the layer on layer of infinitely varied primitiveness which constitutes its buried foundation), something impelling a Hindu towards the simpler in preference to the more complex, towards the unemerged in preference to the emergent, and towards the general in preference to the particular. According to some of the noblest teaching of Hinduism, the manifested universe is an illusion, the ultimate reality attribute-less, and man's supreme happiness lies in putting an end to the cycle of births and deaths, or, in other words, in eliminating precisely those particular forms possessing sensible attributes which confer qualities and values on reality, and clothe it with attractiveness for us. With such a philosophical background it is not surprising that a Hindu should tend to ignore distinctions.

p. 448.

28

definitely, certainly sufficiently to fill a book. I shall mention only three more examples, the operation and significance of which are manifest over large areas and yet widely ignored in the consensus literature. These instances are sanctity of cattle; an authoritarian tradition; and a certain physical and mental inactivity or torpor.

The sanctity of cattle has been a prominent and pervasive feature of much of Indian life for millennia. This attitude is in part related to the belief in the inviolability of sentient animal life but it largely derives from the attachment to their cattle of the Aryans who reached the Gangetic plain around 1000 B.C. in the course of their migration from Europe through the Middle East.[20] The deep emotion for cattle and the worship of the cow have been embedded in Hindu culture for many centuries. Since 1949 the sanctity of cattle has been reinforced by legislative prohibitions on its slaughter (affecting non-Hindus as well) first in some major Indian States, and later extended to almost all India. The sanctity of cattle has far-reaching adverse effects on material progress. But its enforced termination, inconceivable in the absence of external conquest, might well bring about a spiritual collapse in the country.

For centuries or even millennia the individual person in Africa and Asia has been much more closely subject to authority, both to political authority and to that of the traditional society, than in Europe. The much greater strength of the authoritarian tradition of Africa and Asia is reflected in many aspects of personal life including the choice of one's spouse. An authoritarian tradition emphasizes functions rather than achievements and obligations rather than rights. Moreover such a tradition discourages enquiry, experimentation, self-reliance and personal provision for the future; and conversely it encourages lack of curiosity in the activities and achievements of other societies, that is a cultural insularity or even xenophobia. These results of an authoritarian tradition are reinforced by a belief in the supernatural which is still relatively strong in Africa and much of Asia.

A distinct mental and physical lassitude of the majority of the local population in many underdeveloped countries, notably so in the Middle East and South Asia has also often been noted both

20 According to Mr. Chaudhuri: 'Throughout their existence in India the Aryan Hindus have never wavered in their loyalty and adherence to four things. In fact, they have worshipped all four in different ways, and these loyalties are basic to their way of life. The Vedas, fair complexion, the rivers, and cattle.' *The Continent of Circe*, London 1965, p. 151.

29

by foreign observers and those indigenous observers who have had some basis of comparison.

It is not clear how far this inertia and some of the other traits and attitudes unfavourable to material progress reflect the operation of biological, cultural, climatic or other geographical factors. The climate almost certainly plays a substantial role whose importance has been underrated in spite of the obvious concentration of material poverty in extreme climates.

19. The connection between climate and material backwardness is especially pronounced in the case of some of the poorest groups within the underdeveloped world, notably the desert peoples, the Eskimos and the pygmies. These numerically substantial groups are rarely mentioned in the development literature partly because they contain no articulate or politically effective groups, or because their presence throws into relief both material inequality within the underdeveloped world, and also many defects of the current development literature, such as the neglect of differences within the underdeveloped world, and the patent irrelevance or inadequacy of such general policy proposals as industrialization or comprehensive central planning.

However, quite apart from these extreme cases the connection between climate and economic performance is suggested not only by the concentration of material poverty in non-temperate climates, but also by the insistence of Western organizations operating in tropical or sub-tropical climates that their employees spend frequent and prolonged spells in temperate climates.

The neglect of the influence of climate in the contemporary development literature is *prima facie* surprising since it would seem to lend itself fairly readily to systematic examination and perhaps even to a measure of appropriate quantification. The neglect may be explained in part by the fact that the influence of the climate normally affects people only after prolonged exposure. Much of the development literature is written by people who stay in underdeveloped countries only briefly and spend much of their visit in sheltered conditions including air-conditioned buildings. The obvious impossibility of modifying climate substantially in the immediate future may also have conduced to the relative neglect of a factor not readily susceptible to influence by political action.

20. The presence and operation of influences adverse to material advance in the underdeveloped world and the presence of more

favourable influences in the West, are of long standing. This conclusion is suggested by such evidence as the extensive use of comparatively sophisticated instruments and of relatively advanced methods of construction in medieval and Renaissance Europe, and also by the volume and direction of travel for centuries before the industrial revolution, which was so largely from West to East.

21. Some of the major determinants of development are either ignored altogether in the development literature, or are often treated parametrically, that is their presence is recognized but disregarded in the particular context. The significance of the disregard of these factors is enhanced by their frequent and extensive interrelations with the variables conventionally discussed.[21] For instance in many underdeveloped countries (as elsewhere) foreign contacts are often restricted in order to influence the volume and direction of domestic investment. External contacts have usually been prime agents of material change throughout the world. They have been major influences in undermining values and attitudes damaging to material progress, as well as with new wants, crops and methods of production. The restrictions on external contacts are correspondingly damaging. Such repercussions (examples of which can be readily multiplied) often affect development more than do the direct and intended results or the ostensible objectives of the policies designed to operate on the conventional variables; these repercussions are perforce overlooked if the determinants themselves are disregarded.

The neglect of the major determinants of development in the more widely canvassed models has also prevented the fruitful use of abstraction. Appropriate abstraction promotes precision in social studies, as in other disciplines. In development economics the opposite has been brought about by the combined result of the neglect of major determinants, the reliance on abstract concepts, and of the shifting interpretation of the abstract concepts.

22. The significance of personal and cultural factors underlines the inappropriateness of negative definition in development economics,

---

21 This problem posed by the interaction of variables and parameters is related to important methodological issues in social studies, namely the appropriateness and limitations of the examination of specific variables isolated from other factors and conditions. This procedure is unavoidable in systematic study in the social sciences because of the simultaneous presence of countless factors and influences affecting the phenomena under observation. But the dangers and limitations of the procedure are often insufficiently recognized.

i.e. of treating the underdeveloped world as being much the same as the developed world, but only poorer, and of envisaging the peoples of underdeveloped countries as being substantially similar among themselves and different from the peoples of the developed world solely in being poorer. This practice obscures the differences in the operation of the determinants of development not only between the peoples of the so-called developed and the so-called underdeveloped world, but also within each category. For instance, there are substantial differences in economic capacities, attitudes and institutions between say the Chinese of South East Asia, the Indians in South East Asia, the Hindus in India or the tribal peoples of Central Africa.

The insistence on the sharp distinction between underdeveloped and developed countries and the assumption of basic homogeneity of the underdeveloped world reflect a procedure analogous to the treatment of locomotives, sailing ships, carts and horses as substantially identical means of transport because none of them uses the internal combustion engine. Quite apart from other implications on the differences between these different means of transport, their performance even for specified purposes cannot be improved by substantially similar methods. Indeed application of the same method – say the injection of additional supplies of water, can lead to diametrically opposite results. And the same applies to the conditions of underdeveloped countries.

Recognition of the significance of personal and cultural factors in economic performance and of the differences in these factors both between people in developed and underdeveloped countries and also within the underdeveloped world, is not intended to suggest that economic analysis is inapplicable in underdeveloped countries. It implies only that the major determinants of material progress are not the variables of conventional economic analysis, and that the skills of the economist are of only limited use in indicating how these determinants can be most effectively influenced.

23. The neglect of personal and cultural determinants of development and the emphasis on income differences derive in part from the attraction of the quantifiability of income differences. However, there are also other substantial political influences behind these intellectual attitudes. The suggestion that the only relevant differences between people are those in incomes or wealth merges readily into the suggestion that people by virtue of being born have

the right to substantially the same incomes, because they are similar in all other respects, except for differences in incomes; and that material inequality as expressed by conventional statistics is therefore inequitable.

If all men are created equal, and their conditions are substantially unequal, then something must have occurred to pervert the natural and just state of affairs; international inequality can then be identified with inequity, and inequity which moreover is comparatively easily rectifiable. Thus, according to these ideas, justice can be restored with relative ease, effectiveness and permanence by a redistribution of incomes. However, once the reality of the depth and extent of differences in capacities, attitudes, objectives and mores are recognized, the case for standardization of conditions becomes more doubtful, and its difficulties and problems much more obvious. In particular, it is bound to be recognized that if there are pronounced and tenacious differences in the faculties, habits and conditions of the groups whose incomes and living standards are to be substantially equalized, the process involves vast extension of coercive power to carry out the postulated standardization of conditions, with consequent increase in inequality of power between rulers and ruled. And the greater the international differences in the relevant factors and conditions, the closer and more extensive are the powers required to promote uniformity, let alone achieve it. Disregard of differences other than those in income thus enhances the attractions of the aims of international redistribution of wealth and of social engineering, while simultaneously obscuring the objections of such policies and the resistance they encounter. Hence the importance of underplaying the significance of the determinants of economic performance and of the differences in them.

V

24. In both academic and popular discussion, the acceptance of the spurious consensus has been promoted or reinforced by a failure to appreciate certain relevant problems of methodology. As so often happens, apparently recondite matters are issues of much political and practical significance.

While an inappropriate disregard of the historical background is a characteristic of the consensus literature which has helped to promote its popularity, there is also present a pronounced historicist element in the consensus which has substantially contributed to its acceptance.

Sir Karl Popper has coined the term historicism to denote:

> an approach to the social sciences which assumes the *historic prediction* is their principal aim, and which assumes that this aim is attainable by discovering the 'rhythms' or the 'patterns', the 'laws' or the 'trends' that underlie the evolution of history.[22]

Historicism in this sense has had great political and psychological appeal for decades if not centuries. This appeal is still very strong perhaps stronger than ever. The main sources of the appeal are plain: promise of the establishment of universal laws analogous to those of natural science, and which are expected both to explain the past and to foretell the future course of history and perhaps make possible conscious control of the future course of events through the manipulation both of people and of the environment. The appeal of these notions is particularly pronounced when the prestige of natural science is high, and also at times of rapid social change and of widespread apprehension about the future.

The predictions of historicism have been complete failures and its logical, scientific and methodological claims conclusively refuted many times by prominent historians and philosophers, most extensively and conclusively perhaps by R. G. Collingwood and Popper, especially the latter.

As Popper has rightly insisted, quite apart from the operation of random and external events, the progress of knowledge in itself prevents rational prediction of the future development of society, since future knowledge cannot be anticipated in the present.

But even readily demonstrable failures of prophecy and conclusive refutations in logic do not affect the emotionally based appeal of historical prophecy. Its espousal by prominent representatives of the consensus has accordingly assisted in the influence of the consensus.

In contemporary development economics the appeal of historicist prophecy has been compounded by certain specific factors, notably the meliorist bias of some of its major conclusions, especially the suggestion of the long-term progress to be expected in under-

22 *The Poverty of Historicism*, London 1957, p. 3.

developed countries as the result of the policies proposed by the consensus. And the attraction and prestige of historicist prophecies have been enhanced yet further by a combined use of scraps of historical information, usually rather simple statistics, and of certain concepts of macro-economics, especially aggregate capital output ratios, as basis for extrapolation. To the lay public, whose opinions have much influenced contemporary discussions on development economics (including ostensibly academic discussions), these prophecies seem to combine the merits of historical scholarship, scientific prediction and awareness of reality.

Such beliefs and claims are unfounded. Many of the concepts used in this exercise, notably capital output ratios, are exceedingly vague. But even if they were more precisely defined they could not serve as basis for scientific prediction as they are only simple descriptions of past occurrences and not variables between which functional and causal relationships have been established. And casual collection of a few statistics is not serious historical study, nor does simple extrapolation of arbitrarily chosen trends reflect scientific activity.

25. Economic development is an aspect of the historical process of the development of societies. Both the methods of enquiry appropriate to the explanation of historical development and the formulation of the conclusions differ in so many ways from those appropriate to the natural and social sciences, especially the former.[23] The following are among the major aspects and elements of historical process which differentiate the phenomena studied by the historical sciences from those examined by the natural sciences, and to a considerable extent also from those of the social sciences: the dependence of the results of historical processes on the manner in which these processes are initiated and conducted; the non-repetitiveness of major elements of the historical process, and also the growth of skills and knowledge; the multiplicity of interwoven and variable influences (variable in the sense that the strength of their operation differs and varies in place and time) simultaneously affecting the development of societies; the problems posed by the time lag in the operation of different factors and the different problem of the time

23 There are also certain differences in the methods of analysis and the testing and formulation of conclusions within the theoretical sciences, especially between the natural and social sciences. But these are probably less significant than the relevant differences between the theoretical sciences on one hand and the historical sciences on the other hand.

35

span of the manifestation of the response;[24] the often unpredictable nature of the response of human beings to major changes in conditions, which is especially important when a relatively small number of agents exercise a disproportionate effect on the course of events as is usually the case in historical process. Thus in the study of historical process we cannot foretell whether a change in conditions will occur; and even where this is possible we cannot always confidently predict the response of human beings. These factors and complications are either absent from the phenomena, relationships and situations studied by the natural and social sciences, or are present to a much lesser extent only.[25]

For these reasons it has certainly not been possible as yet, and it may never be possible, to establish firm generalizations or laws with predictive value about the course of historical developments; that is, laws which can be formulated as hypotheses testable by scientific procedures, capable of refutation, and suitable for embodiment and expression in analytical systems. Because economic development is a major aspect of the historical process, it is not possible to formulate a theory of economic development analogous to the theories of the natural and social sciences which embody testable hypotheses. This conclusion does not imply that there are no valid generalizations in development economics. The contrary is patently clear. But there is a substantial difference between the discernment of uniformities and the application of the conclusion to specified conditions on one hand, and attempts to forecast the future evolution of whole societies on the other hand, an evolution which even apart from the operation of random factors, depends on variables which have not been incorporated into systematic analysis, and which may not lend themselves to it.

24 The reference is to the problems posed by the lags between both the impact of a change and the response to it, and also to the lag between the response and its manifestation. These lags make it extremely difficult to observe causal or functional relationships between variables when a situation is affected simultaneously by a multitude of past and present influences, as is practically always the case with the phenomena of economic development. And these lags differ in time and space, which is an aspect of the non-repetitive nature of historical processes.

25 It is sometimes thought that these difficulties can be overcome by the application of the law of large numbers. This objection is insubstantial. The law of large numbers is clearly altogether irrelevant to the problems posed by the non-repetitive nature of the historical process, and it is largely irrelevant to the operation of the other factors listed in the text.

36

VI

26. The inadequacies of the historicist elements of the consensus, and indeed of the consensus generally, have often been masked by forms of presentation which have managed to convey suggestions of a rigorous scientific method of approach. Familiar instances include the employment of simple mathematical techniques and of algebraic symbols, the emphasis on quantification, and the use of correlation analysis.

In some major branches of development economics covered by the consensus, notably the discussion of the determinants of development, and discussions of planning techniques and of investment criteria, the use of mathematical formulae has for various reasons obscured the primary issue. To begin with it has obscured the very underdeveloped state of this branch of economics, in the sense that development economics has as yet discerned few valid uniformities. In a discipline dealing with real world phenomena (as distinct from philosophical subjects) a useful analytical system, which can be embodied or expressed in formal mathematical terms, reflects the discernment and systematization of a number of uniformities. This stage has not yet been achieved in development economics. The uniformities discerned, such as the significance of human capacities and attitudes, or the importance of external contacts, or of the maintenance of some law and order, are hardly suitable as bases of a system likely to benefit from the use of mathematical techniques. Further, the concepts of the mathematical development models are also much too vague to serve as bases of analytical systems, a limitation or defect obscured by the use of mathematical symbols: the use of capital output ratios and of investment functions are familiar instances.

Preoccupation with mathematical or quasi-mathematical models has also introduced an inappropriate bias into the choice of variables in favour of those most tractable by the mathematical methods, such as the volume and pattern of saving and investment in the monetary sector, the level of consumption and the volume and composition of foreign trade. Political motives have almost certainly played a part in this choice of variables, in favour of those more readily susceptible to government action because, in this literature, development is regarded as dependent largely on state action, and on the expansion of government activity, rather than on the capacities and activities of the members of the society. However, analytical tractability and susceptibility to formal analysis have almost certainly contributed to the choice of the variables and to the neglect of the prime determinants of material progress.

The use of the mathematical models of development also obscures a significant difference between functional relationships and historical processes: the outcome of historical process is invariably affected by the manner and method by which it is brought about, which does not usually apply to the functional relationships of development models.

These criticisms do not, of course, apply to all uses of mathematics in development economics. For instance they do not apply to demography where the basic concepts and ideas (though not necessarily the available statistical information) are sufficiently firm for effective use of mathematics. But this situation is rather exceptional. Mathematics is extensively applied in development economics especially by exponents of the consensus, in contexts in which the basic concepts are so vague that they are often quite empty of specific content. And even when attempts are made to define the concepts with some precision the available empirical evidence is usually insufficient to put substance into the formal relationships.

27. It is often urged that criticism of the use of mathematics in development economics, or elsewhere in economics, reflects obscurantism usually related to a failure to understand the uses and potentialities of mathematics. This often heard contention is unsubstantial. It is akin to the suggestion that only artists can act legitimately as art critics. Moreover, if only those qualified in a technique can judge its relevance and potentialities in a discipline it is difficult to see who can assess the relative merits of widely different methods of enquiry for the purposes of the particular discipline, as for instance the use of mathematics, anthropology and history for the purpose of development economics. Assessment of the value of criticism of a method or of a technique depends properly on the cogency of the criticism, especially of the reasons advanced for suggesting that a technique has not proved illuminating. The technical qualifications of the critic (in the sense of a capacity to perform the functions or activities whose performance he examines) are irrelevant.

However, criticism is likely to gain in effectiveness if the critic is an unquestioned master of the method to the use of which in a particular context he objects. For this reason I shall quote certain observations by the late Norbert Wiener who, whatever his eccentricities, was undoubtedly one of the great figures of modern mathematics. Some of his remarks are most pertinent to the use and display of mathematical symbols in development economics. Because of the special relevance of his remarks to development economics, the eminence of the source and the unfamiliarity of the work, I shall quote at some length.

The success of mathematical physics led the social scientist to be jealous of its power without quite understanding the intellectual attitudes that had contributed to this power. The use of mathematical formulae had accompanied the development of the natural sciences. Just as primitive peoples adopt the Western modes of denationalised clothing and of parliamentarism out of a vague feeling that these magic rites and vestments will at once put them abreast of modern culture and technique, so the economists have developed the habit of dressing up their rather imprecise ideas in the language of the infinitessimal calculus.

In doing this, they show scarcely more discrimination than some of the emerging African nations in the assertion of their rights. Very few econometricians are aware that if they are to imitate the procedure of modern physics and not its mere appearance, a mathematical economist must begin with a critical account of these quantitative notions and the means adopted for collecting and measuring them.

To assign what purports to be precise values to such essentially vague quantities is neither useful nor honest, and any pretense of applying precise formulae to these loosely defined quantities is a sham and a waste of time.[26]

If development economics succeeds in discerning sufficient uniformities for the establishment of an analytical system with

26 *God and Golem*, Cambridge, Mass. 1964, pp. 89–90.
Wiener also explains (*ibid* pp. 87 f.) that he deliberately refrained from emphasizing the possibilities of cybernetics in economics and sociology because he was convinced that the mathematical practitioners of these subjects would misuse it through misapprehension of the proper application of mathematics and of the limitation of mathematical techniques in the social sciences.
Wiener was, of course, not the only critic of mathematical economics with high credentials. Keynes's and Stigler's remarks on this subject are familiar and easily accessible.

firm unambiguous concepts there may well be scope for the proper application of mathematics in this field, even beyond such specialist areas as demography and some branches of macro-economics. Such advance may well take place. However, there are grounds for believing that mathematics will continue to be of limited applicability in development economics. The application of mathematics has been most successful in those disciplines where the variables are relatively few, their interaction comparatively readily ascertainable and the parameters stable. Development economics examines whole economic systems, or at least large parts of systems, in the process of change. Both the system and its interrelated components are affected by countless past and present factors which are again interrelated. Further, many of the major or even dominant influences, notably human capacities and attitudes, can neither be readily incorporated into formal analysis, nor can they be readily quantified. An economic system and its components are all the time affected by the simultaneous operation of the countless interwoven past and present influences, the force of which differs in space and varies through time. Even if the operation of these interrelated influences can be described in formal mathematical terms, the relevant information is practically never available for an assessment of the relative importance of the different past and present influences; and even if the information is available in some instances, the relevant magnitudes would not be constant in space and time. 28. The liberal use of mathematical symbols in some expositions of the consensus has enhanced the prestige of the authors and of the consensus by conveying a misleading idea of rigour and objectivity of approach and method. A similar influence has been exercised by the use of unwarranted quantification and of inappropriate classification. A neglect of non-quantifiable determinants of development, and an uncritical reliance on correlation analysis are two facets of the uncritical belief in quantification. The former factor has already been noted. Brief reference may be in order to the inappropriate use of correlation analysis. Development economics is cluttered up with spurious correlations (such as the correlation between the relative importance of the manufacturing industry and the level of real income; or between changes in the price level and the rate of development) partly because so many practitioners do not distinguish between a functional relationship and an unanalysed statistical correlation; the discussions on the relation between manufacturing industry and economic development provide familiar instances.[27]

Many of the classifications which are prominent in the consensus literature convey inappropriately the presence of clear distinctions which can serve as basis for analysis or policy. The division of the world into developed and underdeveloped countries, or of economic activity into primary, secondary or tertiary activities, are familiar instances. The distinctions implied by these classifications are arbitrary and blurred. Yet the process of classification suggests by inappropriate analogy with the classifications in natural science that clear differences of analytical and practical significances have been established. Perhaps even more important has been the role of inappropriate classification in inducing disregard of connections and interactions, the recognition of which is necessary for an understanding of the sequence of events. An example is provided by the sharp distinction between consumption and investment in conditions where a higher level of consumption induces a higher level of economic performance, including additional investment. The various types of interaction between variables and parameters, already instanced in this paper especially in Section IV, tend also to be obscured by arbitrary classifications. The process of classification often serves unavowed political purposes, as for instance the promotion of the collection of activities arbitrarily classified as manufacturing, or the pursuit of income and wealth transfers in favour of countries designated as underdeveloped.

29. These considerations of methodology do not warrant the conconclusion that historical study cannot be objective, or that in this field one opinion is as good as another, or that illuminating insights cannot be gained, or specified generalizations established. But the methods by which insights are gained and generalizations established in the study of historical processes differ from those of the sciences, especially of the natural sciences. The methods required include the

27 There is so much confusion on this subject in development economics that a simple example may be useful. There is almost certainly a very high statistical correlation over any period of a few decades in the twentieth century between the population growth of a randomly selected country (a), the general level of prices in a randomly selected country (b), and the growth of GNP of a similarly selected country (c). It has not yet been suggested that these correlations reflect functional relationships.

And even when a correlation does reflect a functional relationship, statistical correlation by itself cannot distinguish between a dependent and an independent variable.

observation of phenomena and events likely to prove representative or influential, the tracing of significant connections by observation or the use of documentary material, the collection of evidence from various sources, and the relation of the conclusions to such evidence, including evidence normally handled by disciplines other than history or economics, especially cognate disciplines such as social anthropology. Such procedures need not lack objectivity, rigour or depth. The conclusions reached, on the other hand, differ in character from the generalizations of the theoretical sciences; in particular however successful and illuminating they are they cannot be subject to the test of refutability.

Recognition that the method of obtaining the insights and establishing uniformities differ in some respects between disciplines, that the methods of study and the test procedures appropriate to some disciplines are inappropriate elsewhere, does not justify either the assumption of anti-intellectual attitudes, or the suggestion that only the methods closely analogous to those used in the interpretation of nature are intellectually respectable.

The failure to appreciate the relevance of the methods and tasks of historical interpretation, and the problems confronting the historian, has much affected the substance and tenor of discussion in development economics, and has led to much misdirected effort. In particular it has contributed to the inappropriate emphasis on quantification and classification and also to the prestige both of long-range historicist forecasts and the employment of quasi-mathematical methods. By the same token it has also discouraged the adoption of the methods of serious historical study in development economics including reliance on first-hand evidence and primary sources, the assessment and comparison of different types of evidence and the tracing of connections. It has promoted the timeless approach to development problems and the amputation of the time dimension from the discussion.

The pursuit of political, administrative, commercial or personal interests has often been responsible for the use and the acceptance of inappropriate methods of study and discussion in development economics. But the presence of deep-seated and often unrecognized problems of methodology has contributed both to the adoption of irrelevant and misleading methods and approaches and to the acceptance of the invalid conclusions and results derived from them.

The difference between the methods of historical interpretation and the methods of the theoretical sciences extends to the formulation of their results. The conclusions of the historical sciences are usually more tentative and cannot be generally expressed so categorically as can scientific laws, especially those of the natural sciences. This difference in presentation enhances the intellectual attraction and popular influence of the natural and social sciences compared to those of historical study.

VII

30. Thus a whole range of mutually interacting political and intellectual forces has promoted the spurious consensus in development economics, a consensus the conclusions of which are unrelated to reality. Moreover, the operation of many of these influences has encouraged inappropriate methods of study and presentation, in the sense of methods yielding unilluminating results, and has simultaneously discouraged or even obstructed more appropriate forms of enquiry.

The adverse effect of adoption of inappropriate methods of enquiry may prove to be especially damaging to the intellectual and practical value of development economics, including its potential contribution to the material welfare of the populations of poor countries. The latter may indeed suffer more from the indirect results of the spurious consensus than from the direct results of the application of its invalid conclusions.

It is a matter of some moment both for the prospects of development economics and for its potential contribution to the material welfare of underdeveloped countries that the appropriate scope and limitations of the subject should be more clearly understood than they seem to be at present, especially in the expositions of the consensus. And because inappropriate methods and invalid conclusions in a major branch of the subject are apt to affect other branches as well, the relevance of this issue extends beyond development economics.

31. The insistent demand for the services of economists working in the area of underdeveloped countries and of economic development derives from the belief that economists can assist substantially in the promotion of material progress, a belief which is reflected and encouraged by the use of the term economic development to denote

material progress. This belief is at best over-sanguine, if not largely unfounded.

The public believes, or at least believed until recently, that economics is a more or less exact subject which can and should provide definite answers to a wide variety of questions and demands. And in development economics many of us confirmed readily what people wanted to be told, and what was agreeable and lucrative to the profession, namely that we largely have the answers; and by implication that the important variables are those which we can readily analyse and the politicians can readily influence. What the public and the politicians want to hear is intellectually and materially congenial to us. Indeed quite often the policy proposals of development economists, notably so of the exponents of the consensus, reflect primarily what the governments and the international agencies wish to see proposed. The implications of such a situation for the intellectual standards and prospects of development economics are manifest.

By acquiescing in the belief that development economics can appreciably promote the material progress of underdeveloped countries we have to some extent come to live beyond our intellectual incomes, and perhaps have even come to live on false pretences. Some have certainly gone as far as this, if not further. For instance a prominent writer in development economics said in a widely publicized paper that one of the many vicious circles which afflict underdeveloped countries is a lack of qualified economists for their development planning. In its claim for economists this suggestion comes very near to an intellectual confidence trick. Confidence tricks can be profitable for different indeterminate and usually unpredictable lengths of time. It is impossible either to predict the likely persistence of public confidence in development economics, or to identify the prospective beneficiaries. But the cost of the continued promotion of unwarranted expectations is certain to be very high. The soul of a profession, as well as that of persons, can be lost in attempts to gain the world.

The application of economic reasoning in this general area is of definite but limited value. Economic reasoning can help in the explanation and prediction of certain phenomena and thereby in the assessment of the probable results of certain policies which appreciably affect the prosperity of poor countries. Familiar examples include the effects of relative prices and of price changes on the output of different groups; the effects of incidence of various forms of taxation; and the effects of different monetary policies. These instances of the usefulness of the application of economic analysis have been notably neglected, obscured or even disavowed by the exponents of the development consensus. On occasions economists can even in the present state of knowledge legitimately go beyond these familiar areas and examine the effects of certain policies on the supply of incentive goods or on international economic contacts, as well as the repercussions of these matters on people's behaviour or on certain social institutions.

Moreover, economic analysis has shown considerable promise in recent years in unexpected directions as for instance in the unravelling of some of the factors behind economic nationalism, in the investigation of the factors behind the emergence of certain types of property rights, and also in the analysis and implications of important categories of collective action. Further progress in these various important directions is probable, especially if the work is designed primarily to promote knowledge, rather than to advance particular political results. However, even such results are still very far from the discernment of uniformities about the major determinants of material progress, let alone their incorporation into systematic analysis, especially economic analysis. And it is still further away from the possibilities of influencing substantially the major determinants of development, notably the faculties, beliefs and attitudes of the populations.

The contribution of economics to the material progress of under-developed countries is through the illumination of the scene by disciplined search for truth, an activity of much practical value in this context as in others. It is impossible to predict the extent to which this process can be carried. I believe the scope is already considerable, and that it is probably capable of substantial extension in width and depth.

However, it is improbable that formal economic analysis will in the foreseeable future contribute substantially to the explanation, let alone to the modification, of major determinants of material progress.

45

Is Economics the Science of Choice?*
James M. Buchanan

'. . . from time to time it is probably necessary to detach one's self from the technicalities of the argument and to ask quite naively what it is all about.'
F. A. Hayek, 'Economics and Knowledge'.

Robert Mundell commences his Preface to *Man and Economics* with the assertion: 'Economics is the science of choice.'[1] Most professional scholars who check off the box marked 'Economist' on the Register of Scientific Personnel find no quarrel with Mundell's statement. Despite some danger of once again being called iconoclastic, I propose to examine this assertion seriously and critically. In the process, I shall not discuss what economics is or is not, should or should not be, at least in any direct sense. My question is more elementary and its answer is obvious once it is asked. I want to ask whether a *science* of *choice* is possible at all. Are we not involved in a contradiction in terms?

There is no need to go beyond the everyday usage of the two words. I am neither competent nor interested in detailed etymological inquiry. 'To choose' means 'to take by preference out of all that are available,' 'to select.'[2] Choice is the 'act of choosing,' or 'selecting.' In particular, 'choosing' should be distinguished from 'behaving.' The latter implies acting but there is no reference to conscious selection from among alternatives. Behavior can be predetermined and, hence, predictable. Choice, by its nature, cannot be predetermined and remain choice. If we then define science in the modern sense of embodying conceptually refutable predictions, a 'science of choice' becomes self-contradictory.[3]

---

* I am indebted to David B. Johnson, Roland N. McKean, Gordon Tullock, and Richard E. Wagner for helpful comments.
1 New York, 1968.
2 *Oxford Universal Dictionary*, 1955.
3 In a wholly determinist universe, choice is purely illusory, as is discussion about

47

This elementary proposition is recognized by those who accept the Mundell position. If this is the case, what are the reasons for adherence to what, at first glance, seems glaring methodological inconsistency? To the economist, choice seems to be imposed by the fact of scarcity. Given an acknowledged multiplicity of ends and a limitation on means, it becomes necessary that some selection among alternatives be made. It is in such a very general setting that economics has been classified as the study of such selection, or choice. Once this is done, replacing the word 'study' with the word 'science' becomes a natural extension of language. Is the science so defined devoid of predictive content? Some scholars might answer affirmatively, but surely there are many others who, at the same time that they acquiesce in Mundell's statement, busy themselves with the empirical testing of hypotheses. Are such professionals unaware of their methodological contradictions? It seems useful to try to answer these questions in some detail.

I The Categories of Economic Theory

1 *The Logic of Economic Choice*

The legitimacy of a 'science of choice' may be questioned, but there should be no doubts about the usefulness of a 'logic of choice.' Much of orthodox economic theory is precisely this, and is, therefore, concerned with choice, as such. This logical theory provides students with the 'economic point of view' and it can be posed in either a normative or a positive setting. In the former, the logic reduces to the economic principle, the simple requirement that returns to like units of outlay or input must be equalized at the margins in order to secure a maximum of output. In this most general sense, the principle is empirically empty. It instructs the chooser, the decisionmaker, on the procedures for making selections without requiring that he define either his own preference ordering of output combinations or the resource constraints within which he must operate. Empirical emptiness should not, however, be equated with useless-

---

choice. I do not treat this age-old issue, and I prefer to think that the subject discussed as well as the discussion itself is not illusory.

ness. If a potential chooser is made aware of the principle in its full import, he will weigh alternatives more carefully, he will think in marginal terms, he will make evaluations of opportunity costs, and, finally, he will search more diligently for genuine alternatives. The norms for choice can be meaningfully discussed, even if the specific implementation takes place only in the internal calculus of the decision-maker. Instructing the decision-maker as to how he should choose may produce 'better' choices as evaluated by his own standards.

There is a positive counterpart to the logic of choice, and this extends theory to the interaction among separate decision-makers. Commencing with the fact that choosers choose and that they do so under constraints which include the behavior of others, the economist can begin to make meaningful statements about the results that emerge from the interaction among several choosers. Certain 'laws' can be deduced, even if conceptually refutable hypotheses cannot be derived. Analysis makes no attempt to specify preference orderings for particular choosers. The 'law' of choice states only that the individual decision-maker will select that alternative that stands highest on his preference ordering. Defined in purely logical terms, this produces the 'law of demand.' In this way, trade or exchange can be explained, even in some of its most complex varieties. Characteristics of equilibrium positions can be derived, these being defined in terms of the coordination between expected and realized plans of the separate decision-takers.

In the strictest sense, the chooser is not specified in the pure logic of choice. Under the standard assumptions, the analysis applies to the individual. But the logic requires no such limitation; it applies universally. The norms for efficient choice can be treated independently of the processes through which decisions are actually made. It is not, therefore, explicitly in error to present decision-making norms for nonexistent collective entities who do not, in fact, choose. Under some conditions, it may be helpful to discuss the economizing process 'as if' such entities existed, although, as we shall note in Section II, this is the source of much confusion.

In its normative variant, the logical theory of choice involves the simple principle of economizing, nothing more. This is the mathematics of maxima and minima. Much of modern economic theory is limited to various elaborations on this mathematics. By modifying the formal properties of the objective function and the constraints, interesting exercises in locating and in stating the required conditions for insuring satisfaction of the norms can be produced. Whether or not such exercises command too much of the professional investment of modern economists remains an open question.

The logical theory of interaction among many choosers may also be classified as pure mathematics. But this mathematics is not that which has attracted major interest of the professionals in that discipline, and there is some legitimacy in the economists' pre-emptive claim. Game theory, as one part of a general theory of interaction, owes its origin to a mathematician, but the elegant theory of competitive equilibrium was developed by economists. Major strides are being made in this purely logical theory of inter-action among many choosers, some of which are aimed at relating game theory, more generally the theory of coalition formation, to the theory of competitive equilibrium. The marginal productivity of mathematically-inclined economists in this area of research appears much higher than that which is aimed at working out complex variations of the simple maximization problem.

2   The Abstract Science of Economic Behavior

In the logical theory summarized, no objectives are specified. Choice remains free, and because of this, it remains choice. As we move beyond this pure logic, however, and into economic theory as more generally, if ambiguously, conceived, choice becomes circumscribed. Specific motivation is imputed to the decision-maker, and it is seldom recognized that, to the extent that this takes place, genuine 'choice' is removed from the theory. What we now confront is *behavior*, not choice, behavior that is subject to conceptually predictable laws. The entity that acts, that behaves, does so in accordance with the patterns imposed by the postulates of the theoretical science. The actor is, so to speak, programmed to behave in direct response to stimuli. The abstract science of economic behavior, as I have here classified this, has empirical content that is wholly missing in the pure logic of economic choice. This content is provided by restricting the utility function. Several degrees of restrictiveness may be imposed. Minimally, nothing more than a specification of 'goods' may be introduced. From this alone, conceptually refutable hypotheses emerge. The acting-behaving unit *must* choose more of any 'good' when its 'price' relative to other 'goods' declines.[4] Additional restrictiveness takes the form of specifying something about the internal trade-offs among 'goods' in the utility function of the behaving unit. This step produces the *homo œconomicus* of classical theory who must, when confronted with alternatives, select that which stands highest on his preference ranking, as evaluated in terms of a *numéraire*. The pure economic man must behave so as to take more rather than less when confronted with simple monetary alternatives. He must maximize income-wealth and minimize outlays. He must maximize profits if he plays the role of entrepreneur.

Confusion has arisen between this abstract science of economic behavior and the pure logic of choice because of ambiguities that are involved in the several means of bounding the utility functions of the acting units. In the pure logic of choice, the arguments in the utility function are not identified; 'goods' and 'bads' are unknown to the external observer. In any science of economic behavior, the 'goods' must be classified as such. But under minimally-restricted utility functions, specific trade-offs among these may remain internal to the acting units. The individual 'chooses' in the sense that his selection from among several desirable alternatives remains unpredictable to the observer. What we have here is an extremely limited 'science' of behavior combined with an extensive 'logic' of genuine choice. We move beyond this essentially mixed framework when the trade-offs are more fully specified. Additional 'laws of behavior' can then be derived; and, more importantly, predictions can be made about the results of the interaction processes. These predictions can be conceptually refuted by empirical evidence. If internal trade-offs among 'goods' in utility functions are fully specified, behavior becomes completely predictable in the abstract. Normal procedure does not, however, involve the extension to such limits.

As noted earlier, the pure logic of choice may be interpreted in either a normative or a positive sense. If choice is real, it is meaningful to refer to 'better' and 'worse' choices, and the simple maximizing principle can be of some assistance to the decision-taker. By relatively sharp contrast, there is no normative content in the

---

4 This approach may be associated with the work of A. A. Alchian and his colleagues. *Cf.* A. A. Alchian and W. R. Allen, *University Economics*, Belmont, California, 2nd edition 1967.

abstract science of economic behavior. The reason is obvious. The acting unit responds to environmental stimuli in predictably unique fashion; there is no question as to the 'should' of behavior. The unit responds and that is that. Failure to note this basic difference between the pure logic of choice and the pure science of behavior provides, I think, an explanation of the claim, advanced especially by Mises, that economic theory is a general theory of human action.[5] The logical theory is indeed general but empty; the scientific theory is nongeneral but operational.

At this point, it seems useful to refer to the distinction between the 'subjectivist economics', espoused by both Mises and Hayek, and the 'objectivist economics' which is more widely accepted, even if its limitations are seldom explicitly recognized. In the logic of choice, choosing becomes a subjective experience. The alternatives for choice as well as the evaluations placed upon these exist only in the mind of the decision-maker. Cost, which is the obstacle to choice, is purely subjective and this consists in the chooser's evaluation of the alternative that must be sacrificed in order to attain that which is selected. This genuine opportunity cost vanishes once a decision is taken. By relatively sharp contrast with this, in the pure science of economic behavior choice itself is illusory. In the abstract model, the behavior of the actor is predictable by an external observer. This requires that some criteria for behavior be objectively measurable, and this objectivity is supplied when the motivational postulate is plugged into the model. An actor behaves so as to maximize utility, defined in a nonempty sense. It becomes impossible, in the formal model, for an actor to 'choose' less rather than more of the common denominator units, money or some *numéraire* good, when he is faced with such alternatives. Cost, in this objectivist theory, the pure science of economics, is measurable by the observer. This cost is unrelated to choice, as such, since the latter really does not exist. The opportunity cost of using a resource unit in one way rather than another consists in the *money* earnings of that unit in its most productive alternative use. These earnings may be object tively estimated and quantified. In this setting, the cost of a beaver is two deer, and there is no relationship between cost and sacrifice.[6] To say here that nonpecuniary elements may affect choice is to con-

5 *Cf.* Ludwig von Mises, *Human Action*, New Haven 1949.
6 For an extended discussion of the concept of cost in contrasting methodological settings, see my *Cost and Choice* (forthcoming).

52

fuse the model of pure economic behavior with the model of the logic of choice. In so far as nonpecuniary non-economic elements actually enter the resource owner's calculus, the behavioral model is falsified.[7]

The motivational postulate, the behavior of *homo œconomicus*, effectively converts the purely logical theory of choice into an abstract science of behavior. It accomplishes this by replacing the subjectivity of the logical theory by objective payoffs. Generality in explanation is and must be sacrificed in crossing this bridge. But this is replaced by predictability. The abstract science of economic behavior is the familiar world of *ceteris paribus*. This science provides the analyst with tools for discussing the complex interaction of market processes to the extent that individual participants behave economically. Equilibrium characteristics can be objectively described in terms of quantifiable, measurable relationships among variables, among prices and costs. It is this abstract theory upon which most economists rely in making rudimentary predictions about reality. When asked: 'What will happen when an excise tax is placed on Product X?', the professional responds: 'The price of X to consumers will rise, and less will be demanded, provided that other things remain unchanged, and provided that men behave economically.' The last qualifying phrase 'provided that men behave economically' shifts the analysis into the science of behavior and enables conceptually refutable predictions to be advanced. By this qualifier, the economist states that he is preventing actors from behaving other than economically in the theoretical model that he is constructing. As we all recognize, many professionals do not go further than this; they do not consider it a part of their task either to examine the psychology of behavior more fully or to test empirically the predictions that the abstract science enables them to make.

Such methodological aloofness is acceptable only so long as the severe limitations of the scientist's role are appreciated. Failure to

---

7 To avoid ambiguity here, I should note that nonpecuniary 'goods' can be introduced in individual utility functions in the minimally-restricted limits that were discussed above. Given the specification of such 'goods,' conceptually refutable hypotheses about individual behavior can be derived. Nonpecuniary 'goods' tend to be different for different individuals, however, and the limits of any predictive science are reached when those 'goods' which are common to all persons are exhausted. This provides the basis for reliance on the strictly pecuniary motivation in the general model of the economic interaction process.

recognize these limitations leads naive professionals to claim far too much for the science and with such claims they infuriate those critics who concentrate attention on the non-economic content in human choice patterns.

3 The Predictive Science of Economic Behavior

The abstract science is restricted to the derivation of propositions or hypotheses that are conceptually refutable. The realm of predictive science is entered only when these hypotheses are subjected to empirical testing against real-world observations. One of the features of modern economic research has been its shift toward the rigorous testing of hypotheses. The pound of *ceteris paribus* no longer protects the scientist; he must, through imaginative construction of hypotheses and through exhaustive search for appropriate data, try to corroborate the predictions that the theory allows him to make. Because of empirical constraints, the range of his efforts must be more limited than that allowed to the free-floating abstract theorist. Data are difficult to come by, and even when these can be assembled, the hypotheses-tester must be prepared for frustration and failure. Data can, at best, reflect the results of genuine choices made by participants in a very complicated interaction sequence. The economic behavior implicit in these choices may be nonexistent in some cases, and swamped in effect by non-economic considerations in many others. The predictive hypotheses may be refuted at the initial levels of testing. But the scientist cannot readily use such refutation for overthrowing the general laws of behavior derived from the central structure of his theory. He must normally acknowledge his probable failure to isolate the economic from the non-economic elements of choice, and, accordingly, he must acknowledge the continuing challenge of empirical testability for his theoretically-based hypotheses.

This amounts to saying that, despite his efforts, the predictive scientist remains chained to the vision of the economic universe produced in the abstract theory of economic behavior. He can, when successful, show that indeed 'water runs down hill', but, with contrary results, he can rarely, if ever, refute the economic analogue to the law of gravity. At best, the predictive science is an extension of the abstract science. It must incorporate the basic motivational postulate of *homo œconomicus*; indeed this provides the source for deriving the hypotheses to be tested. The paradigms are unchanged over the two subdisciplines.

There are, however, significant differences. In some strict sense, the abstract science treats only of pure economic man, unalloyed by non-economic behavioral traits. Accordingly, the theorems are simple, elegant and aesthetically satisfying. But the real world is a grubby place, and it is this world that must be the raw source for any science that aims at operational validity. In the face of the apparent divergence of the real world from the paradigms of the abstract science, the empirical corroboration of many predictive hypotheses is perhaps surprising.

The fact that his hypotheses refer to the behavior of *many* actors greatly facilitates the predictive scientist's efforts. He need only make predictions about the behavior of average or representative participants in the processes that he observes; he need not hypothesize about the behavior of any single actor. Hence even if non-economic elements dominate the behavior of some participants, and even if these enter to some degree in the choices of all participants, given certain symmetry in the distributions of preferences, the hypotheses derived from the abstract theory may still be corroborated. For example, given comparable institutional constraints, the wage levels for plumbers and carpenters may tend toward equality even if a substantial proportion of plumbers exhibit strong non-economic preferences for their chosen occupation and even if a substantial proportion of carpenters exhibit similar preferences for their own occupation. So long as some sufficient number of persons indicates some willingness to make the occupational shift on purely economic grounds, the hypothesis about wage level equality is supported. The multiplicity of participants generates results that are identical to those predicted in the model that embodies the strict assumption that all actors behave economically.

4   The 'Behavioristic' Science of the Economy

Unless he is able to call upon the motivational postulate of the abstract science, the predictive scientist can scarcely derive the hypotheses that he seeks to test. It is folly for him to abandon this postulate deliberately in some misguided attempt at imitating the methods of the natural scientists who find it impossible to introduce comparable behavioral postulates. 'Scientism' of this sort has been

55

effectively criticized by Hayek[8] and others, and this approach need not be examined in detail here. It seems clear that with no behavioral basis from which to begin his search for uniformities and regularities in the data that he observes, the pure 'behaviorist' is reduced to massive efforts at observation with very limited prospects of successful results. He confronts a universe of prices, quantities, employment levels, measures for national aggregates. He presumably remains aloof from the behavior that generates these data as results, whether this behavior be economic or not. This is not to suggest that such efforts should be wholly abandoned. It seems clear, however, that the deliberate sacrifice of the directional hypotheses provided by the paradigms of economic science should be made with great caution.

A somewhat different behaviorist approach (and one that fits the terminology considerably better) involves an attempt to specify non-economic elements that enter into the individual's choice calculus. This approach, which we may associate with the work of Herbert A. Simon and his colleagues,[9] calls upon psychological insight to assist in the development of motivational patterns that may be considerably more complex than the simple postulates of standard economic theory. Ultimately, the objective parallels those of orthodox economic science, the ability to make predictions about human behavior in the social interaction process. And, to the extent that the hypotheses of standard theory are refuted, such an approach as this offers the only avenue of advance for social science. This approach may proceed by relaxing or modifying the restrictions placed on individual utility functions, or, alternatively, the procedure may involve dropping the utilitarian framework.[10]

II   The Confusions of Economic Theory

Economics, as this discipline is currently interpreted, embodies elements of each of the four categories listed. The confusions arise

8 *Cf.* F. A. Hayek, *The Counter-Revolution of Science*, Glencoe, Ill. 1955.
9 *Cf.* H. A. Simon, *Models of Man*, New York 1957.
10 This summary review does not do justice to the approach under discussion. For the most part, the contributions here have been made by social scientists in disciplines other than economics. Indeed, to the extent that social 'science' other than economics exists at all, it must be produced by those who adopt the approach summarized here.

from the failure of economists to understand the categorical distinctions. Many of the continuing and unresolved arguments over particular methodological issues can be traced more or less directly to this source.

1   The Derivation of Policy Norms

One of these arguments concerns the relevance of theory for deriving policy conclusions. I shall illustrate some of the confusion here through the familiar prisoner's dilemma of game theory, interpreted variously in terms of the categories of Section I. The pedagogic advantages of this construction are immense; properly employed the dilemma allows us to introduce in a two-person interaction model many of the relevant issues of economic policy in the large.

Figure 1 presents the dilemma in a form slightly modified from its classic setting. The game depicted is positive-sum. The first term in each cell indicates the payoff to A, the player who chooses between rows. The second term shows the payoff to B, the player who chooses between columns. Each player's result depends on the behavior of the other, but, for each player, there is a dominating strategy shown by the second row and second column. The independent-behavior solution, shown in the south-east cell of the matrix, depicts the dilemma; the combined payoffs are larger in the north-west cell.

With nothing more than the payoff matrix of Figure 1, something has been said about the interaction of the two players. Their choice behavior has been related to the structure of the game itself, and

Player B

Player	50, 50	20, 60
A	60, 20	30, 30

Figure 1

57

the possible conflict between the independent-adjustment solution and the combined-payoff potential outcome has been shown. None the less, it should be noted that, to this point, nothing has been said about the nature of the payoffs. These have been treated strictly as numerical indicators of that which motivates choice behavior. In some respects, these payoffs may be thought of as being defined in utility units, so long as the purely subjective nature of utility in this context is kept in mind. In this setting, we have remained strictly in the pure logic of choice. There is absolutely no predictive content in the analysis.[11]

We move from this pure logic of choice into the abstract science of economic behavior when we define the payoffs objectively. To do this, we need only to put dollar signs in front of the numbers in the matrix illustration of Figure 1. The solution seems to remain as before, but it is now limited to those situations where players do, in fact, behave economically. There will be no convergence to the south-east cell if players in the real world should choose to behave co-operatively rather than independently. The abstract theory of economics says that they will behave economically, that the south-east cell is the 'solution' to the game. This prediction may be falsified, at least conceptually.

At this level, it becomes legitimate to derive limited policy implications from the analysis. As they behave in the real world, individuals are observed to adopt the dominating strategies, as these are identified in the eyes of the observer. In the objectified payoff structure imputed to the participants, there appears to exist a conflict between the independent-adjustment outcome and the jointly-desired optimal outcome. Given nothing more than the potentiality of this conflict, it becomes plausible for the political economist to consider modifications in the choice structure that would enable individual participants to eliminate such a conflict, if indeed it should exist. If ways and means can be found to remove the restrictions of the potential dilemma, if institutional rearrangements can be made which will allow independent behavior of the participants to produce results that may be mutually more beneficial than those observed under present environmental conditions, these should, of course, be suggested. (In the strict prisoner's dilemma example, and limiting attention to the world of the two prisoners only, the

11 *Cf.* John C. Harsanyi, 'A General Theory of Rational Behavior in Game Situations', *Econometrica*, 34 (1966), 613 f.

58

introduction of communication between the two persons represents such an institutional change.) This point was recognized and well expressed by Sir Dennis Robertson when he called upon the economist to suggest ways to minimize the use of 'that scarce resource Love.'[12] Since Adam Smith, economists have been within the bounds of methodological propriety when they have proposed organizational-institutional arrangements that channel behavior that may be, but need not be, economically motivated in the direction of promoting what may be, but need not be, mutually desired economic objectives.

This very general policy position, which I shall call Smithean, requires minimal empirical backing along with minimal ethical content. All that is required is the conceptual possibility that payoffs relevant for individual behavior should be directionally linked with those emerging from the postulate of economic science. So long as a person may, other things equal, respond to the change in stimuli, as objectified, in the direction suggested by the central postulate of the theory, the economist is justified in his search for institutional arrangements that will remove the restrictiveness of the dilemma, should it exist. In a very general sense, this amounts to little more than opening up avenues for potential trades which participants may or may not find it advantageous to exploit. The policy prescription is, in effect, limited to suggestions for widening the range for potential choice.[13]

To the extent that the empirical testing of hypotheses supports the central behavioral postulate of the abstract theory, the productivity of Smithean institutional reforms is enhanced. But the corroboration of the behavioral postulate by empirical evidence implies much more than the *ceteris paribus* limits of the abstract theory. Such corroboration indicates that economic behavior dominates all non-economic elements of choice in the specific context examined. This offers a temptation to go much beyond the general institutional reforms implied by the Smithean position. If man can be shown to behave in some more direct relationship to an objectified payoff structure than the *ceteris paribus* potentiality

12 D. H. Robertson, 'What Does the Economist Economize?', in *Economic Commentaries*, London 1956.
13 For an earlier and somewhat different statement of this position see my 'Positive Economics, Welfare Economics, and Political Economy,' *Journal of Law and Economics*, II (October 1959), 124–138. Reprinted in *Fiscal Theory and Political Economy*, Chapel Hill 1960.

implied by the abstract theory, direct manipulation of his behavior seems to become possible through the appropriate modification in the conditions for choice. It is one thing to say that, when given the opportunity, an individual will choose more rather than less provided other elements affecting his choice remain unchanged. It becomes quite a different thing to say that the representative individual will choose more rather than less in terms of objectified units in the *numéraire* without regard to non-economic influences on his choice situation. Rarely will the multidimensional complexity of real-world choice allow results of such simplicity to be adduced. But, if it should do so, specific control of individual behavior through imposed changes in the payoff structures might be possible.

It is precisely at this point that a pervasive and fundamental error emerges. The false step is taken when the explicitly objectified payoff structure that is postulated for use in the abstract theory of economic behavior is translated into direct guide lines for the explicit manipulation of choice alternatives. This procedure must assume that the actual *choice-maker* in the real world *behaves* strictly as the pure economic man of the theorist's model. Markets are held to 'fail' because of the dilemma-type situations that are confronted by the idealized man of the theorist's analytical model. As a follow-up to this, policy suggestions are made which incorporate this rarified behavioral postulate as reality. In a genuine sense, this whole procedure is absurd.

The point can be illustrated with the matrix of Figure 1. The abstract theory bases its elaboration of the interaction processes on the postulate that individuals behave economically in the sense that they respond to objectified and externally measurable payoffs. In this context, it is meaningful to say that, in the model, Player A selects Row 2 rather than Row 1 because of the $10 difference in payoff, regardless of what he predicts about B's behavior. It is meaningful to say that, in this model, the opportunity cost to Player A, 'that which could be avoided by his not taking Row 2', is $10 in foregone payoffs. But this opportunity cost, embodied in the theoretical model for behavior, cannot then be taken as the specific basis for policy prescription aimed at manipulating A's actual choice behavior. This violates the purpose and meaning of the abstract theory and, as suggested, has little or no empirical base. Despite this, such procedure is manifest in a substantial part of modern economic policy discussion.

60

It is not caricature to say that modern policy discussion, which I shall call Pigovian, proceeds as follows, still within the matrix illustration of Figure 1. The economist proposes a 'corrective' tax on Player A, a tax designed to make the costs that he privately confronts equivalent to those that are confronted by the collectivity in the two alternatives that are faced. The general welfare criterion becomes equality between *private* and *social* cost. To implement this result, private costs must be modified; but in order to know by how much, some assumption must be made about private payoff structures. The orthodoxy proceeds as if the purely economic man exists. The criterion calls for a tax of $10+ to be imposed on A's returns in Row 2 (or a subsidy of $10+ on his returns in Row 1). Given this change in his alternatives, Player A (similarly for Player B) will be motivated to 'choose' that alternative that is jointly desired. The efficient collective outcome will be generated. The emphasis has been subtly shifted from the exploitation of potential gains-from-trade to the attaining of specifically defined results.

As the construction shows, if either A or B should behave non-economically the suggested modification of the payoff matrix may not produce the desired results. Suppose, for example, that both players value independent action highly and are willing to sacrifice economic gain to secure this objective. In this instance, the independent-adjustment solution in the south-east cell remains dominant, regardless of the imposition of the suggested corrective tax or subsidy. Some tax (or subsidy) will, of course, result in behavioral change, but the outcome may be less rather than more desirable in some 'social' sense. The dilemma indicated to be present in objectified payoff structure may not exist when payoffs relevant to genuine choices are incorporated in the matrix. The artificiality of any objectified payoff structure, as conceived by the external observer, tends to be overlooked with the consequence that 'dilemmas' which exist only in the mind of the observer may be imputed to actual participants in an interaction process.

The point of emphasis is clear. The costs that influence 'choice' are purely subjective and these exist only within the mind of the decision-maker. The economist may, within limits, discuss this 'choice' provided that he remains within what we have called the 'logic of choice.' He cannot, however, plug in the *homo œconomicus* introduced in his abstract models of economic behavior and then use this as the basis for constructing specific choice-influencing

61

constraints aimed at welfare improvements. Individuals choose on the basis of their own preference orderings; they may, within limits, behave as the abstract theory of economics postulates. But rarely do they behave strictly as the automatons of the analytical models. Yet this is precisely the unrecognized assumption that is implicit in most modern policy discussion.

The critical distinction to be made is that between what I have called the Smithean policy position and what I have called the Pigovian policy norms. In the former, organizational-institutional changes, modifications in the structure of property rights, require only that possible conflicts between individually-adjusted behavior and mutually-desired collective outcomes be recognized. Specific definition of 'efficient' or 'optimal' results is not needed. Such results are allowed to emerge from the choice process itself. In the Pigovian framework, by contrast, property rights are normally assumed to be fixed exogenously. Corrective measures take the form of specific modifications in the choice conditions that are confronted by individual participants. Clearly, this approach to policy requires much more knowledge about the actual preference orderings of individuals. Efficiency in outcomes is no longer defined by the observed absence of further gains from trade as revealed by the behavior of traders. This Smithean definition is replaced by the objectively defined set of equalities central to theoretical welfare economics.

The error extends through much of modern economics. This was at the base of the debate over the possibility of socialist calculation that took place in the 1930s. Mises and Hayek were, I think, indirectly making essentially the same point that I have tried to make here. Their arguments failed to convince their fellow economists; most economists continue to think that efficiency, at least ideally, can be produced by the enforcement of output and pricing *rules*, that these can effectively substitute for the modification in *property rights* dictated by the particular economic setting.

2 *'Scientific' Decision-Making* for *the Collectivity: Systems Analysis, Operations Research, Cost-Benefit Analysis*

The confusions embodied in the Pigovian norms are complemented by an even more elementary set of confusions when the economist extends his range to the 'choices' of the collectivity. He tends to be trapped in the scarcity-choice maximization nexus, and it is not at all easy for him to accept the fact that a collective 'decision-maker' or 'chooser' is nonexistent. Failing this, he tends to conceptualize some supra-individual entity which makes effective 'choices,' which maximizes some objective function subject to appropriately defined constraints. This procedure allows the analyst to produce interesting and self-satisfying results. But error arises when either the analyst or his interpreters consider such results applicable to real-world issues.

Analysis of this sort is two dimensions away from real-world relevance. In the first place, the 'logic of choice' for the single decision-maker is applied to a situation where no such person or entity exists. Since there is no maximizer, analysis is of questionable value when it is based on the assumption that one exists.[14] In the second place, the costs and benefits of alternative courses of action must be objectified if the analyst is to do more than present his own value orderings. This objectification runs into the same difficulty as that noted in connection with the Pigovian approach. There may be little or no relationship between the objectively defined costs and benefits and the evaluations that individuals place on alternatives in actual choice situations.

In this latter respect, the analyst has even less to fall back on than the Pigovian welfare economist. The abstract science of economic behavior with its embodiment of economic man does provide some basis for considering modifications in the conditions of choice, as faced by acting persons. For the cost-benefit analyst, however, there is no prospect of modifying the alternatives facing individual choosers. He must advance norms for choice itself. He is advising the collectivity quite specifically concerning how it 'should' choose. Even if the complexities of group decision-making are ignored, the subjective evaluations of individuals are of a different dimension from the objectively quantifiable measurements placed on alternatives by the analyst. And it should be emphasized here that this difficulty is not removed by allowing the careful analyst to introduce 'nonquantifiable' elements into his calculus. In point of fact, the more subjective that his own calculus becomes, the *less* relevant become his efforts. At best, he may be able to place values

14 These comments apply only to the orthodox analyses under discussion here. It is possible to advance understanding of actual processes of group decision-making through an extension of the pure logic of choice applied to individual participants in these processes. In this approach, there need be no presumption that the collectivity, as such, maximizes anything, or indeed itself exists.

63

on cost and benefit streams that would characterize the world in which all men behave economically. This calculus would be of limited, but perhaps of positive value. Once this standard drawn from the behavioral postulate of the abstract science is left behind, however, there is nothing that the analyst can provide that assists in the understanding of actual collective decision processes.

III Conclusions

Modern economics, as practiced by professional scholars, embodies confusions that are fundamentally methodological. These have their historical foundations in the failure of economists to establish an effective synthesis between the objective and the subjective theory of value. The issues did not emerge with clarity, however, until efforts were made to extend the applicability of economic theory beyond its traditional limits. So long as the task of theory remained that of 'explaining' the functioning of a market system, objective and subjective elements could exist side by side without open contradiction. During the past half-century, however, theory has been called upon to do much more than this. It has been employed to derive norms for policy aimed at making allocation more 'efficient'. Economists have, in other words, proceeded as if theirs were a 'science of choice'.

It is in such extensions that the confusions that I have stressed in this paper have emerged. The critical methodological oversight was that which Hayek emphasized, with clarity but to little avail, in several of his fundamental papers in the late 1930s and early 1940s. The failure of economists to recognize that the sense data upon which individuals actually choose in either market or political choice structures are dimensionally distinct from any data that can be objectively called upon by external observers led directly to the methodological chaos that currently exists. Economics seems unlikely to escape from this chaos for many years, if indeed it survives at all as an independent discipline. Few economists are wholly free of the confusions that I have discussed. For myself, I advance no claim that my own thinking has yet fully rid itself of the paradigms of neoclassical orthodoxy.

Wage-Push Inflation Once More
Gottfried Haberler

Professor Hayek has consistently held the view that labor unions have become an increasingly serious threat to price stability and full employment and that they tend seriously to endanger the working of the individualistic price economy. He has criticized Keynes for assuming that workers and their unions are subject to strong money illusion and he has pointed out that union leaders as well as the rank and file are becoming more and more price conscious and concerned with *real income* rather than nominal wage rates. He also has analyzed the dangers inherent in this development of collective bargaining.[1]

It is clear that prolonged inflation has the effect of making people more and more price conscious and to erode money illusion. What is really surprising is that it takes so long and that it is apparently still possible to revive the faith in money fairly rapidly by comparatively short periods of price stability.

In the present essay I shall, however, not explore for how long we can count on money illusion to survive, nor shall I try to analyze what will happen after it has been destroyed. I shall rather discuss once again the more modest question whether unions really are a threat to price stability. On this question, liberal economists – using the word 'liberal' in the traditional sense of *laissez-faire* and not in the modern perverted sense – are not all of the same opinion. Hayek

1 See e.g. his 'Unions, Inflation and Profits,' in Philip D. Bradley (ed.), *The Public Stake in Union Power*, Charlottesville, 1959, reprinted in F. A. Hayek, *Studies in Philosophy, Politics and Economics*, London and Chicago 1967.
The same criticism of Keynes has been made by the late Albert Hahn, and James Tobin, a good Keynesian, has pointed out (see *The New Economics* edited by S. E. Harris, New York 1947) that Keynes assumes contradictory behavior of the same individuals in their capacity as savers (in which they are supposed to be swayed entirely by real income) and in their capacity as bargainers for wages (in which they are supposed to be concerned with money wages only).

believes, along with William Fellner, Friedrich Lutz, the present writer and others, that modern collective bargaining by powerful labor organizations confronts the monetary authorities with the disagreeable dilemma either to permit enough inflation to maintain full employment at the higher, union-imposed money wages, or to keep prices stable at the expense of a certain amount of unemployment.[2] (This does not imply, it should be observed, acceptance of the theory of the Phillips Curve in the sense that there exists a *stable long-run* trade-off between inflation and unemployment.)

A much more cheerful and relaxed view about the monetary impact of labor unions is offered by Milton Friedman and some other economists in the liberal camp.[3] Friedman and his followers deny that there is such a thing as 'wage- (or cost-) push inflation' as distinguished from a 'demand-pull inflation.' There is no trade-off between unemployment and inflation (except perhaps in the very short run). The power of labor unions to push up the wage level has been greatly exaggerated and, if the monetary authorities stood firm and refused to increase the quantity of money by more than, say, 3–5 per cent a year, the economy could be set on a smooth growth path – very mild fluctuations apart – with substantially full employment and stable prices, unions or no unions.

This is indeed a very different and much more encouraging picture than the awkward dilemma of unemployment or inflation visualized by the other group. But it must not be overlooked that the two schools agree on a number of very important points. For both of them inflation is fundamentally a monetary phenomenon in the sense that it could not go on for long without an ever growing money supply. They agree that labor unions have no power to push up the long-run trend in *real* wages, and Friedman does not deny that well organized unions of certain groups of workers (craft unions) are able to raise the rate of nominal and real wages of their members.[4] Friedman also concedes that unions have

2 Hayek goes, of course, beyond this and gives good reasons why eventually it would require inflation at an accelerating rate to stave off indefinitely any depression or recession. But I shall not go into that problem in the present paper.
3 See e.g., M. Friedman, 'What Price Guideposts?', in George P. Shultz and Robert E. Aliber (eds.), *Guidelines, Informal Controls and the Market Place*, Chicago 1966, and Allan Meltzer, 'Is Secular Inflation Likely in the U.S.?' in *Monetary Problems of the Early 1960s*, Georgia State College, Atlanta, Georgia 1967.
4 Whether the real income of the group as a whole can be raised depends, of course, on the elasticity of demand for the product and the elasticity of substitution

helped to make money wages almost entirely rigid downward.[5]

Furthermore, it is generally agreed that the replacement of competition by monopoly, be it in labor or commodity markets, will have the one-shot effect of pushing up wages and prices. This is not denied by the critics of the cost-push theory. Thus Milton Friedman himself shows that 'from 1933 to 1937, the NIRA, AAA, Wagner Labor Act and the associated growth of union strength led to *increasing* market power of both industry and labor and thereby produced upward pressure on a wide range of wages and prices.' He points out that 'the concomitant rapid growth in nominal income at the average rate of 14 per cent per year from 1933–1937 . . . reflected a rise in the quantity of money of 11 per cent per year.' This rise in nominal income (expenditure) cannot be explained, he says, by the cost push. But 'the cost push does explain why so large a part of the growth in nominal income was absorbed by prices' and only a correspondingly smaller part reflected by rising output and employment. 'Despite unprecedented levels of unemployed resources, wholesale prices rose nearly 50 per cent from 1933 to 1937 and the cost of living by 13 per cent. Similarly, the wage cost-push helps to explain why unemployment was still so high in 1937, when monetary restriction was followed by another severe contraction.'[6]

This was, indeed, an extreme case of wage and cost-push inflation[7] and the reader may ask what is then the difference between the two schools? The difference is that the critics of the cost-push

5 Downward rigidity of wages can conceivably bring about inflation all by itself, but it is probably not a serious threat to price stability unless downward rigidity of wages is combined with an upward wage push. Suppose overall demand rises in proportion to the gradual growth of output; there is, thus, no inflationary pull. Now assume that there occur from time to time shifts of demand from one group of commodities to others. Then wages will rise where demand increases, but will not fall where demand declines. Thus in the long run it is possible that through this ratchet mechanism the price level will be jacked up. A theory of inflation along these lines was put forward by Charles L. Schultze. See his widely quoted study, *Recent Inflation in the U.S.*, Study Paper No. 1, Joint Economic Committee, 86th Congress, 1st Session, Sept. 1958, and my criticism in *Inflation: Its Causes and Cures*, 1966 edition, p. 86.

6 *Loc. cit.*, p. 22.

7 Friedman calls it 'the only example he knows of in the U.S. history when such a cost push was important.' (*Ibid.*) He probably is right that there exists no other case of similar magnitude. But in much milder form wage push is no rarity, as explained in the text below.

between different factors of production and types of labor which together determine the price elasticity of demand for labor and the volume of employment.

67

theory believe that the price-raising power of trade unions and other monopolies is a one-shot affair when market power is first introduced or strengthened, while the wage-push theorists regard it as a continuing force. Thus when the New Deal policies greatly strengthened the market power of unions and business cartels, the newly formed or strengthened monopolies were put in a position to give a strong boost to wages and prices. But it would have required a further increase in monopoly power, the critics of the cost-push theory say, to carry forward the inflationary price boosting.

I am prepared to accept this argument for industrial monopolies; in fact, I have put it forward myself years ago,[8] but I do not believe that it applies to labor unions. The reason is that business monopolies and labor unions cannot be assumed to operate according to the same rules. This is obscured by calling trade unions 'labor monopolies.' They are, of course, monopolies in the sense that they eliminate competition in the labor market and make a group of workers speak out with one voice. But their rules of conduct are quite different from those of industrial monopolies or oligopolies.[9]

Industrial monopolies and oligopolies try to maximize their

8 See my 'Wage Policy and Inflation,' Philip D. Bradley (ed.), *The Public Stake in Union Power*, Charlottesville 1959, p. 75, and *Inflation: Its Causes and Cures*, 1966 edition, pp. 71–73.

9 The basic difference between industrial monopolies and labor unions is often overlooked or ignored. When talking about cost-push inflation many economists feel the urge to demonstrate their social impartiality by blaming industrial monopolists and oligopolists along with labor unions. That there is a difference between the two has, however, been clearly recognized by a group of leading economists representing a cross section of experts from left, right and center who wrote the remarkable report, *The Problem of Rising Prices* (OEEC, Paris 1960). They unanimously reached the conclusion that in the United States in the late 1950s wage push played a major role. 'With demand pressures (in the United States) less intense than in Europe, round after round of wage increases have weakened the competitive position of American industry' (p. 62). They also agree unanimously that there is no counterpart to continuous wage push on the business side. 'We believe that the danger of aggressive pricing to raise profit margins is a limited one. It can add fuel to the fire in an inflationary situation. But it is not likely to be the starting cause, nor can it be a cause of continuously rising prices. In this respect, an increase in profit margins differs from an increase in wages; there can be a wage-price spiral but there cannot be a profit-price spiral' (p. 70). The Committee thus rejected the theory, very popular at that time in the United States, that large corporations in oligopolistic industries continuously 'push up' prices in the same way as unions push up wages.

It is not surprising that the group split on policy recommendations. The majority, including Bent Hansen and Richard Kahn, recommended incomes policies while W. Fellner and Friedrich Lutz were in favor of dealing with the evil at its root by curbing the power of industry-wide labor unions.

profits making allowance, of course, for various constraints – the danger of competitors from at home or abroad entering the field, the risk of government intervention and antagonizing public opinion, etc. Monopoly prices are always higher than prices would be under competition. Hence when competition is replaced by monopolies – as happened on a large scale under the early New Deal policies – prices of the monopolized commodities go up. If the monetary authorities were sufficiently firm, the price *level* could remain stable and in the competitive sphere of the economy prices would fall offsetting the rise in monopoly prices.[10] If total expenditure – nominal income as Friedman calls it – is allowed to go up, the price level will rise, monopoly prices rising faster than competitive prices. Thus the introduction of numerous monopolies in the early 1930s explains, as Friedman points out, why the increase in nominal income was reflected to an abnormally large extent in rising prices and to an abnormally small extent in expanding output and employment.[11] Once, however, monopoly prices have been established and equilibrium is restored, there is no tendency for monopoly prices to go higher and higher unless the underlying situation changes, that is to say monopoly power is further increased. Hence the substitution of monopoly for competition has a one-shot inflationary effect and is not a steady force exerting continuous upward pressure on the price level.[12]

Labor unions behave differently. True, they too seek gains, i.e. higher incomes, for their members and raise the price of labor. But they are out for large *annual* wage increases and not merely for a once-for-all substitution of a higher monopoly wage for the lower

10 Except if wage or price rigidities prevent the price decline.

11 The result was abnormal in view of the large amount of unemployed resources then existing. From 1933 to 1935, over 20 per cent of the labor force was unemployed. In 1936 it was still 16·9 per cent, in 1937 14·3 per cent and in 1938 again 19 per cent. This analysis is fully acceptable, in principle at least, for Keynesians. Thus Alvin Hansen in his *A Guide to Keynes* (New York 1953) points out that 'to the extent that this occurs (viz., that money wage rates rise before full employment is reached) the increase in aggregate demand is unnecessarily dissipated in higher prices with correspondingly less effect on output and employment' (p. 193). It is true, however, that few other Keynesians have stressed this point as much as Hansen has.

12 Naturally, this does not exclude that it takes some time until a newly created or strengthened monopoly has tested the market, evaluated the various constraints mentioned above and found the price that suits it best. Thus during a transitional period prices may rise for a certain period of time after a monopoly has been created or strengthened.

69

competitive wage. The fact that even in the absence of any labor unions, that is in a perfectly competitive labor market, real wages would rise in a progressive economy in accordance with the growing (marginal) productivity of labor, that furthermore money wages would rise even if the price level were kept stable and that money wages rise faster than prices under inflationary conditions[13] – all this makes it a perfectly natural objective for union policy to push continuously for money wage increases that are higher than is compatible with full employment equilibrium at stable prices. There can thus be no question about the wage objectives of labor unions. What can possibly be questioned is the actual importance of this factor.

But, in my opinion, there cannot be the slightest doubt that unions very often, probably in most cases, succeed year after year (or from one contract to the next) in pushing up money wages beyond the level of competitive, full-employment equilibrium at stable prices. At the higher wage, employment will, of course, be lower as a rule than it would be at a lower wage. But the effect on employment is usually not immediately clear and may well be delayed for a considerable period; at any rate, it is strenuously denied by labor leaders. In some cases, however, unions pay the price of lower employment consciously and deliberately.[14] Thus it is generally agreed that the United Mine Workers under the leadership of John L. Lewis traded rapidly increasing wages for dwindling employment in the coal industry. It is hardly open to doubt that in public utilities and in progressive industries, where

13 It is true that inflation strengthens the hand of trade unions, because it offers them an opportunity to secure large increases in money wages which bolsters their prestige and reinforces their hold on the workers, even though a part of these increases is not real. It also stands to reason, as was pointed out earlier, that the transition to a non-inflationary situation is made difficult because when inflation is stopped labor unions have to get used to the fact that in a non-inflationary situation money wage increases cannot be so generous as under inflation. But this does not alter the fact that, apart from any transitional intransigence, unions quite naturally wish to achieve larger wage increases than are compatible with stable prices and full employment.

14 The close connection between wages and employment becomes quite clear in export industries, especially in small countries where exports constitute a large proportion of output and a small fraction of the world market so that the elasticity of demand for the product is very large. For example, in the Netherlands or Switzerland workers know that exports would fall drastically and they would lose their jobs if wage costs were to rise more than elsewhere. That is probably the main reason why wage discipline is so well maintained in these countries.

output rises rapidly and profits and quasi-rents are high, unions are in a specially strong bargaining position and often are able to secure wage increases way above the level at which wages in the economy at large can rise, if full employment at stable prices is to be preserved. That the same is true of steel and automobiles and many other manufacturing industries is only slightly less clear.[15]

A little reflection will convince the reader that, once labor unions have acquired strength, cohesion and discipline, either as a consequence of changed legal status or otherwise, we can expect continuing wage push without any further acquisition of 'market power.' If it is true that unions invested with great monopoly power by the New Deal legislation were able to push up wages and prices from 1933 to 1937 in the face of 'unprecedented unemployment,' we must conclude *a fortiori* that they are able to do the same when unemployment is much lower. No increase in 'market power' is required; in other words, to give a little more precision to that vague term, none of the following changes were needed: more complete unionization of labor, more aggressive union leadership, or more lenient public policy either because of further changes in the legal status (extended privileges or exemptions accorded to unions) or more sympathetic interpretation of the unchanged law or a more favorable attitude of public opinion towards unions. All that was necessary for continued wage push was continuing exercise of the 'market power' created or greatly enhanced by the New Deal legislation.

The experience of 1933–37 was, to repeat, an extreme case of wage push caused by a sudden vast increase in market power. As far as labor is concerned, the market power conferred by the New Deal legislation has never been lost, although it was slightly

---

15 It is generally agreed among economists that in a growing economy, if the price level is to remain stable, prices of the products of progressive industries, where rapid technological improvements take place and cost of production declines more quickly than elsewhere, have to fall. If this price decline is prevented by strong unions being able to capture, as it were, the fruits of technological progress for themselves instead of letting them be passed on to the consumer, the chances are that the price level will eventually be jacked up. The required price differential between fast and slowly progressing industries is in the end restored, at least to some extent, but in the form of prices of progressive industries rising less fast than other prices, not in the form of such prices actually falling. This process, of course, requires that the wage increases obtained in the progressive industries spread, at least to some extent, to the less progressive industries. This is in fact very likely the case.

71

diminished by the Taft-Hartley legislation under the Eisenhower administration.[16] There are, however, many cases of milder wage push on record. For example, during the recession from July 1957 to April 1958 wages and prices continued to creep up in the face of substantial unemployment. It would, furthermore, not be difficult to cite cases where unions were able to secure large wage increases through strike and intimidation in particular industries despite the fact that there was a good deal of unemployment in that particular industry at the time (steel is a notorious example). If unions are able to push up wages in periods of slack, we have a case of overt wage push. But we must assume that they are in an even better position to do it in boom periods when employment and profits are rising and industries operate at high and rising rates of capacity. This means that we must assume that wage push reinforces demand pull.

The upshot is that wage push is a reality even though its influence on the price level (inflation) is often swamped or overshadowed by demand pull, that is, by open monetary inflation. The reality of wage push is sometimes denied on the ground that in the United States only a fraction of the labor force (some 25 per cent) is actually unionized. But this does not disprove the existence of the wage push. In the first place, in most industrial countries other than the United States the percentage is much larger. Second, in the United States non-union wages tend to follow the rise in union wages because employers find it necessary to adjust non-union wages, at least approximately, to union rates, either because differentials have to be maintained for the sake of morale and efficiency, or in order to forestall rapid unionization.

The fact that in periods of rapid open demand-inflation the rise in union wages often lags behind that in some non-union areas such as the service industries, does not prove that unions have no influence in pushing up the level of money wages. It only means that because of the cumbersome process of collective bargaining, especially when large unions are involved, and the length of con-

16 By contrast, the New Deal policy fostering industrial monopolies was discontinued and was later replaced by more vigorous antitrust policies. Moreover, the liberalization of trade in the postwar period and the rising competition from abroad has strongly operated to reduce monopoly power in many industrial areas. In the field of agriculture, however, guaranteed prices for the major products, limitation of production, etc. which can be regarded as monopoly power exercised through government policies, have been continued undiminished.

tract periods of one or two years, wage push may, so to speak, temporarily be overtaken by swift demand-pull inflation. But we can be sure that when unions find they have been napping they will lose little time to make up for opportunities lost, or unauthorized wildcat strikes and breaches of contracts will speed up wage adjustment. The basic fact of wage push is not altered by minor lags and frictions.

I conclude that Hayek is quite right when he sees in labor unions and their policies a threat to price stability. He is probably also right when he foresees serious dangers for the free-enterprise system resulting from the increasingly explicit concern with *real* wages and the erosion of money illusion. This development is highlighted by the spread of cost-of-living clauses in wage and salary contracts and the fact that everywhere many of the so-called 'fixed' incomes – incomes of government officials, policemen, firemen, etc. – have become flexible upward being pushed up by threat of strike and actual work stoppage or work slowdown ('working to the letter of the rules') organized by unions of policemen, firemen and other public servants.

There can be little doubt that union power has been steadily increasing and expanding despite occasional attempts to curb it. The rapid spread of lawlessness and the rise of extreme left radicalism in the universities and elsewhere strengthen the position of unions by giving them an aura of responsibility, conservatism and respectability. These leftist movements, irrational and anarchistic though they are in stark contrast to most unions (even communist-dominated ones), have been trying again and again, more or less successfully, to make common cause with labor unions and they often support unions in their strikes and struggles by organizing boycotts or in more direct ways involving force and violence. It is true that these developments have not yet interfered seriously with the working of the economy, except in France. Moreover, the process of erosion of money illusion has been, to repeat, slower than one might have expected and up to now it has been surprisingly easy to revive faith in money by comparatively short spells of stable prices.

But it surely is too early to discount the worry and concern about these developments as false alarms. The French upheaval in May and June 1968 and its economic aftermath may not remain an isolated event.

Will Market Economies and Planned Economies Converge?
George N. Halm

The Convergence Thesis

Recent developments in the centrally planned and market economies suggest to many observers a convergence of economic systems. This belief contrasts with the previously held conviction that the two systems could not even co-exist for very long. Orthodox Marxists expected the breakdown of capitalism while many Western observers thought that the Soviet experiment would eventually fail. Both parties were victims of wishful thinking.

Not many socialists will support Paul M. Sweezy's[1] statement that the economy of the United States is 'plagued by ever growing problems of unemployment, poverty, and waste.' On the contrary improvement of the centrally-planned economy is now being sought through the application of measures that actually try to emulate important features of the market economies – even at the danger of violating Marx's labor theory of value. On the whole, Marxists have become less extreme, though they express themselves in terms that cannot be interpreted as suggesting anything as mild as convergence. Jan S. Prybyla[2] is probably right in saying that admission of co-existence is, for the time being, the most that can be expected from the Russian side. This makes the convergence thesis a predominantly Western interpretation of development trends.

Western observers of the Soviet economy had to give up ideas of a Russian breakdown at the latest when the Sputnik success made it irrefutably clear that a centrally-planned economy could achieve

1 Paul M. Sweezy, 'Obstacles to Economic Development,' in C. H. Feinstein (ed.), *Socialism, Capitalism and Economic Growth. Essays Presented to Maurice Dobb,* Cambridge 1967, pp. 193–194.
2 Jan S. Prybyla, 'The Convergence of Western and Communist Economic Systems. A Critical Estimate', *The Russian Review*, 23, No. 1 (1964), p. 4.

75

impressive results in priority areas while simultaneously keeping low-priority branches of the economy in rough balance through bureaucratic integration. Indeed, even Ludwig von Mises,[3] the most outspoken critic of socialism, never said that a centrally-planned economy could not operate at all; he merely stated that without price and cost calculations, there could be no economic behavior *'in our sense of the word.'* He pointed out that, without the aid of genuine market processes, a centrally planned economy would suffer from inadequate motivation and factor allocation – the very criticism which in 1965 became the basis of Kosygin's reform proposals.[4]

For many years now there has been little doubt that the two opposed systems are possible in the sense that both are obviously going concerns with a fair chance of survival for the foreseeable future. The Western market economies have managed after World War II to maintain high employment levels (even though at the expense of creeping inflation) and the Soviet economy has succeeded in developing, by trial and error, a modicum of balance between inputs and outputs. Both systems performed better than their opponents expected. 'Co-existence' and 'growth-competition' replaced the waiting for the other system's early demise.

But co-existence need not last. The winner in the systems' growth competition could bring about a one-system world, either peacefully, by inviting emulation, or forcefully, by preponderance of power. This would not be convergence. Convergence implies that the improvements which take place will be due to a softening on both sides. The central planners will make increasing use of prices and profits, and the market system will introduce some sort of government planning. Market and planning are not seen as mutually exclusive organizing principles; they are economic instruments that can be used simultaneously, once the champions of pure systems have divested themselves of their ideological blinkers.

Convergence, supposedly, has already gone quite far. Both systems are making use of formerly forbidden or rejected instru-

3 Ludwig von Mises, *Socialism: An Economic and Sociological Analysis*, New Haven, Conn. 1951, p. 122. (My italics.)
4 A. N. Kosygin, 'On Improving Industrial Management, Perfecting Planning, and Enhancing Incentives in Industrial Production', in Myron E. Sharpe (ed.), *Planning and Profits and Incentives in the USSR*, Vol. 2: *Reform of Soviet Economic Management*, New York 1966, pp. 3 ff.

ments and are becoming more alike every day, until finally the symbiosis of market and plan produces very similar economic structures everywhere. While preconceived opinions and ingrained ideologies may delay this process, irresistible forces are expected to lead both systems together.

Market Economies and Convergence

Characteristic for the convergence trend of market economies we are told is, first of all, a continuous relative growth of the public sector. Not only does the government claim an increasing share of the national product for the satisfaction of collective wants, it also makes itself responsible for an aggregate demand that is neither too large nor too small. Monetary and fiscal policies try to control both inflation and deflation. But these undeniable trends do not prove the growth of central planning in the Western market economies if by central planning is meant the conscious integration of all inputs and outputs from the center. When the government influences the economic climate of a market economy through its credit, tax, and expenditure policies, it does not tell industrial managers what and how to produce and to whom to deliver, nor does it allocate productive resources in a predetermined way. Monetary and fiscal policies, when correctly applied, leave private industry free to make its own decisions.

It was unfortunate that John Maynard Keynes[5] referred to deficit spending as a 'somewhat comprehensive socialization of investment,' an expression that conjured up vague fears of comprehensive and, therefore, central industrial planning. The context, however, made it clear that he did not advocate state socialism. He was exclusively concerned with the regulation of aggregate demand and felt that, once this was successfully accomplished, there was 'no objection to be raised against the classical analysis in which private self-interest will determine what in particular is produced, in what proportion the factors of production will be combined to produce it, and how the value of the final product will be distributed between them.' Keynes was opposed to Soviet-type central planning which to him

5 John Maynard Keynes, *The General Theory of Employment, Interest, and Money*, New York 1936, pp. 376, 378–379, 380.

implied the loss of personal choice 'which is the greatest of all the losses of the homogenous or totalitarian state.'

Nationalization has lost most of its appeal in Western market economies precisely because the government can exercise the necessary indirect controls over aggregate demand and investment without having to aim for public ownership of industry. When consistently applied, monetary and fiscal policies are not aimed against the market, they are compatible with the private enterprise system, they are what Walter Eucken[6] called *systemgerecht*. As Friedrich A. Hayek has emphasized: 'our evaluation of any particular measure of policy will have to depend not so much on its particular results, all of which in most instances we shall in any case not know, but on its being in conformity with the whole system.'[7]

The convergence thesis is not convincing where it misinterprets a mere percentage growth of the public sector or the use of fiscal policies as a growing core of *central planning*. However, there is a second argument.

To John K. Galbraith[8] 'convergence begins with modern large-scale production, with heavy requirements of capital, sophisticated technology and, as prime consequence, elaborate organization. These require control of prices and, so far as possible, of what is bought at those prices. This is to say that planning must replace the market.' The requirements are the same for socialist and capitalist economies. 'In the Soviet-type economies control of prices is a function of the state . . . With us this management is accomplished less formally by the corporations, their advertizing agencies, salesmen, dealers and retailers. But these, obviously, are differences in method rather than purpose. Large-scale industrialism requires, in both cases, that the market and consumer sovereignty be extensively superseded.'

However, the trend is not one-sidedly a trend towards *central* planning. The large-scale organization in industry requires autonomy as much as control over markets. The Soviet system, therefore, is forced to give more freedom to the enterprise, to decentralize, to 'allow the firm autonomy over its planning'.

Galbraith comes to the conclusion 'that convergence between the two ostensibly different industrial systems occurs on all fundamental

6 Walter Eucken, *Grundsätze der Wirtschaftspolitik*, Hamburg 1959, p. 163.
7 F. A. Hayek, *Studies in Philosophy, Politics and Economics*, London, Chicago, 1967, pp. 263–264.
8 John Kenneth Galbraith, *The New Industrial State*, Boston, Mass. 1967, ch. 35.

points.' The cause is the technostructure of modern society in which 'the erstwhile capitalist corporation and the erstwhile communist firm come together as oligarchies of their own members.'

For the capitalist economy Galbraith speaks of 'the socialization of the mature corporation.' His use of the term in this context is more objectionable than Keynes' use of 'socialization' for government control of aggregate demand. Keynes instantly emphasized that this socialization would help strengthen the private enterprise system while Galbraith's use of the term blurs the fundamental difference that separates market economies from centrally-planned economies.

Galbraith follows a long line of economists who have in common that they all failed to see the basic difference that separates the two economic systems. This line leads back to theorists like Gustav Cassel and Frank H. Knight who belittled the importance of public or private ownership of the material means of production with the argument that the same economic problems would have to be solved both in socialism and capitalism. Knight[9] stated that the bare fact of substituting a collectivist for a competitive individualist organization 'does not logically or necessarily imply any change whatever in the empirical course of economic life,' while Cassel[10] tried to show that the principles of pricing hold good for an economy 'in which the State has assumed control of production and reserved for itself the ownership of the material factors of production.' In particular, he wanted to make clear how untrue it is that free competition is a theoretically necessary condition for giving effect to the principle of cost.

Since neither Knight nor Cassel cared to show how cost accounting and factor allocation could work in practice in a centrally planned economy, we cannot be surprised that economists with a lesser grasp of these basic problems felt free to shift from one extreme of the systems-spectrum to the other when the similarities on the surface veiled the fundamental issues. It made no longer any difference whether a given policy or institution belonged to the United States, Nazi Germany or Soviet Russia. The use of market prices here and of central planning there did no longer suggest a basic difference in the economic systems.

9 Frank H. Knight, 'The Place of Marginal Economics in a Collectivist System', *American Economic Review*, 26 (March 1936), pp. 255–266.
10 Gustav Cassel, *The Theory of Social Economy*, New York 1932, pp. 132–133.

Most important among the phenomena that suggested convergence seemed the concentration of economic power in the giant corporation. Even Joseph A. Schumpeter[11] believed that 'the individual leadership of the entrepreneur tends to lose its importance and to be increasingly replaced by the mechanized team-work of specialized employees within large corporations.' Together with 'the shifting of economic activity from the private to the public sphere' this increasing 'bureaucratization of economic life' would lead to a change of the economic system to either socialism or guided capitalism, depending on what terminology we prefer. Obviously, Schumpeter believed in convergence.

Centrally-Planned Economies and Convergence

Soviet experiences, too, seemed to support this special convergence theory through the creation of a 'new managerial class'[12] whose emergence was for some observers the exact counterpart of the 'managerial revolution'[13] in the market economies. That there are many similarities between the giant corporations of the Western market economies and Soviet industrial collectives is obvious. Both are intricate bureaucracies with an advanced internal division of labor; in both, specialized functions are performed by hired experts. But this comparison neglects the most important problem, namely, whether investment, output and factor allocation follow the command of a central plan, or result from essentially free entrepreneurial or corporate decisions based on market data.

As far as prices are concerned, the believers in convergence point out that prices are used in both systems and are 'set' in either case: set by the government in the centrally planned economies and by monopolistic groups and the government in the market economies. But a closer look at the performance of the Soviet economy will show that superficial similarities veil basic differences.

More recently, the Liberman plan and the Kosygin reforms have, indeed, emphasized the role of prices, profit norms and profit rates in the centrally planned economy. The new proposals seem to

11 Joseph A. Schumpeter, 'Capitalism,' in *Encyclopaedia Britannica*, Vol. 4, 1946, pp. 801–807.
12 See Milovan Djilas, *The New Class*, New York 1957.
13 See James Burnham, *The Managerial Revolution*, New York 1941.

revolutionize the Soviet system. It had become increasingly clear that the Soviet economy suffers from the implicit weakness that 'the primary data used for planning and decision-making purposes are generated largely by individuals and groups whose performance is evaluated, and whose rewards and punishments are determined, on the basis of the same data.'[14] The enterprises' estimates are usually much lower than their capacities while they ask for superfluous capital investments and overstate their need for materials, tools, and manpower. This situation, in turn, necessitates the strictest supervision from the center, but the auditing process cannot be very effective because the task simply is too big and the information of the central authorities incomplete and often wrong. These are the main points of Liberman's[15] criticism. The latest reforms try to remedy this situation. Now 'the enterprises are presented with plans with respect to the volume of output and the assortment,' but the new system will 'relieve centralized planning of the petty tutelage over enterprise, of the expensive attempts to influence production not by economic measures but by administrative techniques.'

The change from bureaucratic commands to 'economic levers' is to be brought about through the use of a profit system in which a profitability rate that expresses enterprise profits as percentage of production capital is to be compared with a profitability norm for every branch of production. It is to be assumed (though Liberman is not very clear concerning this point) that the enterprises will now work out their own production 'plans' by trying to maximize their share in the excess of profit rate over profit norm. The new incentive system is to combine central planning with the greatest possible scope for local initiative. If workable, the new system would support the convergence thesis. However, it can be shown that it will meet with enormous difficulties. The following points must be considered:

(1) A profit system must rest on a consistent price structure. Since, according to Liberman, *all* prices are to be set centrally, we have to assume that the planning authorities will be able to create a consistent network of millions of prices and to adjust these prices continuously to changes in government priorities, consumers' preferences,

14 John P. Hardt, Dimitri M. Gallik, and Vladimir Treml, 'Institutional Stagnation and Changing Economic Strategy in the Soviet Union,' in *New Directions in the Soviet Economy*, Joint Economic Committee of the United States Congress, Washington, D.C., 1966, pp. 33–34.
15 Evsei G. Liberman in Myron E. Sharpe (ed.), *op. cit.*, Vol. 1: *The Liberman Discussion; A New Phase in Soviet Economic Thought*, pp. 79, 82, 217.

81

technological changes, and changes in factor supplies. The whole Liberman discussion has not produced one single suggestion as to how this price-setting problem can be solved without the aid of genuine, competitive markets.

(2) In order to apply profit norms and profit rates to 'rubles invested' it will be necessary to know in each case the value of invested capital. But capital values are not known and can be set only arbitrarily.

(3) Liberman suggests the setting of different profit norms for industries with different priority rating and violates, therefore, from the start, the idea of a uniform capital allocation according to opportunity costs.

(4) The co-operation of the managers with the planning authorities will be less wholehearted than the proposal assumes. The managers will be afraid of a stiffening of the profit norms as a result of good performance and, accordingly, will still misinform the center. As before, the managers are in sole possession of the technical knowhow. The earlier fight for low output quotas and high input allocations will now become an argument about prices and profit norms. Where the managers have leeway to substitute profit calculations for their former participation in the formulation of the operational plans, production will be misguided as long as the price guidelines are wrong.

Since it is patently impossible for the Soviet authorities to produce a consistent network of prices, a decisive improvement of the Soviet economy can be sought in two opposite directions:

(1) The system could be decentralized so that the producing units could compete in real markets for productive resources and base their decisions on genuine prices that would emerge from this competitive process:

(2) Centralized controls could be stiffened and commands could become even more detailed. In this way the system would be made immune against wrong prices and against unreliable managerial behavior.

Past experience suggests that an even greater emphasis on central command would strain the capacity of the planning authorities to the breaking point. But escape via decentralization seems to be equally impracticable. As R. V. Greenslade[16] has pointed out, two

16 R. V. Greenslade, 'The Soviet Economic System in Transition,' in *New Directions in the Soviet Economy, op. cit.*, pp. 14–15.

institutions – the market and the central plan – 'cannot perform the same function at the same time, and enterprises cannot simultaneously produce the mix of output that the market wants and the one that planners want.' On the other hand, we cannot assume that the central plan will give way to a full-fledged market system since 'it is difficult to picture the party and the planners presiding over the dissolution of planning' because 'neither the economic bureaucracy nor the local party apparatus is likely to accede gracefully to its own withering away.'

But has, what the Russian authorities reject, not already been accomplished in Yugoslavia?

Plan and Markets in Yugoslavia

The Yugoslav system rejects detailed planning from the center as clumsy and inefficient, but the government outlines in terms of broad estimates the desired development of the main branches of the economy and the rate of accumulation and economic growth. The enterprises are *not* given commands concerning output, nor do they receive input allocations. Their workers' councils, managing boards, and directors formulate operational plans on the basis of profit expectations that rest on a complete set of price data. The system is far more decentralized than the Soviet economy would be even after a full implementation of Kosygin's reforms.

The Yugoslav mixture of planning and freedom permits of many combinations. For instance, the central plan could be reduced to a determination of the rate of accumulation and the state preference schedule. All the rest would then be left to price formation on genuine markets and decentralized production decisions on the basis of these prices. But it is more likely that the government interferes with the pricing process than determines the actions of the enterprises. Indeed, in Yugoslavia most prices are set by the government and even the prices that are free to adjust may be raised only with government permission, that is, when increased costs justify the move. Since Yugoslav prices deviate in most instances from the prices that would have corresponded to given market conditions and since these prices are used as guidelines, we are forced to assume that misdirections and disproportionalities will result because it exceeds the capacity of any central bureaucracy to manage a consistent set of price controls in line with government preferences, the consumers' wishes and a factor allocation according to marginal productivity.

The Yugoslav system tries to achieve the advantages of central planning by substituting price controls and a compartmentalization of the credit market for detailed central commands and allocations. While the enterprises are free to base their decisions on profit expectations, the cost of additional capital will depend on the priority status of the industry. The compartmentalization of the credit market violates the consistency of the allocation process much like Liberman's and Kosygin's setting of different profitability norms. However, since the Yugoslav firm is not subject to central command, the danger is even greater that major distortions will result from this permanent interference with interest rates and other costs. Furthermore, owing to the greater decentralization, the economy will be exposed to some of the potential shortcomings of an unplanned system. As in Western market economies, monopolistic forces can produce inflation and unemployment. In Yugoslavia's system of workers' management, enterprises may try to increase the workers' income by monopolistic price policies and the raising of wages at the cost of reduced accumulation. These policies tend to be inflationary. Unemployment may result not only from misdirected production but also from the reluctance of the firm to hire workers who are difficult to fire and would reduce the individual's share in the profit.

The Yugoslavs can hardly claim that their highly interesting blend of market and plan has proved to be so superior to the purer systems' performances that it can be considered as a preview of the advantages to be expected from the latter's convergence.

Soft Planning and Convergence

While the centrally planned economies try to make use of prices and profits, market economies can try to superimpose a central plan on their market structure. But just as mere reference to government price setting is no proof that a real market mechanism can be combined with central planning, so does mere reference to planning in a market economy fail to be convincing unless it can be shown that this planning means more than a growing public sector or monetary and fiscal controls of aggregate demand.

An interesting attempt to superimpose central planning on the market structure of a Western economy is France's case of 'soft' or 'indicative' planning. Pierre Massé[17] believes that reliance on given market prices is not enough. Needed are 'generalized markets' in which future developments find adequate expression, needed is an overall picture of the economy that shows in advance how private productions will gear into each other in the future. Once private firms know how other private firms will act, the common knowledge of this interrelated growth of all industries together will provide a general feeling of security and the foundation for rapid and balanced economic expansion.

Massé's 'generalized markets' are neither real markets nor mere forecasts. They are output programmes on the basis of tentative growth rates and imply steering by the government with instruments such as substantial government controls over investment funds of the nation, selective tax policies, price controls, and the encouragement of monopolistic practices in private industry. These instruments and policies differ basically from indirect controls through monetary and fiscal measures to influence aggregate demand. *Direct* controls are used to induce private corporations to fulfill their share in a programme that, resting on artificial prices and inducements, differs from the course that unfettered market forces would have brought about. 'Generalized markets' obviously are markets whose prices have been 'doctored' to mirror developments which the government wants to foster. But since we deal here with soft planning, the government cannot command; it can only tempt private industry away from the path that genuine market prices would have suggested.

According to Massé, 'every branch of activity is promised the possibility of acquiring its production factors and selling its goods on a balanced market. The promise, however, is only kept when everybody plays the game. The promise acts merely as an incentive. It is not binding on anybody. Firms are not dispensed from working out their valuations and choosing their own attitudes. But they can do so in a better informed way.' The basic weakness of soft planning

17 Pierre Massé, 'French Methods of Planning,' *Journal of Industrial Economics*, 11 (November 1962), pp. 1–17.

85

could hardly be better stated than in this circuitous praise. What if some important firms do not play the game because they believe the whole program to be over-ambitious and inflationary? What if the whole program must be interrupted by stabilization policies? What if monopolistic organizations do not care to co-operate with a proposed 'incomes policy'? What if, in spite of the promised softness of the plan, the government supports its program by direct controls which conflict with clear price signals in real markets?

Since soft planning has already led to repeated inflationary difficulties, it is fascinating to speculate on what would happen under soft planning that would be so obviously tied to price inflation that, knowing this fact and acting accordingly, all participants in the economic process would adjust their actions to the prospective rate of inflation.

Considering these unanswered questions, we must conclude that soft planning has not proved to be a desirable compromise between market and plan. It may do more harm than good through monopolistic policies, direct controls, and price inflation. Instead of improving the markets it will interfere with their proper functioning.

Conclusion

Economic systems do not converge – unless we mean by convergence merely that superficial similarities are on the increase. Of course, no system is pure. The market economies were never really *laissez-faire* and the centrally planned economies make use of markets, prices and, more recently, the profit motive. Many institutional similarities exist, similarities produced by the increasing technical complexities of modern industrial production as well as by the internal division of labor in giant producing units. Furthermore, with growing wealth we find strong pressure toward greater freedom of consumption in the centrally planned economies and a trend toward a more than proportional increase in collective want satisfaction in the market economies. If these similarities and trends constitute convergence, convergence exists.

However, if convergence means a symbiosis of market and central plan, with the implication that the emerging system will combine what is good and eliminate what is bad in the pure systems, convergence is not in progress. Most attempts to decentralize the central plan or to centrally control the market economies on the basis of arbitrarily set prices will, as a rule, produce undesirable mixtures, that is, economies whose production processes are not clearly guided by either central command or private decisions.

Friedrich A. Hayek rejected the convergence thesis already in 1944 when he wrote:

It is a revealing fact that few planners are content to say that central planning is desirable. Most of them affirm that we can no longer choose but are compelled by circumstances beyond our control to substitute planning for competition. The myth is deliberately cultivated that we are embarking on the new course not out of free will but because competition is spontaneously eliminated by technological changes which we neither can reverse nor should wish to prevent. This argument is rarely developed at any length – it is one of the assertions taken over by one writer from another until, by mere iteration, it has come to be accepted as an established fact. It is, nevertheless, devoid of foundation. The tendency toward monopoly and planning is not the result of any 'objective facts' beyond our control but the product of opinions fostered and propagated for half a century until they have come to dominate all our policy.[18]

Thus Hayek argued a quarter of a century ago (and long before it became fashionable to talk about convergence) that we should 'free ourselves of that worst form of contemporary obscurantism which tries to persuade us that what we have done in the recent past was all either wise or inevitable.'[19] The way to improve our system is not to combine principles and policies that are incompatible; rather, we must try to understand the implications of these principles, grasp the basic structure of each system, and achieve our major economic aims by policies that 'conform.' As far as the market economy is concerned, much can be done. Keynes' planning for the correct amount of aggregate spending is as important as Hayek's planning for competition. Both types of control can be so designed that the policies involved do not unduly interfere with the market and private initiative. These policies concern 'the nature

18 Friedrich A. Hayek, *The Road to Serfdom*, Chicago, Ill. 1944, p. 43.
19 *The Road to Serfdom*, p. 240.

of the environment which the free play of economic forces requires if it is to realize the full potentialities of production;[20] they erect around the existing market mechanism 'so to speak, a system of laws and institutions' within which it may be made to work in the right way;[21] and they create 'conditions under which the knowledge and the initiative of individuals are given the best scope so that *they* can plan most successfully.'[22]

20 J. M. Keynes, *General Theory*, p. 379.
21 Lionel Robbins, *The Economic Problem in Peace and War*, London 1947, p. 83.
22 Hayek, *The Road to Serfdom*, p. 35.

Methodological Individualism and the Market Economy
Ludwig M. Lachmann

I

For over a century and a half, from David Hume to Gustav Cassel, the defenders of the market economy were able to draw intellectual strength no less than moral comfort from the existence of a body of economic thought which supported their cause and which appeared to show that interference with the free play of market forces would, at least in the long run, do more harm than good and prove ultimately self-defeating. During this period an attitude favourable to 'interventionism' almost invariably went together with an attitude critical of the doctrines of classical economics. In the *Methodenstreit*, Schmoller appears to have felt that what his opponents were really defending was not so much a methodological point of view as the principle of the market economy – '*Das Manchestertum*'.

In the course of this century all this has changed. Today economic theory, encapsulated in an artificial world of 'perfect competition', coherent plans, and instantaneous adjustments to change, has come to rest so heavily on the notion of equilibrium, embodied in a system of simultaneous equations, that the significance of its conclusions to the real world is more than dubious. In a sense it is easy to explain what has happened. The notion of equilibrium which makes very good sense when confined to individual agents, like household and firm, is less easily applied to the description of human interaction. It still has its uses when applied to a very simple type of market, such as Marshall's corn market. But 'equilibrium of the industry' is a difficult concept to handle. Equilibrium of the 'economic system' is a notion remote from reality, though Walras and Pareto showed its logical consistency. Equilibrium of an economic system in motion, 'equilibrium growth', borders on absurdity. What

89

has happened is that a notion which makes good sense in the description of human plans, within the universe of action controlled by one mind, has illegitimately been extended to a sphere where it has, and can have, no meaning. A formalistic methodology which uses concepts without a proper understanding of their true meaning and natural limits is apt to defeat its own ends and bound to lead us to absurd conclusions.

Professors Mises and Hayek have taken a prominent part in emphasizing the implications of this unfortunate state of affairs. They have both underlined the shortcomings of the notion of equilibrium when employed out of context. Mises in 1940[1] described this notion as 'an auxiliary makeshift employed by the logical economists as a limiting notion, the definition of a state of affairs in which there is no longer any action and the market process has come to a standstill. . . . A superficial analogy is spun out too long, that is all'.[2]

Hayek has twice dealt with the same problem. In Chapter II of *The Pure Theory of Capital* he pointed out why capital problems cannot be discussed within the framework of traditional stationary equilibrium theory.[3] And in 'The Meaning of Competition' we were told that 'competition is by its nature a dynamic process whose essential characteristics are assumed away by the assumptions underlying static analysis'.[4]

Today the defenders of the market economy are finding themselves in a difficult position. The arsenal of economic thought, which served their fathers so well, no longer provides what they need. In fact it now often happens that what it has to supply proves more useful in the hands of their enemies than it does in their own. Their enemies will hardly fail to point out, for instance, that actual market competition, as distinct from 'perfect competition', is bound to fall short of the high ideal of 'Pareto Optimality', an equilibrium notion which occupies a prominent place in modern 'welfare economics', another spurious offshoot of contemporary economic thought.

In these circumstances upholders of the market economy are confronted with two tasks which are as unenviable as they are inevitable. They must, in the first place, be ready to turn themselves

1 In the original German edition of *Human Action.*
2 L. von Mises, *Human Action*, New Haven 1949, p. 352.
3 F. A. Hayek, *The Pure Theory of Capital*, London 1941, p. 14.
4 *Individualism and Economic Order*, London and Chicago 1949, p. 94.

into stern and unbending critics of the economic doctrines currently in fashion, ever ready to point out the aridity of their conclusions, the unreality of their assumptions, the artificial nature of their procedure. Secondly, and even more important, they must henceforth be able to forge their own weapons. What follows in this paper is offered as a modest contribution toward the achievement of these aims.

II

The fundamental question, i.e. in what form we should conceive of the market economy, once we have rejected the general equilibrium of the economic system, has already been answered by Mises and Hayek: The market is a process of continuous change, not a state of rest. It is also clear that what keeps this process in continuous motion is the occurrence of unexpected change as well as the inconsistency of human plans. Both are necessary conditions, since without the recurrence of the first, in a stationary world, it is likely that plans would gradually become consistent as men come to learn more and more about their environment. The recurrence of unexpected change by itself, on the other hand, would not suffice to generate a continuous process, since the elements of the system might respond to each change by a finite process of adjustment to it. We would then have an 'open system' on which external change impinges in the form of 'random shocks' each of which the system, possibly with variable time lags, contrives to 'absorb'. But the existence of human action consciously designed to produce certain effects, prompted by expectations which may, and often do, fail, makes it impossible to look at the market process in this way. Conscious action oriented to a certain state of the market cannot possibly be conceived as a 'random event'. Nor is the inconsistency of the plans of different agents, without which there can be no competition, to be regarded in this manner without doing violence to the facts. For such plans have to be drawn up and carried out with great care if they are to have a chance of success. To speak here of 'random shocks' would mean to profess ignorance where we have knowledge.

We now have to consider the significance of these facts for the methodology of the social sciences. It seems to us that they provide the justification for 'methodological individualism' and the 'compositive method'.[5]

Let us retrace our steps. We have rejected the conception of the market economy as a closed system in a state of equilibrium, or at least with an inherent tendency towards it. We are unable to conceive of it as an open system on which random shocks impinge from 'outside'. Mere outside shocks without the inconsistency of plans would not necessarily generate a continuous process, certainly not the market process with which we are all familiar. This requires the inconsistency of plans prompted by divergent expectations, an inevitable concomitant of human action in an uncertain world. But in these plans the future as image affects the present as action in a way which makes nonsense of the notion of 'random events'. Hence, if we wish to explain the nature of the forces which propel the market process, we have to explain the nature of the relationship between action geared to the future and plans embodying a mental picture of the future.

The case for methodological individualism, for the method which seeks to explain human action in terms of plans conceived before action is actually taken, thus rests on a positive as well as a negative reason. The negative reason is, of course, that an event designed to take place in a certain situation, but not otherwise, cannot be regarded as a random event. The positive reason, on the other hand, is that in the study of human action we are able to achieve something which must for ever remain beyond the purview of the natural sciences, viz. to make events *intelligible* by explaining them in terms of the plans which guide action.

The scope of this principle of explanation is, of course, much wider than the area of significant action in a market economy. Needless to say, the fact that plans often fail and hardly ever are completely successful, provides no argument at all against our postulate. In fact it is only by comparing the outcome of action with the plan which guided it that we are able to judge success, another achievement which is beyond the reach of the natural sciences. The alternative principle of explanation is, of course, that of 'response to stimulus'. It is perhaps unnecessary to stress that the kind of entrepreneurial action mainly responsible for keeping the market process in motion, i.e. innovation and the formation and dissolution

5 F. A. Hayek, *The Counter-Revolution of Science*, Glencoe, Ill. 1955, pp. 38–39.

of specific capital combinations, does not lend itself to this type of explanation. Spontaneous mental action is not a 'response' to anything pre-existent. Neither is it a random event. One might think otherwise of the process in the course of which, in a market economy, large numbers of producers are 'learning by doing', and gradually find out more and more efficient, and cheaper, methods of producing goods, or ways of improving the quality of their products. Here, a formalist would speak of 'adding a time dimension to the production function'. But in reality this process is no more a response to stimulus than is spontaneous action in the form of innovation. The process is part and parcel of the general process of competition in the course of which even those who were unsuccessful in improving their own methods of production can benefit by adopting those of their more successful rivals. In any case, the continuous nature of the process reflects continuous acts of human will and effort, and emulation of the successful is here just as important as in the process by which innovations are diffused.

The method which explains human action in terms of plans, constituted by mental acts and linking an imagined future to an active present, has two aspects of which one is forward-looking while the other is backward-looking.

What Hayek has called the 'Compositive Method'[6] denotes the forward-looking aspect. Here we start with the plans of the individuals, those mental schemes in which purposes, means and obstacles are welded together into a whole and, as it were, projected on a screen. We then ask whether the plans made by different individuals are consistent with one another. If so, the conditions of success do exist, a 'general equilibrium' is possible, though in reality, of course, for a large number of reasons it may never actually be reached. If not, inconsistency of plans is bound to generate further changes. In this case we have to argue from the divergence of plans to their disappointment and hence to their revision. But while we can say that disappointed expectations will lead to a revision of plans, we never can tell what new expectations the acting individual will substitute for those which were frustrated by the course of events. It may be impossible to use a durable capital good for the purpose for which it was designed. That may happen for a large number of reasons. It will then have to be turned to 'second best'

6 *The Counter-Revolution of Science, loc. cit.*, pp. 39, 212.

purpose. But what this will be depends on the new expectations of its owner at the moment of the turning decision, and about that we can say nothing.

But we can also employ the method in the reverse order. Instead of asking what are the implications of a number of plans simultaneously carried out, we can reverse the procedure and ask what constellation of plans has given rise to an existing situation. This is the real meaning of the method of *Verstehen*, which is also, of course, the historical method. There appears to be no reason why the theoretical social sciences, when they pursue their enquiries into the typical causes of typical social phenomena, should not make use of it.

Methodological individualism, then, in its backward-looking form, means simply that we shall not be satisfied with any type of explanation of social phenomena which does not lead us ultimately to a human plan. This entails that explanations couched in terms of so-called 'behaviour variables' are not satisfactory explanations of human conduct. We have it on Hayek's own authority that the main task of the theory of capital is to explain why existing capital goods are used in the way they are. But we may also enquire how the existing capital structure came into existence, i.e. in the pursuit of which plans the existing capital resources came to assume their present form. In fact, it is hardly possible to explain present use without answering these questions. But this means that we analyse an observed phenomenon in terms of the plans in the pursuit of which it came into existence. This is the obverse of the compositive method.

Such analysis of observed phenomena in terms of pre-existent plans has nothing to do with psychology. We are here concerned with purposes, not with motives, with plans, not with the psychic processes which give rise to them, with acts of our conscious minds, not with what lies behind them. As soon as our thoughts have assumed the firm outline of a plan and we have taken the decision to carry it out over a definite period of future time, we have reached a point outside the realm of psychology, a point which we can use either as the starting point or as the final goal of our enquiry. In the former case we make use of it as the starting point of the application of the compositive method, in the latter as the final point to which we carry the method of *Verstehen*. In neither case are we trespassing on the domain of psychology.

III

We must now make an attempt to look at our principle of explanation (hereafter referred to as *Subjectivism*)[7] in the perspective of the history of economic thought.

Hayek has given it as his view that 'it is probably no exaggeration to say that every important advance in economic theory during the last hundred years was a further step in the consistent application of subjectivism'.[8] Naturally one thinks of marginal utility and expectations. But in exactly the same way as in writing the history of a realm an historian would not be entitled to confine himself to reciting the triumphs of its kings, soldiers, and statesmen, but must also deal with the vicissitudes they faced and the failures they suffered, the historian of thought has to record the defeats as well as the triumphs of subjectivism.

It seems to us that, from the point of view of methodology, the history of economic thought of the last 100 years has to be seen as a continuous struggle between subjectivism and its opponent (hereafter referred to as *Formalism*). In this long drawn-out battle success has by no means always been on the side of the subjectivists. They confronted a formidable foe with whose general character we are already familiar. The same late classical formalism which, as we saw, has brought about the alienation of modern economic theory from the market economy, is also responsible for the vicissitudes of subjectivism. Acts of the mind do not fit easily into the formal apparatus of a body of thought the main purpose of which is to produce a closed system within which it is possible to assign numerical values to a large number of magnitudes. But plans are products of mental activity which is oriented no less to an imagined future than to an experienced present. No wonder there were difficulties.

The story of the 'subjective revolution' of the 1870s offers an instructive example of the vicissitudes which befell subjectivism. Its main thrust was directed against the classical theory of labour value. To the Ricardians value was a kind of economic 'substance', a property common to all economic goods. The subjectivists were able to show that value is not a property inherent in goods, but constitutes a relationship between an appraising mind and the object

7 *The Counter-Revolution of Science, loc. cit.*, p. 38.
8 *Ibid.*, p. 31.

appraised, a manifestation of mental activity. But most of the fruits of their victory were subsequently lost when neoclassical economics contrived to 'absorb' subjective utility within the framework of its formal apparatus. 'Tastes' were embodied in its system as a class of 'data', a status which they came to share with resources and technical knowledge. Naturally the successful counter-revolution of neoclassical formalism raised problems of its own. Tastes can, and often will, change in an unpredictable fashion. Whenever this happens, the other elements of the system, i.e. the dependent variables, must adjust themselves accordingly. To be able to speak at all of 'the system having an inherent tendency towards equilibrium', we should therefore have to assume that the velocity with which the other elements adjust themselves to changes in tastes is always so high that no new change will occur before a full adjustment to the previous change has taken place. It is difficult to imagine such circumstances.

From our point of view it is most important to realize that formalism, by assuming all tastes to be 'given', whether in the form of utility functions or of indifference curves, is in fact evading the whole problem of how plans are made, a problem which is of crucial significance to subjectivism. The indifference curves which are imputed to consumers are in reality comprehensive lists of alternative plans to be put into operation if and when opportunity offers. In other words, what is really assumed here is that individuals never need make actual plans, because from the start they are equipped with such a large number of alternative plans that all contingencies are covered! The question how these lists of alternative plans ever came into existence is then ruled out of order as falling outside the sphere of economic questions! The whole purpose of the subjectivist revolt, which was to show that prices and quantities are the indirect results of the decision-making acts of millions of individuals who are renewing or revising their plans every day, is thus thwarted. Consumers' preferences, separated from the mental acts which daily shape and modify them, are turned into independent variables of a system in which there is no scope for planning and plan revision. Spontaneous action has been transformed into a response to stimulus. The formalists are able to claim that they have incorporated into their system the contribution of subjectivism, albeit in an emasculated form.[9] Robertson's famous *bon mot* on Keynes' theory of

9 The Austrians alone stubbornly resisted this trend and retained a wholesome

interest fully applies to the formalist theory of consumers' action: 'The organ which secretes it has been amputated, and yet it somehow still exists – a grin without a cat'.[10]

When we turn to expectations, our second instance of subjectivist success during the last 100 years, we see a very different picture.

In the first place, the problem of expectations did not make its appearance on the stage of economic thought in one thrust, as did marginal utility between 1871 and 1874, but rather by gradual infiltration. As a result it is virtually impossible to date its appearance. If we were to set the date e.g. in 1930 ('bullishness' and 'bearishness' in Keynes' *Treatise*), we should be ignoring the fact that the problem was clearly foreshadowed in the work of Schumpeter and Knight, as well as in the early writings of Lindahl and Myrdal in the 1920s. But on the other hand, before 1930, at least in Anglo-Saxon economics, the problem was hardly recognized at all. It remains true that it began to make its impact in the 1930s.

From our point of view, the crucial significance of the emergence of expectations as a problem rests in the fact that, by contrast to what happened to utility, they have thus far proved refractory to all attempts to incorporate them into the formal apparatus of the late classical economics of our time. The reason is not far to seek. Expectations refer to processes of change. (In the stationary world of Walras-Paretian equilibrium they are in any case of no significance). It is hard to see how they can be treated as elements of a system. They are not constants, since they are bound to change, while tastes can at least be conceived of as constants. Expectations, that is, always refer to a future point of time which we approach more closely as time passes. But neither can they be treated as variables. We cannot regard them as dependent variables since we

10 D. H. Robertson, *Essays in Monetary Theory*, London and New York 1948, p. 25.

distrust of indifference curves in particular and the whole Lausanne approach in general. Unfortunately, they never were able to show, with the cogency their case required, the incompatibility between the idea of planned action, the very core of Austrian economic thought, and an analytical model which knows no action, but only reaction.

See Hans Mayer, *Der Erkenntniswert der funktionellen Preistheorien*, Vienna 1932.

See also: Ludwig M. Lachmann, 'Die geistesgeschichtliche Bedeutung der österreichischen Schule in der Volkswirtschaftslehre,' *Zeitschrift Für National-oekonomie*, 26 (1966), esp. pp. 158–62.

cannot specify any mechanism of response. Different men's expectations will react differently to the occurrence of the same event. And if we regard them as independent variables, very little will be left of the rest of the system. Changes in expectations would then come to overshadow all other causes of change.[11] J. Schumpeter[12] and E. Lundberg[13] saw this very clearly already in the 1930s and reacted with characteristic vigour.

This does not mean that, if we compress our period of decision-making to a point of time, to 'market day equilibrium', expectations could not be used and regarded as data. In this case they clearly can, but any conception of equilibrium over time, of 'moving equilibrium', is incompatible with changing expectations. It is therefore hardly surprising that most of the authors of those macro-economic growth models which have gained prominence in recent years, such as Sir Roy Harrod and Joan Robinson, have on the whole preferred to keep the problem of expectations at arm's length. Only G. L. S. Shackle has been a vigorous and indefatigable exponent and student of its implications.

It is of some interest to cast a cursory glance at Keynes' contribution in the perspective of the continuous struggle between subjectivism and formalism. Fundamentally, Keynes was a subjectivist, aware of the contrast between the variability of expectations and the determinateness required of any formal system, such as his own short-term equilibrium model.[14] He mocked at long-period equilibrium ('In the long run we are all dead'), but then had to use what Marshallian tools lay most readily at hand for the purpose of giving unity to his thought. So he cast it in the mould of a short-period equilibrium system. Moreover, the *General Theory* was largely written as a polemic against what Keynes regarded as the neo-classical orthodoxy of his day. Since his argument relied so heavily on expectations, the polemical effect would certainly have been marred had the contrast between the rather

11 This is, of course, what happened to Keynes' liquidity preference theory.
12 *Business Cycles*, New York and London 1939, Vol. I, p. 140.
13 *Studies in the Theory of Economic Expansion*, London 1937, p. 175.
14 'There is an arresting contrast between the method and the meaning of Keynes' book. The method is the analysis of equilibrium, the endeavour to account for men's actions as a rational, calculated and logically justifiable response to circumstances which in all relevant essentials they thoroughly know. The meaning is that such rationality is in the nature of things impossible and baseless, because men confront an unknown and unknowable future'. G. L. S. Shackle, *A Scheme of Economic Theory*, Cambridge 1965, p. 44.

98

indistinct character of the expectations he used to support his argument and the ostensible rigour of his model been too clearly revealed. In these circumstances he found himself compelled somewhat to 'underplay' the significance of expectations. He introduced them where he needed them for his immediate purpose, as e.g., in the theory of investment and in liquidity preference theory, but left them out where he did not, as in multiplier theory.

But, when seen in the historical perspective which concerns us here, Keynes certainly was on the side of the subjectivists. As Professor Shackle has said so well:

> The whole spirit of Keynes' book insists on the unfathomable subtlety, complexity and mutability of the influences which bear upon the decision to invest. To build a self-contained dynamic model would have been, for him, to contradict the very essence of what he was trying to say, namely, that it is uncertainty, the feeling of a helpless inability to know with assurance how a given course of action will turn out, that inhibits enterprise and the giving of full employment.[15]

No wonder that his successors found themselves somewhat embarrassed when they attempted to distil macro-economic growth models from his work.

Within the confines of this paper we are unable to do more than record a few episodes of the great struggle mentioned. But one such episode of recent years, which constitutes quite a remarkable success of subjectivism, should not go unrecorded.

In 1965 Sir John Hicks, who for many years had been one of the foremost exponents of formal analysis and one of its most skilful practitioners, appears to have changed sides. In an attempt to define the limits of the static method, which is of course *the* method of formalism, he showed that this method is incompatible with the existence of any planned action. 'In statics there is no planning; mere repetition of what has been done before does not need to be planned. It is accordingly possible, in static theory, to treat the single period as a closed system, the working of which can be examined without reference to anything that goes on outside it (in the temporal sense). But this is not possible in dynamics'.[16]

15 *Ibid.*, p. 98.
16 John Hicks, *Capital and Growth*, Oxford 1965, p. 32.

The implications of this passage are far-reaching and intimately concern the matters pursued in this paper. Sir John has not only made clear why it is that expectations, which must transcend the single period, cannot be fitted into any model which employs the static method. He has at the same time shown within what narrow limits the instruments of formalism can be at all usefully employed. And in doing so he has opened up a vast new area for economic research, an area which is of paramount importance to us. For the world 'outside the single period', the world in which men have to act with a sense of the future and a memory of the past, the world of action and not merely of reaction, this world is none other than the realm of the market economy.

IV

At the end of our first section we promised to make a contribution to the arsenal of the market economy. The reader may well be wondering how far the methodological reflections presented in our second and third sections can be said to have furthered this cause. But what we in fact have done is to lay the ground for an attempt to cast what we hope will be new light on two notable features of the market economy which are all too often misunderstood – and not only by its critics.

The first of these is the Stock Exchange, perhaps the most characteristic of all the institutions of the market economy. In fact it is hardly an exaggeration to say that without a Stock Exchange there can be no market economy. What really distinguishes the latter from a socialist economy is not the size of the 'private sector' of the economy, but the ability of the individual freely to buy and sell shares in the material resources of production. Their inability to exercise their ingenuity in this respect is perhaps the most important disability suffered by the citizens of socialist societies, however large their incomes might be, however wide the range of choice of consumption goods that may be available to them.

In the traditional view the chief function of the Stock Exchange is to serve as a channel through which savings flow before they become transformed into additions to the capital stock. Keynes taught us to regard the apportioning of the flow of savings to various investments as a function subsidiary to the constant turnover of an existing stock of securities prompted by divergent expectations. Thus, seeing the importance of expectations in asset markets, and disliking the implications of what he saw, he launched his famous diatribe on the Stock Exchange as a 'casino'.

The Stock Exchange consists of a series of markets for assets, i.e., future yield streams. In each market supply and demand are brought into equality every market day. Demand and supply reflect the divergent expectations of buyers and sellers concerning future yields. Transactions take place between those whose expectations diverge from the current market price. Since as much must be bought as is sold, we may say that the equilibrium price in an asset market reflects the 'balance of expectations'. As without divergence of expectations there can be no market at all, we can say that this divergence provides the substrate upon which the market price rests.

Since all assets traded on a Stock Exchange are substitutes, albeit imperfect substitutes, for one another, these markets form a 'system'. And as equilibrium is attained simultaneously in each market which forms part of it, our system is free of those problems which in the Walrasian system are apt to arise when equilibrium is reached in some markets before it is attained in others.

In this way the market economy accomplishes daily a consistent, because simultaneous, valuation of all its major productive assets. The practical importance of this fact is that it makes possible, whether in the form of 'take-over bids' or otherwise, the transfer of the control of material resources from pessimists to optimists, i.e. to those who believe they can make better use of them than others can. Critics of the market economy who scoff at the continuous and often violent day-to-day fluctuations of share prices, have failed to notice that an equilibrium price which rests on a balance of expectations is bound to be flexible since it must change every time the substrate of this balance changes. For precisely the same reason for which equilibrium in an asset market is reached so smoothly and speedily, it cannot last longer than one day. For expectations rest on imperfect knowledge, and not even a day can pass without a change in the mode of diffusion of knowledge.

The methodological significance of these facts, which is of interest to us here, even transcends their practical importance for the market economy, great as this is. For we are now able to see that the market process in asset markets has a more restricted

101

function than is the case in commodity markets. In the latter, as we said above, the market process is kept in continuous motion by the occurrence of unexpected change as well as the incoherence of human plans. But in asset markets, in which equilibrium is established every day, human plans are made coherent every day. Here the lapse of time between market days serves only to diffuse new knowledge and facilitate the re-orientation of expectations. It does not have to serve to display the inconsistency of, for instance, production plans, which is what must happen between 'market days' in commodity markets if such are to exist. Equilibrium in asset markets, as in the Marshallian corn market, makes sense because it is confined to the exchange of existing stocks. Where these conditions do not exist, as in a flow market, and *a fortiori* in the relations between such markets, it makes no sense, and all there exists in fact is the continuous market process.

The formalists, in extending the equilibrium concept from asset markets, where it makes sense, to the Walrasian system of commodity markets, where it does not, have not only rendered a poor service to economic thought. They have rendered an even poorer service to the market economy by blurring one of its distinctive features. But in doing so, they have unwittingly provided the friends of the market economy with an instructive lesson that they must henceforth forge their own weapons.

A second feature of the market economy, with which we shall deal even more briefly here, is the fact that quantities produced and prices paid apparently depend on the distribution of wealth. We are, for instance, often told that 'The Invisible Hand will only maximize total social utility *provided the state intervenes so as to make the initial distribution of dollar votes ethically proper*'.[17] We shall refrain from comment on the ethical propriety of such statements. But it is perhaps clear that the nature of the market process, which is a continuous process that cannot be interrupted, has here been misconceived. There is, of course, no such thing as an 'initial distribution' before the market process starts. The distribution of wealth in terms of asset values at any point of time is the cumulative result of the market process of the past. In the asset markets, the sources of income streams are revalued every day in accordance with the prevailing balance of expectations, giving capital gains to

17 Paul A. Samuelson, *Collected Scientific Papers*, Cambridge, Mass., 1966, p. 1410. (Italics in the original.)

102

some, inflicting capital losses upon others. What reason is there to believe that interference with this market process is any less detrimental than interference with the production and exchange of goods and services? Those who believe that such a reason does exist (and most of our contemporary 'welfare economists' do!) must assume that asset holders, like Ricardian landlords, somehow stand outside all market processes and 'get rich in their sleep'. Nothing we have said about differences in the *modus operandi* of the market process, in asset and commodity markets respectively, can impair the validity of the simple truth that all these processes form part of an integrated whole.[18]

18 'There is no distributional process apart from the production and exchange processes of the market; hence the very concept of "distribution" becomes meaningless on the free market. Since "distribution" is simply the result of the free exchange process, and since this process benefits all participants on the market and increases social utility, it follows directly that the "distributional" results of the free market also increase social utility.' Murray N. Rothbard, 'Toward a Reconstruction of Utility and Welfare Economics,' in Mary Sennholz (ed.), *On Freedom and Free Enterprise*, New York 1956, p. 251.

On Neutral Money
Friedrich A. Lutz

Hayek remarks[1] that the expression 'neutral money' was first used by Wicksell. I believe, however, that Hayek's own writings were largely responsible for its adoption, nearly forty years ago, as a technical term by economists in the English-speaking world. The problems of how this term should be defined, and of what the conditions are under which money would be neutral, have been the subject of wide discussion which still continues today. And there is no doubt that Hayek's pioneer work in this field has won him a place among the foremost contributors to modern monetary theory.

I

The problem of defining neutral money at once raises serious difficulties. Originally the general idea underlying the concept was that money would be neutral if the real economic quantities were the same *with* the use of money as they would be *without*, i.e. in a barter economy. This idea derived in turn from the notion that in a barter economy Say's law applies, making it impossible for a general depression to occur, so that if such a depression does occur, money, or 'factors on the side of money', must be responsible. It seemed highly desirable, therefore, to aim at making money 'neutral'.

Though the logic behind the idea of neutral money seems clear, the authors who sought to give a precise definition to the concept must be said to have had small success. It does not seem to me that the definition can be derived, as so many writers have suggested it could, from the concept of the barter economy. To illustrate this

1 F. A. Hayek, *Prices and Production*, revised edition, London 1935, p. 129.

105

point I shall consider three attempts to define the neutrality of money with the aid of that concept. The first is due to Wicksell, the second to J. G. Koopmans, and the third to Patinkin.

In Wicksell's view money was neutral so long as the money rate of interest was kept equal to the natural rate, defined as the rate which would emerge if capital were offered on the market *in natura*. This equivalence was supposed both to guarantee stability of the general price level, and to prevent relative commodity prices from being influenced from the side of money. Thus he says: '. . . if money is loaned at this same rate of interest (the natural rate), it serves as nothing more than a cloak to cover a procedure which, from the purely formal point of view, could have been carried on equally well without it. The conditions of economic equilibrium are fulfilled in precisely the same manner. In such a case, there is no occasion for any alteration of the level of prices.'[2] A serious defect of Wicksell's barter-economy model is the impossibility of giving any precise meaning to the idea of a single interest rate determined on a market where the supply of capital takes the form of goods. It is true that Wicksell himself was perfectly aware of this difficulty, as is apparent from his explicit assumption that 'relative prices . . . remain unaltered'.[3] But obviously the assumption that, in a growing economy with capital accumulation, relative prices are constant requires the further assumptions: that all the productive factors, including land, grow at the same percentage rate; that the demand functions for all the different goods also shift up in the same proportion; and, finally, that there is no technological progress. Once we depart from these unrealistic assumptions, and must therefore allow that relative prices do change, we must suppose that, on a capital market where the capital is supplied *in natura*, there will be as many interest rates as goods. The 'natural interest rate' is undefinable, and so therefore is 'neutral money'.

We turn next to the view of Koopmans, who treated the subject in far more detail than any other writer.[4] In his view, what we should understand by the 'ideal type of the pure barter economy' is not the state of affairs that would emerge if money were altogether

2 Knut Wicksell, *Geldzins und Güterpreise*, Jena 1898, pp. 95 f.; English translation *Interest and Prices*, 1936, pp. 103 f.
3 *Ibid.*, p. 103 in English translation.
4 J. G. Koopmans, 'Zum Problem des neutralen Geldes', in F. A. Hayek (ed.), *Beiträge zur Geldtheorie*, Vienna 1933.

eliminated and its place taken by direct barter exchange (or indirect exchange through a chain of barter transactions). For if money were really eliminated, one consequence would be an immense increase in costly 'frictions' in the economy. 'The situation implied by the equilibrium theorem', says Koopmans, 'is . . . a hypothetical one which is inconceivable in reality. It is a situation free both from the frictions which, in the absence of a universally accepted medium of exchange, would hinder the attainment of a state of full equilibrium, and from the special changes which the actual introduction of a such a medium causes in the economic process.'5 One of the younger generation of monetary economists, E. M. Claassen, has interpreted this approach to the problem as meaning that we have to postulate as our ideal type of a 'barter economy' an economy 'in which money exists in so far as it is essential (both as unit of account and as medium of exchange) to the smooth functioning of the economic process, but from which it is eliminated in so far as it acts as a disturbing element'.6

If, as I believe, this interpretation is correct, Koopmans' procedure amounts not to a comparison between a money economy and a barter economy, but to one between an imperfectly working money economy, as this exists in reality, and an, in some sense, ideally working money economy. The exact nature of this ideal system is not directly deducible from the passage that we have quoted from Koopmans. We do not, however, go far wrong perhaps in supposing that the basic notion is the same as that underlying Walras' system of equations, as he developed this for a dynamic economy with capital accumulation. In that system relative prices are determined with the aid of a unit of account, or *numéraire*. But they are not influenced by money either in its function of *numéraire* or in that of medium of exchange. For money in this latter sense is introduced, after the relative prices have been determined, in the shape of a money equation which sets the general price level while leaving relative prices unaffected. Our interpretation of Koopmans' conception of neutral money implies a close link between that conception and what is now called the 'classical dichotomy' between the real and the monetary sector of the economy.

Walras' model obviously cannot be identified with that of a

5 *Ibid.*, p. 230.
6 E. M. Claassen, *Monnaie, Revenue Nationale et Prix*, Paris 1968, p. 25.

107

barter economy. The lack of a unit of account and of a medium of exchange, with the consequent necessity of making direct, or even 'roundabout' exchanges, of goods against goods, are of the essence of a barter economy. And the act of introducing money into such an economy could not possibly leave either relative prices, or the size of the national product, unaffected. Using money, and hence getting rid of the 'frictions' of which Koopmans spoke, means an enormous increase in the productivity of the factors of production. Our examination of Koopmans' definition of neutral money thus leads us to conclude that it is inappropriate to start out from the barter economy.

The third attempt to use this as a starting point, that made by Patinkin, is to my mind just as unsuccessful as the other two. Patinkin starts from the proposition that money is neutral 'if the mere conversion of a barter economy to a money economy does not affect equilibrium relative prices and interest'.[7] He admits that it is difficult if not impossible to establish any sort of equivalence between the two economic systems. But the reason he gives is not that, as we said above, the direct, or else 'roundabout' exchange of goods against goods means that the whole economic process is bound to be different from what it is in a money economy. It is merely that in a barter economy there can be no excess demand for money, and no dependence of an excess demand for goods on the cash balances of the economic subjects. He suggests, however, that the difficulty can be overcome by considering the barter economy as a limiting case of the money economy. We must, he says, enquire what would happen to relative prices and the interest rate if the quantity of money were made to approach zero. But he seems himself to have dealt the death blow to this analytical procedure by admitting that: 'As the nominal quantity of money approaches zero, so does the price level – and at the same rate. Hence the real quantity of money remains unaffected. Thus the limiting position that we have defined as a barter economy is one in which there exists the same *real* quantity of money as in a money economy.' He adds: 'This drawback notwithstanding, there does not seem to be any other meaningful way of comparing the respective equilibrium positions of a barter and money economy.'[8] But if this is so, we are left asking whether this sort of comparison between

7 Don Patinkin, *Money, Interest and Prices*, 2nd edition, New York 1965, p. 75.
8 *Ibid.*, p. 78.

108

a barter economy which *is not really such* and a money economy is in any way meaningful. Again it seems most reasonable to conclude that, in seeking a definition of neutral money, we must give up trying to connect it with a barter economy.

II

Let us now consider the problem from another angle: that of the conditions under which our three authors think that money can be said to be neutral.

When Wicksell speaks of money as being neutral so long as the general price level is stable, he is, of course, not saying more than many other writers who, while not using the term 'neutral', hold that if the price level is stable, money will exert no active influence on relative prices, and hence on the economic process. Hayek cites Cassel and Pigou in this connection.[9] These writers, unlike Wicksell, did not, however, make a special study of the problem of neutral money. Such remarks of theirs as appear to relate to this problem are no more than incidental. What distinguishes Wicksell's treatment is his attempt explicitly to prove the theorem linking neutrality of money with stability of the price level. He tries to show: *first*, that so long as the supply of capital offered on the market comes exclusively from savings, and corresponds to the investment demand, the money rate of interest will be equal to the natural rate; and, *secondly*, that this equality assures constancy of the price level. While his main concern was with the general price level, there are passages in his writings[10] which indicate his recognition that movements in the general price level would entail changes in relative prices, or, in other words, that when the general price level was *not* stabilized, the real quantities in the economic system *would* be affected 'from the side of money'.

A number of economists, and among them Hayek, have criticized Wicksell for failing to see that, in a growing economy, equality between 'saving and investment *ex ante*', as it would now be called, would lead, as they think, not to a stable but a falling price level. Pointing out that an expanding economy requires, as a condition

9 F. A. Hayek, *op. cit.* p. 107.
10 Knut Wicksell, *op. cit.* (English translation) pp. 111 and 154 ff., also: 'Professor Cassel's System of Economics', reprinted in *Lectures on Political Economy*, vol. I, London 1934, p. 251.

109

for stability of the price level, a growing quantity of money, they add that, since the growth must take place through credit creation by the banks, the supply of capital offered on the market will not be confined to savings, but will consist partly of additional bank credit. This, they argue, means nothing less than that the money rate of interest must fall below the equilibrium rate, i.e. the rate which would equate savings with investment (*ex ante*), and the discrepancy will distort the price structure as between consumers' goods and capital goods. It seems to them to follow that what would be required in order to render money neutral is stabilization not of the price level but of the volume of effective demand. This is the conclusion which Hayek drew from the considerations just mentioned.[11] At the same time he added some further considerations which clearly point towards the view of neutral money that has been presented by more recent writers on the subject, and which will be mentioned below.

Koopmans took substantially the same view as Hayek. Given that in the money economy the act of buying (with money) is separate from the act of selling (for money), there exists, he says, the possibility of 'half' exchange-operations. He adds that: 'Such one-sided "half" exchange-operations regularly occur in two sets of cases. The first are those where newly created money enters into circulation for the first time, or where previously circulating money disappears as such. The second are cases of so-called "hoarding" – or more exactly new hoarding – or "dishoarding".'[12] In both sets of cases Say's principle of the equivalence between total supply and total demand becomes inoperative, and inflationary or deflationary symptoms will appear. Accordingly the task of monetary policy is that of 'compensating for any deflation, due to hoarding, by creating a corresponding amount of new money, or of compensating for any inflation, due to dishoarding, by destroying money in like measure'.[13] In other words, Koopmans' condition for the neutrality of money is that the *money outlay stream* should be constant. This condition applies even in a growing economy, where it means that the price level must fall.

It is illuminating to take a somewhat closer look at the difference which separates Wicksell's view from Hayek's or Koopmans'.

11 F. A. Hayek, *op. cit.*, p. 27.
12 J. G. Koopmans, *op. cit.* p. 257.
13 *Ibid.* p. 278.

110

Wicksell was, of course, too good a monetary theorist not to have seen that in a growing economy the quantity of money must increase if the price level is to be prevented from falling. And, what is often overlooked, he gave considerable thought to the case of the growing economy.[14] He tried to show that in this case too his theorem applied; that here too the price level would be stable so long as savings equalled investment. While we cannot on this occasion examine his model in detail, we may briefly consider how it was that his conclusion on this point could be so sharply at variance with Hayek's.

The income-expenditure process as seen by the two authors may be briefly described as follows:

Hayek: The productive factors receive their income for any (short) period at the beginning of that period and spend it partly on consumption goods and partly (via savings) on investment goods at the end. From period to period productivity, and hence national output, rises while the money income of the factors remains constant, so that the price level falls. During each period, transactions on the capital market take place at some time between the payment of the factors and the sale of goods. The supply of funds, which consists exclusively of the savings of the income receivers (there being no additional borrowing from the banks), is equated to the demand by the interest rate mechanism.

Wicksell: The productive factors are again paid at the beginning of the (short) period, but at money rates which have already been raised in proportion to the anticipated increase in the marginal productivity of the factors during the period. The additional money required to finance the rise in money incomes is borrowed by the entrepreneurs from the banks and is passed on at once to the factors. It is borrowed at the rate of interest which is expected to emerge during the period from the equation between the saving (out of the higher incomes) and the demand for investment funds. In real terms Wicksell's case is just the same as Hayek's.

Thus it appears that it is possible for savings to be equal to investment, and the money rate of interest equal to the natural rate, just as well with a falling as with a constant price level, or – we may add – a rising price level. What happens to the price level is thus no criterion for the neutrality of money, or for the 'correct' monetary policy.

14 Knut Wicksell, *op. cit.* (English translation) pp. 151 ff.

111

In anticipation of what we shall have to say in the following sections, we should notice, however, that Wicksell, Hayek, and Koopmans were all agreed that monetary policy should be aimed at keeping money neutral, even if they were not all of one opinion concerning the practical norm that should be applied. They all recognized, too, that the ideal of neutral money can never be exactly reached in practice. For Hayek it remained, none the less, the principal criterion for judging monetary policy. Thus he says: 'The degree by which a concrete system approaches the condition of neutrality is one and perhaps the most important, but not the only criterion by which one has to judge the appropriateness of a given course of policy.'[15]

III

The discussion of neutral money, which had been at its height in the first half of the 1930s, petered out towards the middle of the decade. The reason was, fairly obviously, the publication of Keynes' *General Theory*. Keynes' main thesis was that in a depression effective demand must be increased as a means of nursing the economy back to a state of full employment and a higher national output. He was little concerned with relative prices.

What Wicksell would have recommended as the proper policy to follow in a depression is difficult to say. But both Hayek and Koopmans had denied that a depression should be combatted by increasing money demand. Their view was thus diametrically opposed to that of Keynes, who, far from wanting money to be neutral, believed that it should be made to exert a highly active influence on the economic process.

During the last two decades the discussion of neutral money has been resumed. But both the way of putting the problem, and the supposed solution, are now markedly different from what they were in the earlier writers' treatment. The more recent writers put the problem as one of identifying the conditions under which a change in the supply of, or demand for money will leave *relative* prices, and the equilibrium quantities of goods, unaffected. In their view money is neutral, provided these conditions are fulfilled. Their approach does not require any reference to the notion of a barter

15 F. A. Hayek, *op. cit.* p. 131.

112

economy. And most of them do in fact dispense with that notion. The analytical procedures they adopt, and the answers they give to the question of what is 'neutral money', may be illustrated by two examples.

The first is Patinkin's investigation of the problem, within the framework of comparative statics, of what will happen in response to a doubling of cash balances, assuming that all bonds outstanding (bonds being the only type of security in existence) also double in number. The conclusion to which he comes is that *under certain conditions* all money prices will double, while relative prices and the interest rate will be unaffected. (The details of the logical process by which he reaches this conclusion need not concern us in our present context.) He also shows that *under the same conditions* a change in liquidity preference, or in the demand for money, will likewise leave relative prices, the equilibrium quantities of goods, and the interest rate, unchanged. The conditions required in both cases are the following. First, prices and money wages must be flexible. Secondly, everybody must be free from 'money illusion', in a sense which Patinkin defines. Thirdly, there must be complete absence of 'distribution effects'. Fourthly, and lastly, people must expect the prices ruling in the present to continue in the future, i.e. must have 'static price expectations'.

Our second example is the similar investigation made by Gurley and Shaw. In the view of H. G. Johnson,[16] one of the chief aims of their book, *Money in a Theory of Finance*, is to elucidate the conditions under which money will be neutral or not neutral. The authors have constructed a number of models. To illustrate their procedure we may concentrate on one of these, that in which, starting from a situation of stationary equilibrium, the 'Banking Bureau' (a kind of Central Bank) buys bonds from households with new money. After a doubling of the quantity of money the new equilibrium situation here presents no difference as regards the real quantities, or the relative prices, from the old one. In the author's own words:

Doubling of nominal money is neutral in its effects on the real profile of equilibrium, because differences in nominal money are associated with equi-proportional differences in prices and

16 H. G. Johnson, 'Monetary Theory and Policy', *American Economic Review*, 52 (1962), p. 341.

113

nominal bonds. Consumers and firms are unaffected in their real behaviour by the nominal scale factor applied to the stock of money, the stock of bonds, and the prices for goods and labour. A change in nominal money, therefore, has no effect on the real variables of the economy.[17]

Like Patinkin, these authors make their result dependent upon four conditions: flexibility of prices and wages; the absence of 'money illusion'; static price expectations; and, finally, the absence of *uncompensated* distribution effects. Their own formulation[18] of this last condition is that: 'Aggregate behaviour is not sensitive to possible distribution effects that increase the wealth or income of one private sector at the expense of the other.'[19]

The contrast between the position taken by the three writers just quoted and that taken by Wicksell, Koopmans and Hayek is clear. For the older generation, ensuring the neutrality of money was a task for monetary policy. For the younger generation it is not this, but a matter of creating the four conditions listed above. In their view, were these conditions created, the size of the money outlay stream, and hence monetary policy, would (in a closed economy) be unimportant. John Stuart Mill's oft-cited dictum that: 'There cannot . . . be intrinsically a more insignificant thing in the economy of the society than money'[20] would be correct.

It should be observed that Hayek himself saw two other conditions, besides that of constancy of the money outlay stream, as being necessary for money to be neutral. One was price and wage flexibility, and the other perfectly accurate forecasting of movements in the price level.[21] He did not, however, draw the conclusion of the modern authors that if these, along with some other nonmonetary conditions were fulfilled, it would be superfluous to assign to monetary policy the task of keeping the money outlay stream constant because it would then be a matter of indifference whether money outlay (or alternatively the price level) was constant, rising, or falling.

17 J. G. Gurley and E. S. Shaw, *Money in a Theory of Finance*, Washington, D.C., 1960, p. 56.
18 *Ibid.*, pp. 67–68.
19 The two sectors distinguished by the authors are the 'consumer sector' and the 'business sector'.
20 J. S. Mill, *Principles of Political Economy*, 3rd Book, Ch. VII, § 3.
21 F. A. Hayek, *op. cit.* p. 131.

114

The conclusion that the neutrality or non-neutrality of money cannot be defined by reference to the way in which the general price level moves is one to which we were led by our critique of the views of Hayek and Wicksell in Section I above. We are here on common ground with the new monetary theorists.

IV

How much is left?

We should remember that Wicksell came upon the problem of neutral money by perceiving that the money rate of interest might diverge from the natural rate. And Hayek built his trade cycle theory round this phenomenon. For both authors the primary condition for the neutrality of money was equality between the two interest rates. The further condition of (in Hayek's case) constancy of effective demand, or (in Wicksell's) stability of the price level, was only secondary. Both authors, however, regarded this condition as necessary for defining practical rules of monetary policy. Here they were mistaken. But even if they had left this secondary criterion entirely out of account, they could still have maintained that the aim of monetary policy should be to keep money neutral by following the primary criterion of keeping the money rate of interest equal to the natural rate (when savings equal investment).

It is to be noted that Patinkin, and also Gurley and Shaw, acknowledge the possible existence of cases where an increase in the supply of money (or a decrease in the demand) will lead temporarily to a fall in the money rate of interest and to its divergence from the natural rate. And we might have expected them to identify this possibility with that of the non-neutrality of money, and to conclude that monetary policy should be aimed at preventing a discrepancy between the two interest rates. They do not, however, draw this conclusion. They are concerned only with describing how the fall in the money rate of interest comes about, and what the forces are which finally bring the rate back to the old level. In their analysis the temporary fall in the rate is not supposed to exert any effect on the productive structure.[22] Under the conditions listed in

22 It is true that Gurley and Shaw say that: 'When the inflationary process is over, and the rate of interest has returned to its initial level, the increase in capital

115

Section III above, money remains neutral; and monetary policy has no role to play in keeping it so.

The logic of the argument of these more recent writers is unassailable. They have from the start excluded any possible effect of the reduced money rate of interest on the production process by their assumption of the 'absence of distribution effects'. This assumption allows them to disregard the phenomenon of 'forced saving' (which presupposes a shift in income distribution in favour of entrepreneurs or of profit-receivers), and hence to disregard also the related increase in real capital formation. It means that the problem to which the earlier writers had attached paramount importance is simply dropped out of the picture. Once we assume that there *are* 'distribution effects', the question of what is the right monetary policy if it is desired to aim at the 'neutrality' of money inevitably re-emerges.

---

goods associated with the temporary fall in the bond rate of interest has been eliminated' (*op. cit.* p. 78). If this sentence really means what it says, the falling interest rate exerts at least a temporary effect on the amount of capital goods. Since, however, there is no indication of why or how additional capital goods should have disappeared, we must evidently assume that what is meant by 'increase in capital goods' is really 'increase in the value of capital goods', an increase which would in fact be eliminated by a return to the old (higher) interest rate.

Liberalism and the Choice of Freedoms
Fritz Machlup

Prefatorial note: The first version of this essay was presented in 1955 as one in a series of addresses initiated by Professor Hayek at Claremont Men's College. In the years since then, I have given this paper at numerous convocations in various colleges and universities and have extended it on several issues in response to questions and comments from my audiences. I have saved publication for a suitable occasion; surely none could be more suitable than this anniversary volume for Professor Hayek, with whom I have been bound in friendship for 45 years and to whom my thinking owes more than I can say.

It would be easy to present a collection of statements on 'liberals' and 'liberalism' so contradictory of one another that it would be evident on first inspection either that the authors did not know what they were talking about or had decided to talk about very different men and ideas. The meanings of liberalism have varied over time but differ chiefly among countries. The differences are most pronounced for continental Europe, on the one hand, and the United States of America, on the other.

A Regional Survey

A quick survey will bear this out. Take a look at Swiss papers and journals, for example, the *Zürcher Zeitung* and the *Schweizerische Monatshefte* and you will find that 'liberals' oppose socialism in all forms and are critical of anything that smacks of government intervention in business. Read some German papers and periodicals of any persuasion from the left to the right, and you will confirm that 'liberals' have detested and finally abolished price and production controls. Dr. Ludwig Erhard, German Minister of Economic Affairs for many years and later Chancellor, is called a liberal by his

117

friends as well as his foes because he believes in an uncontrolled economy and has battled against any kind of governmental economic planning and against all sorts of control measures favored by socialists and bureaucrats.

Turn to the north of Europe, to Norway, a country which until recently has had a socialist government, strict price controls, investment controls, and all the rest. The 'liberals' were in the opposition, furiously barking at the majority and claiming that only a free-enterprise economy, free from well-meant but ill-conceived government interventions, could save the nation from ruin. A glance into the 'liberal' weekly *Farmand* or into the socialist papers of Norway, will remove any doubt that the 'liberal' is anti-socialist and the socialist is anti-liberal. It is almost the same story in France, only that none of the numerous political parties there has a 'liberal' program and liberalism is regarded as a largely impractical ideal. Some industrialists support the 'liberal' cause, because the liberal is against strong trade unionism, against high taxes, and against socialism.

The situation is not quite so clear in England, chiefly because there is a Liberal Party and hence a confusion between a Liberal as a member of this party and a liberal in the anti-socialist and anti-interventionist sense. The Liberal Party, though opposed to the Labour Party, has not been anti-interventionist in the twentieth century. Nevertheless, if someone in England is called 'liberal' there is a good chance that he is somehow in favor of more *laissez faire* than there exists in his country.

Turning now to the United States, we find a completely different picture, and a more confusing one at that. Until a generation ago everybody, no matter what his views were, wanted to be regarded as a liberal. But what had long been an honorific has become an epithet designed to arouse suspicion. 'Liberal', in the United States, is now widely used as a name for a political color somewhere between pink and red. Many use it as a synonym for 'communist fellow traveler'. And if some editorial writers want to be particularly derogatory of anybody, they call him a 'liberal-intellectual'. This used to be an everyday occurrence in the *Baltimore Sun*.

But even in the nineteen-thirties and forties, an American was called liberal when he was a New Dealer, an advocate of economic policies to support the underprivileged, to strengthen trade unions, to maintain price and rent controls. In short, the American liberal

118

is just the man whom the European liberal is opposing with all his might. A liberal in America would be an anti-liberal in continental Europe, and a liberal in Europe would be an anti-liberal in the States.

Some people have tried to explain this terminological paradox by literary isolationism, by unfamiliarity with foreign literature. This is an oversimplification. We can find other explanations, historical and semantic. We shall see presently that the history of liberalism reveals some intrinsic contradictions that have given rise to developments in diametrically opposite directions.

A Historical Survey

The term 'liberal' originated in Spain, where in 1812 the conservatives used *vosotros liberales* referring to the constitutional party. The idea, however, was older; John Locke has been called the founding father of the political, economic, and social principles that came to constitute nineteenth-century liberalism.[1]

There can be no doubt that liberalism first stressed freedom from government interference.[2] Liberalism was individualism, emphasizing the removal of coercive restraints by which the state had restricted the individual's freedom in many activities and had thereby reduced his self-reliance, self-responsibility, self-respect, and self-realization.

A major split developed when after the imposing success of 'individualistic liberalism' a so-called 'organic liberalism' began to be expounded. The former had stressed the freedoms of individuals as individuals, the latter stressed the freedom of groups of organized individuals, especially labor organizations. The former – especially the 'Manchester liberals', Cobden and Bright – had fought chiefly for free trade, free markets, free enterprise. The latter – led by writers such as Thomas Hill Green and L. T. Hobhouse – fought chiefly for free coalition of workers. Individualist liberals sometimes

1 Goetz Briefs, 'Staat und Wirtschaft im Zeitalter der Interessenverbände', in *Laisser-Faire Pluralismus*, Berlin 1966, p. 19.
2 One of the best historians of liberalism defined liberalism as opposition to all 'coercive interference, whether in the moral, the religious, the intellectual, the social, the economic, or the political sphere'. And he stated that 'At an early stage of its development . . . the forces of liberalism concentrated on the crucial problem of limiting the interference of the state . . .' Guido de Ruggiero, 'Liberalism' in *Encyclopaedia of the Social Sciences*, New York 1933, Vol. IX.

describe the development of 'organic liberalism' as an attempt of collectivists and egalitarians to steal the attractive banner of 'liberalism' as a front for their objectives.

But there was still widespread recognition of the fact that a harmonious linking of liberty with equality was only possible as long as equality referred to the treatment of people before the law, not to income or wealth. In other words, liberty and equality were regarded as partly complementary, partly antithetical. Even a socialist like Harold Laski refrained from expanding the concept of liberalism to include the idea of income equality, which most of the time may have been closer to his heart than was individual freedom. He once said that in a state of 'distressing inequality . . . freedom is not worth having.' But he kept the two ideas apart, even if he did not see or show a conflict between the two as social goals.[3]

To join the two ideals in one's political program without making it clear that they may conflict with each other, and without deciding which one is to have priority in case of conflict, is bad enough. It is worse if the two are conceptually merged, as it was done by many European socialists and American liberals who changed the concept of freedom from that of non-interference to that of 'effective power'. It started with a French political philosopher, Paul Janet, 1878, became accepted doctrine among many socialists, and was given American philosophical blessing by John Dewey, who stated that 'liberty is the effective power to do specific things'. This fusion of the idea of non-interference with the idea of effective power (which often means buying power) could not but spread confusion. We shall have to say more about it; at this point we merely state that this was one of the chief points from which American and European liberals moved in different directions. To illustrate, I quote Justice

3 See Laski's description of the development of English liberalism from its earlier emphasis on the 'antithesis of individual and state' to its recent acceptance or advocacy of the social welfare state. According to Laski, 'the body of ideas we call liberalism emphasized the undesirability of restraint . . .', and the idea of 'liberty was divorced from the ideas of both equality and justice.' This changed only after most of the aims of liberalism had been attained in England. 'Democratic agitation, which from 1600 to about 1870 had been occupied with the removal of barriers upon individual action, after 1870 began to press for the deliberate creation of equalitarian conditions.' Thus, 'the liberal state of the nineteenth century was gradually replaced by the social service state of the twentieth. This may be described by saying that it again joins the ideal of liberty to that of equality, and this in the name of social justice'. Harold Laski, 'Liberty' in *Encyclopaedia of the Social Sciences*, New York 1933, Vol. IX, p. 443.

William O. Douglas, stating in *An Almanac of Liberty*, (1954, p. vi), that he 'ranks freedom to eat with freedom to speak.'

There are still other elements in the historical development of the liberalist movement that may explain the present terminological paradoxes. I refer chiefly to the identification of the liberal in the nineteenth century with the reformer, the progressive. A liberal was one who favored institutional changes. In the words of John Stuart Mill (1865), 'A Liberal is he who looks forward for his principles of government: a Tory looks backward.'

Surely, Mill did not mean this to be a definition of a liberal. Not every change or reform increases the freedoms of the people, and a liberal must certainly not be favorable to illiberal reforms. In an illiberal society the liberal must be a reformer in order to obtain freedom, in a liberal society he must be a conservative in order to maintain freedom. In the great days of classical liberalism the 'radical reformers' fought for the removal of illiberal restraints and interferences. The idea of the liberal as a perennial radical reformer was strong and has probably contributed to the notion, so widespread in America, that all radical reformers are liberals.

Finally, good liberals respect the thinking of others, and are tolerant of other views; more than that, they have usually come to the defense of anybody who was threatened by state or society because of his non-conformance. A good defense attorney often develops sympathy with his defendant. Thus, the tolerance and defense of socialist and other illiberal views may have made many a good liberal sympathetic with these views and may have blinded him to the incompatibility of the position defended with the position he originally stood for.

'Fuzzy Liberalism'

Thus, we can trace the present-day confusion about the meaning of liberalism to several developments:

1. The liberal demand for freedom of coalition has been extended to the demand for unlimited freedom for groups and unions even where such collective freedom is in conflict with the freedom of the individual; this is the *collectivist* streak in fuzzy liberalism.

2. The liberal demand for equality before the law has been

121

extended to equality of income even where measures to that effect are in conflict with the freedom of the individual; this is the *egalitarian* streak in fuzzy liberalism.

3. The liberal demand for individual freedom has been extended from the mere absence of coercive interference to positive measures to increase and equalize the individuals' effective power to do or get what they want even where such measures are in conflict with the freedom of the individual; this is another *redistributive* streak in fuzzy liberalism.

4. The liberal demand for progressive and radical reforms designed to increase the welfare of society by releasing forces previously restrained has been extended to reforms to increase collective welfare even when in conflict with the freedom of the individual: this is the *radical-interventionist* streak in fuzzy liberalism.

5. The liberal demand for tolerance of dissenting opinions and for the defense of the disseminators of these ideas and their right to advocate communism or anything they like has been extended to the actual support of socialist ideas which are basically in conflict with the freedom of the individual: this is the *fellow-travelling* streak in fuzzy liberalism.

These explanations for the perversion of the original liberal position to what most Americans now call liberalism is not inconsistent with the simple explanation that most of those who sound off – *pro* or *con* – about 'liberalism' are unfamiliar with the classical writings. I do not wish to deny anybody the right to be ignorant. But I believe it is fair to state that, despite all its historical developments and inherent contradictions, American liberalism could not have become quite so fuzzy if the so-called intellectuals had really been intellectuals in the sense of people who read books, including foreign literature. They would have learnt that the collectivist, egalitarian, radical-interventionist and fellow-traveling streaks in American 'liberalism' are incompatible with liberalism in the classical, individualistic sense.

Two Fundamental Errors

Fuzzy thinking about liberalism is fostered by some esoteric concepts of freedom and aggravated by errors of reasoning. The esoteric concepts of freedom shall be relegated to the honored place of a footnote.[4] The more worldly confusions – some merely grammatical and semantic – shall be reviewed here in the simplest possible form.

A relatively simple confusion is that between being *'free to'* and *'free from'*. It is most manifest in the pronouncement of the 'four essential human freedoms' by President Franklin D. Roosevelt. These are four admirable principles; no well-meaning person in our time will ever oppose freedom of speech, freedom of worship, freedom from want, and freedom from fear. The trouble is only that many people see in these principles the foundations of liberalism, each expressing an important freedom or liberty. In fact, only the first two are liberties, the others are not. Freedom of speech and of religion give people the rights to speak, express themselves, and worship in any way they like; these freedoms mean that state and society should not coerce or restrain individuals in the realms of thought expression and religion. Freedom from want and from fear are of an entirely different nature: they express the hope that governments will take measures designed to abolish poverty and war. To be free from want is to be 'rid' of destitution; to be free from fear is to be safe from war and aggression; just as to be free from disease is to be healthy, perhaps thanks to having found effective vaccines. Measures designed to abolish poverty and war are most desirable, but they do not give people any rights 'to do or not to do, as they please'. They do not call for the proscription of public restraints on actions of the individual, but require positive prescription for action by the government.

President Lyndon B. Johnson, in January 1968, added a 'fifth freedom' to the 'aspirations' of the nation, and it is again chiefly designed to make people 'free from', not 'free to': he proclaimed the 'freedom from ignorance', to be secured by better educational

4 Mortimer J. Adler, in his work *The Idea of Freedom*, New York 1958–61, proposed three fundamentally different concepts: the freedoms of 'self-perfection', 'self-realization', and 'self-determination'. The first is an inner freedom beyond the reach of outward circumstances, a capacity to order one's will in accordance with wisdom and goodness; it includes the 'inner freedom' of the slave and the prisoner. The second is the ability to carry out one's intention without outward obstacles, without shackles, threats, or social disapproval. The third is 'free will' in contrast to determinism of one's motives; it means that man's will is not the effect of certain knowable causes and not constrained by outer forces. Only the second of these concepts, the freedom of self-realization, corresponds to the mundane notion of freedom, though it does not sufficiently distinguish the source of the outward obstacles: are they always man-made or can they be natural?

facilities for all. Perhaps, though, in this case, with the history of unequal access to schools, there is a blending of the two ideas, provision of additional services by the government and abolition of legal and illegal restraints that keep individuals from partaking of what is available. To the extent that government is called upon to provide additional educational services, the nation may become better educated and eventually 'free from ignorance'. To the extent that individual children will not be coerced into bad schools and not intimidated from going to better schools, they will be 'free to attend' the latter. Yet, even where the two meanings of 'free' seem to converge in practice, to be 'free from' something is different from being 'free to do' something.

Of course, one may say that we are free to do as we please only if we are free from external coercion and restraint. Thus we could formulate freedom of speech as freedom from restraints on speech and expression; and we could formulate freedom of worship as freedom from restraints on religious or irreligious pursuits. In these cases, the absence of coercion and intimidation secures freedom. On the other hand, in order to make people 'free from' want or ignorance, positive efforts are required, for which, in President Johnson's words, 'Americans have always stood ready to pay the cost in energy and treasure' and which the nation can afford only as it becomes 'wealthier'. Please note that no wealth is needed to secure the freedoms of speech and of worship.

A second fundamental, though related, error may be referred to as the confusion between '*I may*' and '*I can*'. It bears again on the previously mentioned confusion between freedom as non-interference with an individual's actions and his effective power to act. Capacity to act, having the power and the means to do something, is surely not the same thing as having the freedom to do it. The fusion of the idea of effective power with the idea of freedom was obviously proposed by those who held that freedom in the sense of non-interference was of no practical value to those who lacked the power, chiefly the buying power. The sentiment behind this proposition may be illustrated by the grumbling declaration 'I do not care if I *may* do what I *cannot* do. Why should anybody be free to do things which I cannot afford?'

I must admit that the freedom to buy a Rolls-Royce and a luxury yacht has little practical relevance to those who have no money to buy them. But this does not mean that we should expand the concept of 'freedom' to include 'capacity to buy'. I *can* buy illegal drugs if I have enough money, but I *may* not lawfully do so. I *may*, under present law and moral norms, buy the most expensive diamond for my dear wife but, alas, I *cannot* do so within my income. Just as I can understand that many poor people find it uninteresting that they are free to buy what they are unable to buy, I can also understand that many uneducated people find it ridiculous that so much fuss is being made about freedom to teach and inquire, things they cannot do anyhow. Apart from the few who comprehend that they and their children may be indirectly affected, to the masses freedom of scientific inquiry is of little interest. However, would it not be silly to extend the concept of freedom of scientific research so that it includes the capacity for it? Would it not be preposterous if some ultra-pragmatists were to say that Professor X lacks freedom of inquiry since, although no one limits his research activities, his reasoning powers are limited?

I find it difficult to understand what may have compelled learned men and eminent thinkers to take three different ideas – (1) 'I am physically and mentally capable of doing it', (2) 'I have enough money to afford it', and (3) 'I shall not be prevented from doing nor punished for having done it', – and to throw all three into one pot and scramble them into an omelette, which they call 'freedom' or, synonymously 'effective power'. This omelette may be all right for some practical purposes and thus appeal to the pragmatist philosopher. But surely for other purposes, equally practical, we ought to keep the three ideas apart, and this means to use words that help maintain the separation. Unfortunately, too many writers prefer the omelette. D. G. Ingle, a physiologist, wrote this: 'We know many physical and biological limitations on freedom. Man is not free to live without oxygen, water, and food. He cannot jump as much as eight feet into the air or lift a house or become young after once being old. Freedom is extended by the use of tools and knowledge . . . Freedoms are limited by the nature of inborn drives, likes and dislikes . . . The burned child is no longer free to seek the fire . . .'[5]

As an example of the mixing of the second and third of the three ideas, I have earlier quoted Justice Douglas, pronouncing an equivalence of freedom to eat and freedom to speak. In an equally strong pronouncement, Sidney and Beatrice Webb once contended

5 D.G.I.: 'Editorial: The Biology of Freedom', *Perspectives in Biology and Medicine*, VII (Winter, 1964) p. 141.

125

that 'Personal freedom means, in effect, the power of the individual to buy sufficient food, shelter, and clothing.' This confusion between buying power and personal freedom can perhaps be illucidated by the reminder that there may be religious, moral, or legal prohibitions of using existing buying power in particular ways. Even affluent Brahmins may not feel free to eat meat, nor affluent orthodox Jews and Muslims to eat pork. If religious taboos are not sufficiently impressive to drive home my point, let me allude to legal restraints and switch from the 'freedom to eat' to the 'freedom to drink'. The difference between *having the means* to buy gin and whiskey and *being free* to buy such drinks became quite clear to all Americans (or to all drinking Americans, to stay within the confines of pragmatism) when the prohibition laws were enacted. Having money neither gives nor implies freedom; it merely enables you to exercise more of the existing freedoms.

As another example of the mixing of the first and third ideas, let me once more contrast physical incapacity and legal prohibition. If we were to put the physiological incapacity of a mute person and the authoritarian restraint on an advocate of subversion into the same category and declared that neither of the two was 'free' to speak, we would be guilty of badly confusing the issue. The one is unable to speak, say, because of a congenital defect, a disease, an accident; the other is punished if he speaks out and advocates subversion. To include both in the concept of freedom of speech is nonsense.

A definition of freedom which negates the difference between non-interference and effective power (or welfare or want satisfaction) destroys the essential meaning of the word 'freedom'. If it is defined as the capacity or opportunity to get what one wants, we are barred from analyzing the important question whether the development of this capacity or opportunity is better served by restrictionism or by non-interference, by collective control or by individual freedom.

Five Other Errors

Besides the 'fundamental' errors just reviewed, a few other errors concerning freedom and restraints on freedom ought to be mentioned. They are neither grammatical nor semantic, but refer to questions of political theory. Like all questions of theory, these 'corrections of errors' should be presented with reservations and admissions of uncertain knowledge. In the concise formulations attempted here, my statements may sound more apodictic than they are intended. On the other hand, I do not think that my contentions will be terribly controversial. After the two errors discussed, we may continue the enumeration of the next five.

The third error lies in the assumption that the coercive restraints, the presence of which means *negations of freedom, are always effected by the state*, the government, the 'magistrate' (to use the classical term). In actual fact, while the state is usually the most effective negator of freedom, certain coercive restraints may come from all sorts of people or groups in society. At all times have mob violence, clique action and pressure-group manoeuvres been operating to infringe, restrict, or completely eliminate freedoms in several spheres of activity.

A fourth error lies in the belief that *only the state, the government, can effectively uphold freedom* and protect individuals from coercive restraints. Certain types of restraint cannot be restrained by legal prohibition and coercion, but only by moral code and by a strong feeling for tact and manners slowly developed and perpetuated by the upbringing of the young.

A fifth error lies in the belief that freedom implies the *absence of coercion of any sort*. This overlooks that coercion may be required to enforce guarantees of freedom and to protect individuals from certain coercive restraints imposed by other individuals or groups. Of course, all coercive power must be vested in government and must be exercised strictly under the 'rule of law'. This means that all laws apply with equal force to everybody without discrimination and are of such general nature that they can be applied without arbitrary discretion. Under the 'rule of law' no one has a right that is denied to others. But equality before the law involves enforcement of the law, and enforcement involves the use of coercive power by the state.

A sixth error lies in the *identification of liberalism with* laissez-faire. There is a strong presumption for Thomas Jefferson's rule that 'the best government is the one that governs least', but this does not means that individual freedoms are always most securely guarded where government is confined to the prevention of violence, theft, and fraud. The preservation of a maximum of freedom may

127

call for government measures to maintain competition, which private contracts might restrict, to provide services which private enterprise cannot supply, and to prevent misery which private charity cannot cope with.

This error of making liberalism equal to *laissez-faire* was forcefully criticized by one whom careless readers have sometimes accused of having committed it, namely Professor Hayek in his *Road to Serfdom* (London 1944, p. 13). This is what he wrote:

> There is nothing in the basic principles of Liberalism to make it a stationary creed, there are no hard-and-fast rules fixed once and for all. The fundamental principle that in the ordering of our affairs we should make as much use as possible of the spontaneous forces of society, and resort as little as possible to coercion, is capable of an infinite variety of applications. There is, in particular, all the difference between deliberately creating a system within which competition will work as beneficially as possible, and passively accepting institutions as they are. Probably nothing has done so much harm to the liberal cause as the wooden insistence of some liberals on certain rough rules of thumb, above all the principle of *laissez-faire*. Yet in a sense this was necessary and unavoidable. Against the innumerable interests who could show that particular measures would confer immediate and obvious benefits on some, while the harm they caused was much more indirect and difficult to see, nothing short of some hard-and-fast rule would have been effective. And since a strong presumption in favour of industrial liberty had undoubtedly been established, the temptation to present it as a rule which knew no exceptions was too strong always to be resisted.

A seventh error lies in believing that '*freedom is indivisible*'. This is a beautiful and well-meant slogan, but it just is not so. There is not one indivisible freedom, but there are many freedoms, many kinds of human activity to which the principle of non-interference may or may not be applied. Some of these freedoms may be independent of each other, others complementary or competing in the sense that more of one may permit either more or less of another. That is to say, greater freedom in one realm of human action may make it either easier or harder to achieve freedom in another realm of action. Some freedoms support one another, others impair one

128

another; and where there is such a conflict of freedoms it is important to know it and to analyse their comparative value for the pursuit of happiness, present or future.

The hierarchy of freedoms in our systems of value may be highly complicated and uncertain. Depending on our moral and social philosophy, we may regard some freedoms as absolute or ultimate values, others only as instrumental or intermediate values. Moreover, one and the same freedom may be valued both as an end in itself and as a means to other ends. For example, freedom of enterprise may be a means to more material progress and abundance, a means to the preservation of other liberties and, at least for some of its advocates, an end in itself. The same may be said about the freedom of teaching: a means to faster progress, to greater happiness, to the more secure attainment of other freedoms, and an end in itself. At the same time these freedoms may conflict with other goals of society. To close our eyes to these complications would be rather irresponsible. These interrelationships between different freedoms have to be examined in greater detail, but we have several tasks to do before we are ready for it.

Opportunity and Freedom

If, in the discussion of the pragmatists' identification of freedom with effective power, I succeeded in establishing a forward position in the opponents' territory, I must not leave it unprotected from counterattacks. Too often have I seen that, after an initial retreat, the forces proclaiming that freedom requires power came up resurging with new strength and compelled me to resume the battle. Previous arguments had to be repeated and new ones adduced to reinforce the previous. I have realized that the pragmatists' conception of freedom is too firmly ingrained in the thinking on these issues to be uprooted in one try.

I have sometimes resorted to quoting Frank H. Knight as an ally, but found it to be of questionable help. His pronouncement on the central issue is so ambiguous that it may just as easily be used against my position as in its support. Here it is:

Freedom, correctly conceived, *implies* opportunity, unobstructed

129

opportunity, to use power, which must be possessed, to give content to freedom, or make it effective. It is a common fallacy to demand power under the name of freedom, and usage badly needs the expression 'effective freedom' to take account of power and of knowledge and other dimensions in the scope of voluntary action.[6]

I believe Knight means virtually the same that I am trying to say – especially when he offers the expression 'effective freedom' as a substitute for the pragmatists' 'effective power.' However, his statement may easily be misinterpreted – especially where it says that freedom implies power already possessed. This formulation disregards the great fertility of freedom even where the power to take advantage of freedom does not yet exist and the acquisition of such power through special efforts, often in the search for new knowledge, is made attractive precisely because the freedom is still unused or in Knight's phrase 'ineffective'. In other words, certain freedoms may be of great importance for individuals and for society when no knowledge, no opportunity, and no power exist as yet to make use of presumably 'empty' freedoms. Their importance lies in the aspirations and ambitions which they arouse and which may lead to the search for the knowledge, opportunity, and power that are required to exercise the previously unused freedoms. In short, 'ineffective' freedoms can be highly effective.

As a strong believer in the persuasiveness of primitive examples, I propose to offer one that can both expose the fallacy inherent in the notion of freedom as effective power and exhibit the usefulness of the notion of effective 'ineffective freedom' without power. Suppose an automobile capable of doing 100 miles an hour is restricted to a maximum speed of 25 m.p.h. owing to a speed-limit enforced by the police. Suppose further that I, on my bicycle on the same roads, cannot pedal more than about 20 m.p.h. owing to my physical limitations. Does it make much sense to insist on a concept of freedom that makes my freedom 20 m.p.h. and the automobilist's 25 m.p.h.? Is it not more reasonable to admit that our physical powers are different (his 100 m.p.h. against my 20 m.p.h.) whereas our freedom is restricted to the same limit (25 m.p.h.)? And would it not be sensible to hold that an increase

6 Frank H. Knight, 'Laissez-Faire: Pro and Con', *Journal of Political Economy*, 75 (December, 1967), p. 790.

130

or abolition of the legal speed-limit would increase my desire to take advantage of the unused freedom – and acquire a faster vehicle?

The point should be easy to see. As long as the law restricts all traffic on the roads to 25 m.p.h., I can certainly gain no more than 5 m.p.h. by acquiring a car and I do not find it worth while to work harder to earn the money to buy the car. If the speed limit is increased or abolished, that is, if I am free to go much faster, or as fast as I can and wish, then I will make the effort that will eventually enable me to exercise my freedom. In the particular example, the freedom to go fast precedes my 'opportunity' or 'capacity' to go fast. Actual capacity and opportunity are created only after the freedom is established and a potential is made into a reality.

The relationship between actual and potential opportunity, on the one hand, and freedom, on the other, becomes very complicated in the context of the social objective of 'equality of opportunities'. It is a hopeless task to analyze this notion successfully unless distinctions are made with regard to the origin of the opportunities in question. We must distinguish (1) opportunities offered by society, in particular by the government, such as access to facilities (schools, hospitals, police protection) or to jobs or markets, (2) opportunities offered as gifts of nature such as the people's physical and mental endowments, and (3) opportunities offered by the environment into which we were born, including the situation of the parents to whom we were born. Realizing that all three types of opportunity can be very unequal, we ought to contemplate the implications which any attempts to equalize opportunities would have for freedom.

(1) Equalizing the opportunities provided by the state, or society in general, can be a requirement of several freedoms, for example, freedom of access to employment, freedom of entry into trades, or freedom of consumer choice. (2) Opportunities offered as gifts of nature cannot be equalized at all, but can at best be compensated for by deliberate imposition of social handicaps upon persons favored by nature; attempts of this sort constitute reductions of individual freedoms. (3) Inequalities of the third type can be removed only by society providing special assistance to the disfavored. If the cost of this assistance is heavy and is borne chiefly by those favored by their lucky choice of parents or environment, the implied redistribution of income may again amount to a system of assigning handicaps to the more fortunate. But even if the cost is small and the benefits to the assisted are great, the provision of the assistance is

131

not a 'freedom'. Some may see it as an act of 'social justice'; it may serve a widely desired social objective; but it has nothing to do with liberty.

Action designed to provide 'equality of opportunities' has thus three very different relationships to freedom. It may enhance freedom, it may reduce freedom, or it may have no connection with freedom. It depends on the origin of the opportunities that are unequal and about which intervention by the government is proposed.

Limitations by Nature and Restrictions by Man

In the distinctions between types of opportunity the same theme recurred that I previously developed in my criticism of the confusion between 'I can' and 'I may': the difference between limitations by nature and restrictions by man. Perhaps one should not dispute about semantic tastes and linguistic preferences, but I regard it as an obfuscation of thought and a diseconomy of words to expand the meaning of freedom so much that it requires the absence not only of acts of oppression and measures of restriction committed by men but also of limitations of human capacities or opportunities by 'nature'.

There is a gray area between black and white, where it may be possible to differ in judging whether certain limitations are entirely dictated by laws of nature or perhaps to some extent chargeable to human action or failures to act. Limitations on men's opportunities that have not been caused by human action but could with some good will be removed by human effort, at no large cost to anybody, can perhaps, without undue strain, be included, along with the restrictions imposed by men upon fellow-men, among infringements of freedom.

Foremost among the limitations that are neither completely natural nor consciously designed by man are self-grown social institutions possibly leading to results that some groups in society do not recognize as independent of human will. If such recognition or non-recognition is merely a matter of ideology, not subject to evidence and logical argument, the conflict whether a limitation of freedom is involved cannot be resolved objectively. Yet, even if the

132

conflict cannot be resolved without resort to fundamental postulates of social philosophy, it is often possible to engage in immanent criticism and to show the extent to which contentions and convictions bear on the conclusions.

The generalities of the preceding paragraph, however good they sound, will remain empty phrases if we do not offer illustrations of the type of issue in question. I shall try. What effects upon real incomes of industrial labor and agricultural labor can be attributed to (a) all land being owned by the state or community, (b) all land being privately owned but distributed very unequally, most of it being held by large owners, or (c) all land being broadly distributed in only small holdings? The point of the argument is, of course, that many do not accept the given historical situation as a result of an immutable law of nature, even if no man alive had had anything to do with its evolution. There are, however, objective ways of separating the marginal productivities of labor and of land, and of showing that pure labor incomes are independent of the distribution of land property. What is really involved is who gets the rent of land. In the case of public ownership of land, the government may use the rent collected from the producers in any way it likes; it may, in one form or another, use it for the benefit of industrial labor, agricultural labor, or any group in society. Most of the *ideologues* confuse the question of property in land with the question of monopoly in the sale of the produce of land. If such monopolies exist, they can have strong effects upon the incomes of labor as well as of other groups. Such monopolies, moreover, are clearly the result of conscious and deliberate interventions enforced or condoned by the present government and have, therefore, the character of man-made restrictions upon people's freedom of choice.

Another illustration from the gray area: While the laws of nature are independent of human will, knowledge of these laws and the use of that knowledge can surely be influenced by human action. Conceivably, government can restrict the freedom of scientific research and thus reduce the production of new knowledge; it can restrict the freedom of teaching and thus reduce the dissemination of existing knowledge; it can restrict the freedom of applying existing knowledge and thus reduce the use of knowledge in production. These would be examples of infringements of freedoms. The government may also take positive actions to promote scientific research,

133

to promote education (that is, the transmission of knowledge), and to promote practical application of technology (for example, through agricultural field service). While these 'positive' influences on people's choices may extend the scope of producers' and consumers' choices, I see no advantage in characterizing these influences as enlargements of freedom. I see no point in using the findings of economic welfare analysis – that is, findings of whether the increase of material welfare is accelerated or retarded by certain interventions in the allocation of resources – for judgments of whether 'freedom' is being enhanced or restricted. To be free is one thing, to be well off is another, as I am going to argue presently.

My insistence on separating the origins of any limitations on human choices and on regarding as limitations of freedom only those that are the result of restrictions and restraints which man imposes upon man is by no means a position outside the main stream in the history of ideas. I have some rather strange precursors in expressing this position and I am taking the risk of quoting the anarchist Mikhail Bakunin as an ally on this issue. In his *Dieu et l'Etat* (posthumously published in 1876), Bakunin wrote this: 'The liberty of man consists solely in this, that he obeys the laws of Nature because he has himself recognized them as such and not because they have been imposed upon him externally by any foreign will whatever, be it divine, collective, or individual.'

Let me put this in my own way, to express my own point of view. If certain constraints on my actions are suspected by me not to have originated from impartial 'nature' but to have been imposed upon me by some evil power, by a foreign will, by man, then I will feel these constraints as encroachments on my freedom. As long as I cannot blame anybody for the constraints, my freedom is not infringed.

The concept of freedom, I submit, is logically correlated with the concept of suppression, that is with the threat of man being suppressed, restrained, or punished by fellow man. *Actual* existence of freedom presupposes *potential* suppression, for it means that there need not be fear of this suppression actually to occur. To be fully comprehended, the meaning of freedom requires a specification of both the potentially suppressed and the potential suppressors and in addition a specification of the activities of the former which the latter may be inclined to restrain or punish. Hence, there can be no freedom that is not the freedom of a person to do specified things

– which he may or may not be capable of doing – without fear of restraint or punishment by one or more other persons.

Welfare and Freedom

The great protest of the opponents of this concept of freedom is that it is merely *negative*: the absence of restriction, coercion and suppression, and the absence of justified fear of restriction, coercion or punishment. The pragmatist wants a more *positive* concept of freedom, such as that of the effective power to do things. If nature denies me the capacity to do certain things or society refuses me the buying power I would need to afford them, then I am not really 'free' to do what I want – so argues the pragmatist. I have rejected this merger of separate ideas as a violation of good analytic practice.

At one point in the preceding section I objected also to the widespread notion that an increase in one's economic welfare would enhance one's 'freedom'. Some of those who protest against the 'merely negative' concept of freedom as nonrestriction and nonsuppression want to make it 'positive' by having it comprise all the goodies that life provides, the entire bundle of goods and services that make up our economic welfare. Economists will find this a strange case of logical intransitivity. For they are used to a concept of total welfare that includes not only economic welfare but also such nice and satisfying things as being left alone: freedom. Thus, for the economist freedom is included in total welfare; yet, for the pragmatic philosopher welfare is included in freedom. Since formal logic tells us that if A includes B, B cannot include A, we had better start agreeing which is the A and which is the B in our universe of discourse. We need not in the process sacrifice our theories about the possibly mutual effects of freedom as non-restraint upon economic welfare (or upon freedom as effective power). The decision in the Court of Logic, however, must be unanimous: if freedom is a part of welfare, welfare cannot be a part of freedom.

Since even dogs may have strong views about the relative satisfactions derived, on the one hand, from being free to bark and not being kept on a leash and, on the other hand, from being served good and plentiful foods enriched with meat and bones, the dogs surely will take my side: freedom is a part of welfare and its

135

significance is not reduced by being 'merely' negative. In a dog's life the non-punishment for barking and the non-restraint by the leash may be of such utility that he may consider these negatives a fair trade-off for the positive contents of his food tray – apart from the fact that the unleashing may allow him to find some extra tidbits not provided for in his master's plan.

A Catalogue of Freedom

In the discussion of the 'seventh' error of the assertion that 'freedom is indivisible', I advanced the thesis of the multiplicity of freedoms, some of which are reinforcing one another, others conflicting with one another, some are regarded as instrumental values, others as ultimate values.

As an aid in the examination of the relationship among the many separate freedoms, I have prepared a catalogue of freedoms. This catalogue is incomplete in several respects. Apart from my inability to give it adequate comprehensiveness, there must be omissions in the sense that the grant of certain freedoms is out of the question, because they would conflict with other more important freedoms, not only beyond some point, but from the very outset. To give the most obvious examples, a freedom to kill would be incompatible with other people's freedom to live; a freedom to take what belongs to others would be incompatible with the freedom to have property. Or to give an example where we stay within the same kind of activity, a freedom to continue to drive while the traffic light is red would interfere with other people's freedom to drive while they have the green light, and it might even restrict people's freedom to stay whole and alive.

As Herbert Spencer put it, liberalism claims the right of each to the maximum freedom compatible with equal freedom for all others. But since these freedoms may relate to different kinds of human activity, this postulate presupposes a rough quantification of the values of freedoms and sometimes a weighing and balancing of different freedoms of different people.

My catalogue contains two dozens of freedoms, some of them overlapping. All are freedoms 'to do or not to do'; not all exist in our society, and some exist only to a limited extent. We may divide

LIBERALISM AND THE CHOICE OF FREEDOMS

A catalogue of some important freedoms – to do or not to do as we please – which may exist in various spheres of activity

Freedom of	would mean that everybody is free, without restraint, to
Work	work in any kind of occupation, or not to work at all
Enterprise	apply any kind of resources to any kind of business in any field of production
Trade	transport, import, or export any kind and quantity of commodities
Travel	travel abroad and everywhere in the country
Migration	move and make his residence abroad or everywhere in the country
Contract	make any sort of binding contract with anyone, except under duress, or with deceit or fraud
Markets	buy or sell any quantity at any price agreeable to him and to the other party
Competition and entry	enter any industry, trade, or market and compete in any way except with use of violence, deceit, or fraud
Choice of consumption	use his buying power for any goods or services he chooses, with prices reflecting the demand for them and the supply of resources required for their production
Choice of occupation	use his labor power and skills in any occupation he chooses, with wages reflecting the supply of the labor in question and the demand for the products to which it contributes
Coalition and association	combine with anybody for any purpose not involving harm to others
Assembly	convene or attend gatherings for discussion and deliberation of any subject whatsoever
Vote	cast his vote in free and secret balloting in periodic elections and referenda
Revolution	overthrow a government that denies essential freedoms
Thought and expression	think, write, and express in art, music or any other way
Speech	speak privately and publicly on any subject and in any vein whatsoever
Press	Print and publish anything and distribute it in any way
Privacy	work, play, rest, converse, and correspond unexposed to the view or knowledge by any uninvited
Nonconformance and eccentricity	be different in appearance, habits and ways of life, however foolish, perverse or wrong it may look to others
Teaching	teach any subject, facts, ideas, or methods
Research	investigate any subject by any method
Learning	study or attend lectures on any subject
Religion	worship in any way or not at all, if he so wishes
Conscience	refuse to do things against his conscience

ECONOMICS

POLITICAL

INTELLECTUAL AND MORAL

137

them roughly into three groups, again partly overlapping: economic freedoms, political freedoms, and intellectual and moral (or cultural) freedoms.

I cannot take the space to comment on every item on the list. One could spend several hours, perhaps an entire academic term, discussing the interrelationships between the various freedoms. I can select only a few points for discussion here.

Economic Freedoms

Free choice of consumption and occupation, two of the economic freedoms listed, may be understood either in a merely formal way, as a mere absence of rationing restrictions, of prohibitions and other barriers, or in a comprehensive way, as the operation of a price mechanism that assures perfect realization of the law of supply and demand under competition in every market. If the two freedoms of choice were only formal, they would be consistent with the most thorough central planning of the economy by a dictator. Assume the dictator decides on the basis of his judgment what is good for the nation, and how much of each commodity ought to be produced. He can carry out this decision either by coercion or by using the price mechanism: he may set wages so that he attracts no more and no fewer workers than are required in each industry to produce the planned output and he may set prices so that he attracts no more and no fewer consumers than he can serve out of his planned output. The dictator will then find that there are high profits and serious losses in various industries, but he can take care of that through taxes and subsidies. Neither the worker nor the consumer needs to know that he is barred from following his own free choice; yet *we* know that under such a system the consumption and occupation patterns would express only the wish of the dictatorial planner and not the preferences of the consumers and workers. Only when all wage rates and prices are consistent in the sense that they reflect the supply of labor in each occupation and the demand for products in each industry can we say that there is really full freedom of choice. In this case, however, the freedoms of choice of occupation and consumption are so comprehensive in their scope that they include or presuppose several of the other economic freedoms in our catalogue.

138

Another case of overlapping or even duplication is free enterprise and free competition if the latter is understood in the sense of unrestricted entry into the industry (and has no connotation of absence of power or domination over markets, supplies, and prices).

On the other hand, there are some serious conflicts of freedoms within the economic sphere. The freedoms of coalition and of contract may be used to restrict the freedoms of work and enterprise, and thereby the freedoms of choice of consumption and occupation. We know of many instances where workers' or businessmen's combinations have created monopolistic positions restricting entry into occupations or industries.

Mere freedom of coalition could not have created all the strong labor monopolies of our days; active government interventions and failure to suppress private coercive activities have helped in this process. But once labor unions have attained great power, they can maintain it and exercise it (to restrict the freedom to work and freedom to enter the occupation of one's choice) by the mere use of the freedom of combination and contract. Hence, some limitations have been made in the freedom of contract between unions and employers in the hope to increase the freedoms that have been encroached upon. But who can say that the laws to this effect have been successful? Many trade unions use the freedoms of coalition and of contract in ways badly restricting the freedom to work. And no practical solution of this problem is in sight.

The use by businessmen of the freedom of contract, together with a host of governmental restrictions of trade and entry, have resulted in restrictions of free enterprise. Freeing trade and entry by removing the restrictions which governments through tariffs, quotas, licenses, and many other measures have imposed on foreign and domestic competition might solve the problem to a large extent. Without government support, businessmen would probably not be able to use their freedom of contract to restrict very seriously the freedom of enterprise and competition. But there is no sign that governments are ready to do anything in the indicated direction, and thus the conflict of freedoms remains.

Political Freedoms

There is less conflict among the various freedoms in the political sphere; but some of these freedoms have been reduced or abolished even in the United States. The freedom to revolt, to which the founding fathers appealed when they successfully subverted the previous government, was often cited and glorified in the early years of the republic. Several of the state constitutions included the freedom to revolt among the fundamental rights of the people; and Abraham Lincoln, in his First Inaugural Address (1861) reconfirmed this principle in ringing words: 'Whenever the people shall grow weary of the existing government, they can exercise their constitutional right of amending it or their revolutionary right to dismember or overthrow it'.

A 'freedom of revolution' to overthrow a government of which people have 'grown weary' is an odd idea. What percentage of the people must have become dissatisfied? Would the state ever grant to a disenchanted minority a legal right to use violence to remove a lawfully elected government? Could one reasonably expect a government not to attempt to suppress such violence? I suppose what the founding fathers, and later Lincoln, meant by the 'freedom to revolt' and the 'revolutionary right' of the people was a *moral* right to revolt against oppression when all legal means of bringing about change – that is, an end to the denial by the government of essential freedoms – had failed. A freedom to change by violence the form of a lawfully elected and freedom-respecting government cannot be supported by reasonable men. However, since peaceful change should remain possible, insistence on a freedom to *advocate* a change of the government and of the form of government remains a valid position. Such a freedom is, of course, closely linked with the freedom of speech, freedom of the press, and freedom of teaching. And I am inclined to go further and include in these freedoms the right to advocate violent revolution, as long as there is no clear and present danger that the advocacy will be followed by the immediate use of deadly weapons. Advocacy of a violent uprising where there is time for reasoned argument and for countering advocacy of acquiescence, patience, or peaceful procedures of bringing about reforms is among the freedoms which under a truly democratic form of government are granted to the citizens.

My catalogue is woefully incomplete in the area of political freedoms. The freedom of possession of firearms is now much debated in the United States. In early times this was regarded as an important right of the citizen in a democracy; in recent times the

140

possession of firearms by criminal or insane persons has reduced other people's freedom to live, to work, to retain their properties, and so forth. An evaluation of the relative importance of unlimited possession of firearms presupposes estimates of their misuse and of the damage caused. Personal habits, local customs, love of sport, and a few other things will bear on the comparative evaluation of the importance of some people giving up their arms and other people giving up their lives. A compromise between these conflicting values seems imperative and some restrictions on the possession of firearms seem strongly indicated.

Much ought to be said, though little can be said here, about the freedom to vote. My definition makes it a right to cast a vote in free and secret balloting in periodic elections. Secrecy of the ballot is an integral part of the right if it is not to be a fake. But there are serious questions about limitations concerning age, sanity, permanent residence, and literacy. Regarding the last of these, one may on first thought insist on literacy as a condition for the right to vote. But if access to schools has been limited or restricted with the result that large sectors of the population have remained illiterate, should they forever be deprived of the freedom to vote?

In view of the many nations that have recently become independent after decades of foreign rule, the question of individual political freedom and democratic elections for people with limited political experience and a low rate of literacy is of sometimes tragic complexity. Maybe, democracy works only for informed people who can distinguish between deceptive promises and realistic programs. It may also be true that political intelligence can be acquired by practice, and only by practice, so that a costly learning process has to be accepted.

One thought, far too seldom considered, is the possible conflict between collective (national) freedom and individual freedom. Liberation from colonial rule is often associated with severe restrictions on personal liberty. Examples from the New Africa come to mind, where national independence sooner or later led to restrictions on political and intellectual freedoms. If the new 'freedom' for the nation means less freedom for its citizens, it may almost be named the government's freedom to suppress its people. Clean semantic analysis would use the words 'independence' or 'autonomy' for the collective, and reserve the word 'freedom' for the individual. It would then be more clearly understood that national 'liberation' in the sense of achieving independence from some foreign power can lead to 'illiberation' of the people.

I may have given the impression of a serious bias on these questions. May I admit that I really am of two minds? Let me recall Mill's dictum that there can be no liberty for 'savages'. Replace this harsh word by 'politically and intellectually immature people' and reflect on the proposition that full democracy may not be the most suitable system of government for such people; that, for example, the unlimited right to vote and elect the men who will govern the country may lead to the destruction of many other freedoms and also of any real chance for economic development. Communist, socialist, and capitalist countries have resorted to denials of political freedom in order to permit the execution of development programs. Now I am probably giving the impression of the opposite bias. This is intentional, for we must see the difficult choices and the almost inevitable conflicts between different freedoms and between freedoms and other social objectives.

In recent years one of the most fundamental political (and also moral) freedoms, the right to privacy, has been invaded in many ways. Telephone wires have been tapped, mail has been intercepted, pressure has been brought on people to testify on matters they would have chosen to keep secret, and citizens were questioned on their political beliefs, which should be nobody's business where freedom of privacy is respected.

Moral and Intellectual Freedoms

In the moral sphere, the freedom of nonconformance and eccentricity has never been respected to any high degree. John Stuart Mill, more than a hundred years ago complained that the English, who had gone further than most other nations in securing individual liberties, had not seen fit to grant their nonconformers the freedom to be different without being embarrassed or harassed. We have not matured on this score; nonconformance is subject to public disapproval, to social ostracism, and in many instances to legal punishment.

The next three freedoms in my catalogue, the freedoms of teaching, research, and learning are usually discussed under the combined designation of academic freedom. This is a topic on which I published an essay in 1955 (in the *Bulletin* of the American Association of University Professors) and have undertaken to write a comprehensive article (in the forthcoming *Encyclopedia of Education*). It is amazing how much the academic scene has changed in this short period. In 1955, I discussed the major misunderstandings of academic freedom on the part of those who, alarmed by the danger of communist subversion, felt insecure under a system of full freedom to teach. In 1969, the greatest threat to academic freedom is not from conservative trustees and subservient administrators, but from exuberant and militant students suspicious of the 'establishment' and intolerant of academic tradition. Rather than expatiate here on these issues, I may refer the reader to the two publications in which I deal exclusively with the subject of academic freedom.

Perhaps I should say just a word about freedom of conscience. There were times when our society was willing to respect it to a greater extent than it has since the early 1950s. In the McCarthy (Joseph, not Eugene) period in the United States, the refusal of some people to bear arms, to salute the flag, to inform on former friends, and to do other things which the government may require but which their own conscience forbids, subjected many of these conscientious objectors to severe penalties, social and economic as well as legal.

The Choice of Freedoms

I have emphasized the interrelationships among different freedoms: they may conflict with one another or reinforce one another. The conflicts will compel the liberal to choose among liberties or at least among various degrees to which he wants conflicting liberties to be realized. But apart from these 'interlibertarian' conflicts there are the conflicts between various freedoms and other social goals. For example, the objectives of greater income equality, social security, and national security cannot be pursued without sacrificing some of the liberties to some extent. These conflicts compel the liberal to choose between certain liberties, or high degrees of them, and other objectives. The extreme libertarians are not willing to pay much for the attainments of competing social objectives; the American 'liberal' (in the usual sense, described at the beginning of this essay) is prepared to give up most of the economic freedoms in order to get more income equality and social security; some timid liberals are ready to sacrifice economic, political and intellectual freedoms for the sake of national security; and some economic liberals are inclined to restrict intellectual freedoms if these might through political action endanger economic freedoms.

Under these circumstances it is not surprising that we find the adherents of liberalism split in several directions. Perhaps one might say that timidity and liberalism are not compatible and, thus, that those who in the absence of a clear and present danger sacrifice freedoms for increased national security are no liberals at heart. Perhaps one might say that egalitarianism and liberalism are largely contradictory and, thus, that those who sacrifice freedoms for more economic equality and social security are no liberals at heart. But even if one takes such points of view, enough conflicts remain to prevent even the purest liberals or libertarians from agreeing on the 'proper' choice and balance of freedoms.

The most deplorable split, in my opinion, is between those intellectual liberals who have little respect for economic liberties and those economic liberals who have little concern for intellectual liberties. Indeed there are some intellectual liberals who are anxious to restrict, if not altogether strangle, free enterprise and free markets and who wish to introduce more and more central 'planning' in the supply of goods and services to consumers. On the other side, there are some economic liberals who would not mind silencing a teacher of opposite persuasion and who are inclined to see a strong dose of 'planning' introduced in the supply of ideas to university students.

While these illiberal liberals, or demi-liberals, despise each other and call each other such names as 'fascist' and 'communist', their positions can be rationalized by plausible argument. The economic liberal is convinced that economic freedoms provide the most efficient organization not only for creating welfare but also for maintaining political freedoms. I share this conviction. In the long run, a society without a large scope for economic freedom is not likely to retain the political liberties treasured by all liberals. However, from this the pre-eminently economic liberal goes on to argue that the teaching of antiliberal economics will lead to an increasing

144

flow of socialist interventions and to the emergence of central economic planning that can be carried through only when the planners restrict political freedoms. He concludes that in order to prevent such developments it is imperative to suppress what he regards as 'subversive' teaching.

The intellectual liberal is convinced that the existence of abject poverty in the midst of plenty is intolerable for humanitarian reasons and, moreover, will provide a fertile breeding ground for revolutionary movements. I share this conviction. A society that tolerates the existence of misery which it economically could afford to mitigate may not be able to resist movements to overthrow the whole system. However, from this the pre-eminently intellectual liberal goes on to argue that the free-enterprise system is incapable of producing welfare for all and must therefore provoke a hostility that will kill political freedom in order to get rid of economic 'injustice'. He concludes that measures to restrict economic freedoms are imperative for the sake of social justice as well as political freedom.

I submit that both these demi-liberalisms suffer from a lack of faith in liberty. Economic liberals who distrust intellectual freedom and intellectual liberals who distrust economic freedom are equally deficient in their understanding of the fundamental idea of liberty. To be sure, every liberal position must imply some compromise because of the inevitable conflict of competing freedoms. Even the best liberal may recognize a hierarchy of freedoms, attaching, for example, highest importance to civil liberties and giving other liberties a less exalted place in his system of values. But he will never disregard, disparage, distrust, or discard any of the freedoms valued by others.

Does this leave us with a definition of a liberal – a pure, all-round liberal? Not really. Perhaps though we may say that a liberal is one who values liberty above all other social goals and who will never consent to the restriction of any freedom, economic, political, or intellectual, except as the price to be paid for the fuller realization of other freedoms. He must demonstrate that this price is worth paying; he must always be ready to re-examine his and other positions; and he must not place material welfare above liberty.

I do not say that anybody ought to be a liberal; I do not say that one ought to love or promote liberty above material welfare; nor do I say that one ought to neglect promotion of security or welfare for

145

the poor. I only say one ought not to declare oneself a 'liberal' as one promotes such programs. Food is not liberty, and liberty is not food. Medical care is not liberty, and liberty is not medical care. It is admirable to provide food and medical care for the poor – but let us not misuse the term 'liberalism' in advocating these policies.

The Control of Demand
Frank W. Paish

A competitive market system, the best method so far devised for reconciling freedom with service to the community, requires a minimum of three conditions for its effective operation: law and order; the absence of monopoly; and a satisfactorily working monetary system. Without these, the pursuit of individual self-interest will result in harm, instead of benefit, to the economy. Without law and order, some individuals will be able to benefit themselves by theft or fraud rather than by work. In conditions of monopoly, some firms can make larger profits by restricting supplies than by producing more of what the public wants; and in conditions either of inflation or deflation individuals, in quite reasonably trying to safeguard their own positions, tend to intensify the ills from which the economy is suffering. None of the conditions is, of course, absolute. The economy will continue to function even though some robberies and frauds take place, even though competition is less than perfect, and even though the general level of prices is not altogether stable. But the less perfectly they are satisfied the greater will be the loss of social benefit, and if any one of them is wholly absent the whole system will break down.

The maintenance of law and order has been a main function of government since the dawn of history; for many years, and in many countries, it has increasingly assumed responsibility for the control of monopoly; but until very recently it has restricted its responsibility for the satisfactory functioning of the monetary system within very narrow limits. So long as the supply of money depended on the availability of the precious metals, the main monetary function of governments was to maintain the weight and fineness of the coinage – although it is true that they devoted much effort to trying to increase the quantity of money in circulation by ensuring

147

an export surplus of merchandise and an import surplus of gold and silver. With the invention of paper money and bank credit many disastrous experiences showed the danger of inflation, usually as the result of financing heavy government expenditure by the printing press or loans from the banks. From these experiences emerged the doctrine that the government should maintain a strict monetary neutrality, with the budget carefully balanced whatever the state of the economy. But this policy, while maintaining approximate long-run price stability, did not prevent wide fluctuations in business activity, culminating in the great depression of the 1930s. From this experience, and from the teaching of Maynard Keynes, most governments have learned to attempt to use the power which their enormous relative size gives them to take contra-cyclical action.

If we may use a homely analogy, the government is like a very large animal, such as an elephant, in a Noah's Ark of much smaller ones. Experience has shown him the disastrous results of throwing his weight violently about, and from this the doctrine emerged that the right policy for him was to lie as still as possible in the middle of the boat. This was a great improvement; but subsequent experience showed that, even with the elephant lying still, simultaneous rushes of all the smaller animals to one side or the other could still rock the boat dangerously. Keynes' contribution was to point out that, when a combined movement of the other animals was threatening the stability of the boat, the elephant should not merely lie still: *he should lean the other way*. This, of course, is an exercise which takes practice; for if the elephant times his movements badly, or leans too hard, he may easily increase the instability instead of reducing it. But there is at least the possibility that he may make things better.

The many critics of the various governments' efforts to reduce the magnitude of cyclical fluctuations rarely make sufficient allowance for the purely technical difficulties of this operation. Governments share with individuals an inability to foresee the future. Their information about the past is always inadequate, usually late, and frequently inaccurate. Further, the controls available to them for expanding or restricting demand, whether fiscal, monetary or direct, operate with unknown and variable forces and time-lags. A government carrying out a contra-cyclical policy may be compared with the driver of a car who can see, in a distorting mirror, only

148

things a considerable distance behind him, and whose accelerator and brake operate with variable force and with time-lags which may vary from a few seconds to several minutes. It is no wonder that it has difficulty in maintaining a steady course.

In spite of these difficulties, many governments have succeeded in running their economies since the war with considerably smaller and shorter fluctuations than were customary in earlier decades. Their main mistake has been the political, rather than technical, one of trying to run their economies with rather too small a margin of unused resources. The result of this policy has been, not only a persistent tendency to inflation, but also wider cyclical fluctuations and very possibly a slower rate of growth than would have existed if governments (and electorates) had been prepared to tolerate a slightly higher level of unemployment. It is believed that, with a slightly lower employment target, it would be possible for governments to run their economies both with less inflation and with smaller cyclical fluctuations than have been customary since the war.

To enable governments to run their economies both with a margin of unused resources just large enough to prevent inflation and with the smallest possible fluctuations in business activity, it is essential that they should have a satisfactory measure of the pressure of demand in the economy. The indication which has most often been used in the past is the level of unemployment. But this, though published promptly, is unsatisfactory for the reason that it tends to lag, by very variable periods, behind changes in demand. On more than one occasion unnecessary action has been taken, or necessary action has not been taken, because the unemployment figures were slow to reflect changes which had already taken place in the economy.

A better measure of the pressure of demand which has been devised in recent years is the margin between what has actually been produced in the most recent period for which figures are available and what could have been produced in the same period with the fullest possible use of resources. This level of maximum potential output is sometimes called 'productive capacity', but as this term is understood by business men to refer to capital resources only, a better one, now coming into general use, is 'productive potential'. There are many possible factors which might set a limit to productive potential, but in most developed countries since the

149

war the main limiting factor has been labour, and especially skilled labour.

In most developed countries productive potential rises from year to year. There are three main components which influence its rate of increase. The most important is productivity, reflected in the rise of output per man-hour. The second is the number of hours worked per head. A fall in the number of hours worked a week probably has some effect in increasing output per man-hour, although, in present conditions, not enough to prevent some resulting fall in output. And the third is the number of people available for work.

The main cause of the rise in productivity seems to be the gradual improvement in technical efficiency, including not only efficiency in production but also in management. A rise in the amount of capital per head is probably important mainly because it facilitates the introduction of improved methods of production.

All three factors show cyclical fluctuations. To estimate the rate of growth of productive potential, which is, of course, not subject to cyclical fluctuations, it is necessary to find a way of eliminating these. The simplest way is to find two comparable periods, at similar stages of different business cycles, and to measure the rate of growth of output between them. In the United Kingdom there were three clearly marked cycles between 1952 and 1967. Three suitable periods for comparison are the second quarters of 1952, 1959 and 1963. All three had very similar levels of unemployment and all three were just at the beginning of the upturn of a cycle. No such comparison is possible between the second quarter of 1963 and the second quarter of 1968, although the unemployment levels were similar, because, while the second quarter of 1963 was at the beginning of an upturn, the second quarter of 1968 followed a sharply disinflationary budget. We can, however, make a suitable comparison between the last quarter of 1962 and the last quarter of 1967.

We start by calculating the increases in output per man-hour between comparable periods, using the official statistics for output (gross domestic product at constant prices measured from the output side), for the average number of hours actually worked per week, and for the number of persons at work. Quarterly figures of output are not available before 1955, but we can obtain a close approximation for 1952 by breaking down the official annual figure into quarters with the help of the index of industrial production. These calculations are set out in Table 1.

150

Table 1

Increases in Output per Man-hour in the United Kingdom 1952–1967

Year and Quarter	Unemployment (%)	Employment	Weekly hours worked	Man hours worked	Output	Output p.m.h.	Increase in output p.m.h. (%)
1952 - 2	2·21	97·1	98·9	96·0	85·8	89·2	
1959 - 2	2·17	100·4	100·7	101·1	103·8	102·7	+15·1
1963 - 2	2·36	103·9	97·7	101·5	116·5	114·8	+11·8
1962 - 4	2·35	103·7	97·1	100·7	113·7	112·9	
1967 - 4	2·47	104·4	95·3	99·4	133·4	134·2	+18·9

4th Quarter 1955=100

We can now convert the growth of output per man-hour into the growth of underlying productivity by making an adjustment for the change in the number of hours worked. It is assumed that for each fall of 1 per cent in hours worked, 0·4 per cent is offset by a rise in output per man-hour and 0·6 per cent is reflected in reduced output. We can then convert the increase of underlying productivity into the increase of productive potential by adjusting for the change in the number at work and for the remaining 60 per cent of the change in hours worked.

Table 2

Output per Man-hour, Productivity and Productive Potential. (Percentage Changes over Period)

	1952-2 to 1959-2	1959-2 to 1963-2	1962-4 to 1967-4
Output per Man-hour	+15·1	+11·8	+18·9
40% of Change in Hours Worked	+ 0·7	− 1·2	− 0·8
Underlying Productivity	+15·8	+10·5	+18·0
Underlying Productivity per annum	+ 2·1	+ 2·5	+ 3·4
Employment	+ 3·4	+ 3·5	+ 0·7
60% of Change in Hours Worked	+ 1·1	− 1·8	− 1·1
Productive Potential	+20·9	+12·2	+17·5
Productive Potential per annum	+ 2·7	+ 2·9	+ 3·3

It will be seen from Table 2 that, whereas until 1963 the rise in the population at work permitted productive potential to rise faster than productivity, since 1963 the check to the rise in the working population, together with a further fall in hours worked, has reduced the rise of productive potential to below that of productivity. It is these factors, together with the cyclical check to output in 1966–67, which have until recently prevented the effects of the accelerated rise of productivity from becoming apparent.

The acceleration of the rise in productivity becomes even more apparent if we break the rises for periods down into annual increases. Since the increases shown in Table 2 for both 1952–59 and 1959–63 are almost identical with the results for the same periods obtained by W. A. H. Godley and J. R. Shepherd in their paper on 'Long-term Growth and Short-term Policy', published in the August 1964 issue of the *National Institute Economic Review*, we can adopt their estimates of annual increases. These show the rise of productivity accelerating by just under 0·08 per cent a year, from less than 1·8 per cent in 1951–52 to just over 2·6 per cent in 1962–63. It is clear that this rate of acceleration must have increased in 1962–67, for if it had been maintained the total rise in productivity from the last quarter of 1962 to the last quarter of 1967 would have been 14·6 per cent, instead of the 18·0 per cent actually achieved. If we assume a steady rate of acceleration from the second quarter of 1963 onwards, we find that this must have been at a rate of 0·3 per cent a year, increasing the rate of growth of productivity from 2·6 per cent between the last quarter of 1961 and the last quarter of 1962 to 4·0 per cent between the last quarter of 1966 and the last quarter of 1967. If we were to assume that the acceleration started later than the third quarter of 1963, the rise in the later years would be still greater.

Table 3

Annual Increases in Productivity and Productive Potential 1962–1967. (Percentage Changes between 4th Quarters)

Years	Underlying Productivity	25% of Change in weekly Standard Hours	Employment	Productive Potential
1962–63	+2·8	—	+0·4	+3·2
1963–64	+3·1	−0·3	+0·2	+3·0
1964–65	+3·4	−0·5	+0·1	+3·0
1965–66	+3·7	−0·3	—	+3·4
1966–67	+4·0	—	—	+4·0
Total, 1962–67	+18·0	−1·1	+0·7	+17·5

153

In converting the annual rise of productivity into the annual rise of productive potential, we cannot use hours actually worked, since these undergo marked cyclical fluctuations. Since, however, standard hours (which do not fluctuate cyclically) fell by 40 per cent during the period, as compared with a fall of 1·9 per cent in hours actually worked, we can deduct 25 per cent of the fall in standard hours instead of 60 per cent of the fall in hours worked. This concentrates the fall in hours on the middle three years of the period. Similarly, we cannot use actual figures of employment, since these also fluctuate cyclically. As, however, the rise in the population of working age (though not in the total population) slowed down in 1963–65 and ceased in 1966, we are probably justified in concentrating the rise in the population at work on the first three years of the period. As the result of these adjustments, the effects of the steady acceleration of the rise in productivity on the rate of increase of productive potential do not become fully apparent until 1967.

The estimated rise of 4 per cent in productivity in 1966–67 is consistent with the results actually achieved in that year. Between the last quarter of 1966 and the last quarter of 1967 output rose by 3·4 per cent, while the number at work fell by nearly 1·2 per cent and the average number of hours worked per week increased by rather over 0·8 per cent. Output per man-hour therefore increased by 3·7 per cent. Adding back 40 per cent of the rise in hours worked gives a productivity increase of 4·0 per cent.

The extrapolation of the growth of productivity and productive potential beyond the end of 1967 is necessarily tentative, and will remain so until sufficient new evidence has accumulated to permit a new comparison of comparable periods. The acceleration of the growth of productivity may continue, or, on the other hand, the causes of the acceleration in 1963–67 may prove to have been temporary and the rate of growth may decline again. In either case, however, the rate of growth in 1968 is not likely to be widely different from what it was in 1967, and it seems safest to assume a continuation of a 4 per cent rate of growth of productivity until more evidence is available.

It is even more difficult to know how to treat the fall of about 0·5 per cent in the seasonally corrected level of employment in the first nine months of 1968. We can regard the fall as cyclical, in which case it does not affect the rate of growth of productive potential, or as non-cyclical, in which case the growth of productive potential is correspondingly reduced. Pending further evidence, it seems safest to treat it as non-cyclical, and to reduce the estimated increase of productive potential from the last quarter of 1967 to the last quarter of 1968 to 3·5 per cent. It may be hoped that this estimate will prove to be conservative.

If we combine the estimates of annual rates of growth of productive potential shown in Table 3 with those made by Godley and Shepherd for earlier years, we have a continuous series of annual growth rates from 1952 to 1968. It only needs the choice of a common base period to enable us to compare this series with that of output. The base chosen is the last quarter of 1955, when unemployment (seasonally adjusted) stood at only 1 per cent and the economy is regarded as having been fully employed. (More strictly, full employment is defined as a condition similar to that which existed in the last quarter of 1955.) Any gap between the output and the productive potential series is therefore a measure of the size of the margin of unused productive potential. The two series are set out in Table 4 and Chart 1. A curve has been added in Chart 1, as a guide to the eye, to denote a 95 per cent use of potential.

The variations in the gap between output and productive potential provide a good measure of the cyclical fluctuations of demand in the economy. The three business cycles between 1952 and 1967 are clearly marked, with troughs in 1952, 1958–59 and 1962–63, and peaks (or plateaus) in 1954–55, 1960–61 and 1964–66. Each was inaugurated by an expansionist budget and each, after various inadequate attempts at disinflation, was finally brought to an end by a combination of fiscal, monetary and restrictive measures, including severe restraints on hire-purchase transactions. Each left a legacy of permanently increased costs and prices, the cumulative effects of which were seen in the devaluation of November, 1967.

The effects on the rate of rise of income from employment of attempting to run the economy with very little margin of unused potential are shown in Chart 2. It will be seen that the rate of increase of income moves very closely with the percentage of potential in use, rising by about 8 per cent a year with a 98 per cent use of potential, and falling to equality with the 1966–67 rise of productive potential (the necessary condition for preventing inflation) only with a use of potential of 94 per cent or less.

155

The anomalous movements of incomes in 1966–68 are the results of the Government's attempt to impose direct restrictions on wage-rates. The successful 'wage-freeze' of the second half of 1966 caused the increase of incomes from the second quarter of 1966 to the second quarter of 1967 to be much smaller than in the corresponding years of previous cycles, 1957–58 and 1961–62. Unfortunately the increases were only postponed. In spite of subsequent attempts to re-impose wage restrictions, the relaxation in the middle of 1967 was followed by a much faster rise in incomes from employment than in either 1958–59 or 1962–63. As a result, the rise for the two-year period from the second quarter of 1966 to the second quarter of 1968 was almost exactly the same as those in the corresponding periods of the two previous cycles:

Table 5

Income from Employment

(Percentage Increases between 2nd Quarters)

1957–1959		1961–1963		1966–1968	
1957–58	+4·1	1961–62	+5·0	1966–67	+2·5
1958–59	+4·9	1962–63	+4·5	1967–68	+7·0
Total	+9·2	Total	+9·7	Total	+9·7

Before 1966 the respites from a state of excess demand were brief; only in 1966–68 has the continued precarious balance of payments forced the Government to prolong the maintenance of an adequate margin of unused potential for more than about a year. The immediate reasons for the early re-expansion of demand in 1959 and 1963 were largely political – the approach of a general election. But in the background there has always been present a pathological fear of anything but the smallest margin of unemployment – a fear derived from the high level of unemployment which persisted throughout almost the whole of the inter-war period. Since the main limiting factor on output is the supply of labour, a larger margin of unused potential is naturally reflected in a higher level of unemployment. In their 1964 paper referred to above, Godley and Shepherd estimated that fluctuations in the margin of potential

156

were nearly five times as large as the fluctuations in unemployment, so that, if 1·0 per cent of unemployment is correlated with a zero margin of potential, 2 per cent of unemployment would correspond to a 5 per cent margin. Mr. Shepherd has, however, now revised this calculation. In a recent paper[1] he estimates that the 5 to 1 ratio applies only when unemployment is in the vicinity of 300,000, and that when it reaches the neighbourhood of 500,000 the ratio is about 3 to 1. If we assume an intermediate level with a ratio of 4 to 1, we can draw up a rough scale of equivalents at each level:

Table 6

Unemployment and the Margin of Unused Productive Potential

Unemployment Number (thousands)	Per cent	Margin of Unused Potential (%)
233	1·0	0·0
256	1·1	0·5
280	1·2	1·0
303	1·3	1·5
326	1·4	2·0
349	1·5	2·4
373	1·6	2·8
396	1·7	3·2
419	1·8	3·6
443	1·9	4·0
466	2·0	4·3
489	2·1	4·6
513	2·2	4·9
536	2·3	5·2
559	2·4	5·5
582	2·5	5·8
606	2·6	6·1
629	2·7	6·4

In Table 4 and Chart 3 we use Table 6 to compare fluctuations in the percentage of unemployment with those in the margin of unused potential. We see that, when using this scale, the magnitudes of the fluctuations are closely similar, but that there are considerable differences in timing. On the average, fluctuations in unemployment lag about six months behind those in the margin of potential, but the time-lag is very variable. At times, as in 1952–55,

1 'Productive Potential and the Demand for Labour', *Economic Trends*, (September 1968).

157

1962–63 and 1967–68, it is almost non-existent, while at others, as in 1957, 1960–61 and 1966, it is much longer than six months. The current level of unemployment is therefore an unreliable guide for purposes of policy.

In Table 7 and Chart 4 we try to achieve a more precise measurement of the relationships of the margin of unused potential and of unemployment to the rate of increase of employment incomes. From the beginning of 1952 to the second quarter of 1968 there have been sixty-six quarters. For the whole of these, the average use of potential has been 96·7 per cent and the average annual increase of employment incomes 6·6 per cent. Since the average annual increase of output was 2·7 per cent, the average annual increase of labour costs per unit of output was 3·8 per cent. We can also find the averages for all quarters above and below a number of given percentages of potential in use. From these we obtain, in Table 7, a number of annual average increases in income to set against the corresponding average percentages of potential in use and also, with the help of the scale in Table 6, against the corresponding percentages of unemployment:

Table 7

Use of Potential, Unemployment and Rise in
Income from Employment

Number of Quarters	Percentage of Potential in Use		Corresponding Unemployment Percentage	Average Annual Increase in Income from Employment
	Range	Average		
13	95 and under	93·9	2·6	3·8
25	96 and under	94·7	2·3	4·9
30	97 and under	95·0	2·2	5·3
46	98 and under	95·9	1·9	5·9
66	All	96·7	1·7	6·6
53	Over 95	97·4	1·5	7·4
41	Over 96	98·0	1·4	7·7
36	Over 97	98·2	1·4	7·9
19	Over 98	98·7	1·3	8·4

When these values are plotted in Chart 4, we find that they all lie near a straight line running from a 4 per cent rise in incomes with a 94 per cent use of potential and nearly 2·6 per cent of unemployment to an 8 per cent rise in incomes with a 98 per cent use of potential and unemployment at 1·4 per cent. We find, therefore, that if we are to keep the rate of rise of incomes from employment down to 4 per cent, or about the present rate of increase of productive potential, we must be prepared to accept a seasonally adjusted unemployment level of nearly 2·6 per cent, or about 600,000. Of this number, about 180,000, or nearly 0·8 per cent, are, according to a Ministry Of Labour survey carried out in 1964,[2] suffering from various personal disabilities which make them unlikely to be able to obtain work whatever the state of the local labour market. The level of effective unemployment compatible with the absence of inflation may therefore be no more than 420,000, or about 1·8 per cent. For the next two or three years, while the balance-of-payments problem remains urgent, the country will probably have no option except to continue to pay this price for the suppression of excess demand. Perhaps by the end of that time it will have become sufficiently habituated to a slightly higher level of unemployment to be prepared to continue the policy indefinitely.

2 *Ministry of Labour Gazette*, April 1966.

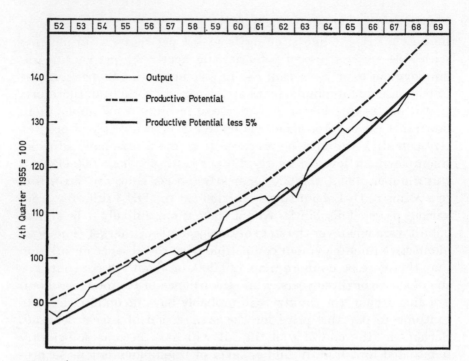

Chart 1 Output and productive potential

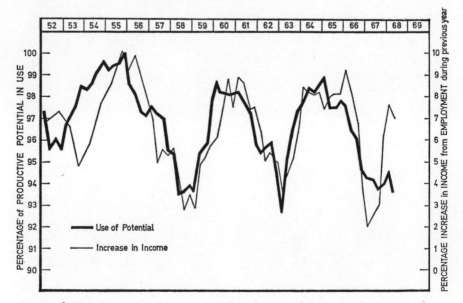

Chart 2 Use of productive potential and annual increase in income from employment

160

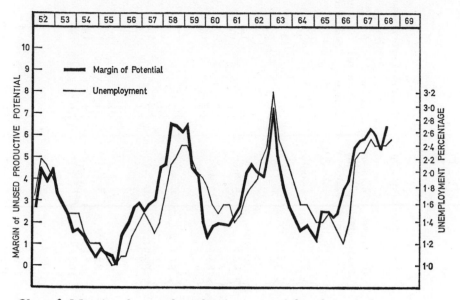

Chart 3 Margin of unused productive potential and unemployment percentage

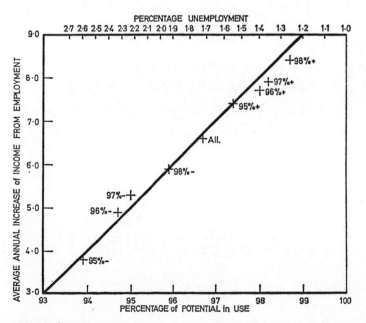

Chart 4 Unemployment, use of productive potential and income from employment

Table 4

Productive Potential, Output, Income and Unemployment

Year and Quarter	Productive Potential	Output	Use of Potential		Income from Employment		Unemployment percentage	
	4th Quarter 1955=100	4th Quarter 1955=100	Percentage in use	Unused margin (%)	4th Quarter 1955=100	Increase over previous year	Calculated from unused margin	Actual (seasonally adjusted)
1952								
1	90·5	88·1	97·3	2·7	77·1	+ 6·9	1·6	1·7
2	91·1	87·1	95·6	4·4			2·0	2·2
3	91·7	88·1	96·1	3·9	79·7	+ 7·3	1·9	2·1
4	92·3	88·2	95·6	4·4			2·0	1·9
1953								
1	92·9	89·8	96·7	3·3	82·3	+ 6·7	1·7	1·8
2	93·5	90·8	97·1	2·9			1·6	1·6
3	94·1	91·8	97·6	2·4	83·5	+ 4·8	1·5	1·5
4	94·7	93·2	98·4	1·6			1·3	1·5
1954								
1	95·3	93·7	98·3	1·7	87·1	+ 5·8	1·3	1·5
2	95·9	94·7	98·6	1·4			1·3	1·3
3	96·5	95·8	99·2	0·8	89·9	+ 7·7	1·2	1·2
4	97·2	96·8	99·6	0·4			1·1	1·2
1955								
1	97·9	97·1	99·2	0·8	93·6	+ 8·6	1·2	1·2
2	98·6	98·0	99·4	0·6	95·6		1·1	1·1
3	99·3	98·8	99·5	0·5	98·0	+10·1	1·1	1·0
4	100·0	100·0	100·0	0·0	100·0		1·0	1·0
1956								
1	100·6	99·2	98·6	1·4	102·2	+ 9·2	1·3	1·1
2	101·3	99·4	98·1	1·9	105·1	+ 9·9	1·4	1·1
3	102·0	99·2	97·3	2·7	106·8	+ 9·0	1·6	1·3
4	102·7	99·7	97·1	2·9	108·0	+ 8·0	1·6	1·4

162

Year	Qtr							
1957	1	103·4	100·8	97·5	2·5	109·4	+7·0	1·6	1·5
	2	104·0	101·2	97·2	2·8	110·3	+4·9	1·6	1·4
	3	104·8	101·7	97·0	3·0	112·8	+5·6	1·7	1·3
	4	105·5	100·7	95·5	4·5	113·8	+5·3	2·1	1·4
1958	1	106·2	101·3	95·4	4·6	115·6	+5·6	2·1	1·7
	2	107·0	100·1	93·5	6·5	114·8	+4·1	2·7	2·1
	3	107·7	100·8	93·6	6·4	115·9	+2·8	2·7	2·2
	4	108·5	101·9	93·9	6·1	117·8	+3·5	2·6	2·4
1959	1	109·2	102·2	93·6	6·4	118·9	+2·9	2·7	2·4
	2	110·0	104·9	95·4	4·6	120·5	+4·9	2·1	2·2
	3	110·7	106·3	95·8	4·2	122·0	+5·3	2·0	2·0
	4	111·4	109·1	97·9	2·1	124·7	+5·8	1·4	1·9
1960	1	112·1	110·6	98·7	1·3	126·2	+6·1	1·3	1·8
	2	112·8	110·8	98·2	1·8	129·7	+7·7	1·4	1·6
	3	113·5	111·4	98·1	1·9	132·7	+8·8	1·4	1·5
	4	114·3	112·1	98·1	1·9	133·9	+7·5	1·4	1·6
1961	1	115·1	113·0	98·2	1·8	137·4	+8·9	1·4	1·6
	2	115·9	113·4	97·8	2·2	141·0	+8·6	1·5	1·4
	3	116·8	113·7	97·3	2·7	142·6	+7·4	1·6	1·5
	4	117·8	112·8	95·8	4·2	143·9	+7·5	2·0	1·7
1962	1	118·7	113·3	95·4	4·6	146·2	+6·4	2·1	1·8
	2	119·7	114·6	95·7	4·3	148·2	+5·0	2·0	1·9
	3	120·7	115·7	95·9	4·1	150·3	+5·4	1·9	2·2
	4	121·7	115·0	94·5	5·5	151·0	+5·0	2·4	2·4
1963	1*	122·7	113·9	92·8	7·2	151·7	+3·7	3·0	3·2
	2	123·8	117·8	95·2	4·8	154·9	+4·5	2·2	2·5
	3	124·7	120·4	96·5	3·5	158·1	+5·2	1·8	2·3
	4	125·6	122·2	97·3	2·7	161·1	+6·6	1·6	2·1

Table 4 continued

Productive Potential, Output, Income and Unemployment

Year and Quarter	Productive Potential	Output	Use of Potential		Income from Employment		Unemployment percentage	
	4th Quarter 1955=100	4th Quarter 1955=100	Percentage in use	Unused margin (%)	4th Quarter 1955=100	Increase over previous year	Calculated from unused margin	Actual (seasonally adjusted)
1964								
1	126·5	123·7	97·8	2·2	164·4	+ 8·4	1·5	1·8
2	127·5	125·4	98·4	1·6	167·5	+ 8·2	1·3	1·6
3	128·4	126·1	98·2	1·8	170·9	+ 8·1	1·4	1·6
4	129·4	127·4	98·5	1·5	174·4	+ 8·2	1·3	1·5
1965								
1	130·3	128·9	98·9	1·1	176·5	+ 7·4	1·2	1·4
2	131·3	128·0	97·5	2·5	180·8	+ 8·0	1·5	1·4
3	132·3	129·0	97·5	2·5	184·8	+ 8·1	1·5	1·5
4	133·3	130·3	97·8	2·2	188·5	+ 8·1	1·4	1·4
1966								
1	134·4	131·2	97·6	2·4	192·7	+ 9·2	1·5	1·3
2	135·5	130·8	96·5	3·5	195·5	+ 8·2	1·8	1·2
3	136·6	131·3	96·1	3·9	197·4	++ 6·8	1·9	1·4
4	137·8	130·3	94·6	5·4	195·3	+ 3·7	2·4	2·2
1967								
1	139·1	131·1	94·3	5·7	196·5	+ 2·0	2·5	2·3
2	140·5	132·3	94·2	5·8	200·5	++ 2·5	2·5	2·3
3	141·9	132·9	93·7	6·3	203·4	++ 3·0	2·7	2·5
4	143·3	134·7	94·0	6·0	207·6	+ 6·2	2·6	2·4
1968								
1	144·5	136·7	94·6	5·4	211·6	+ 7·6	2·4	2·4
2	145·7	136·4	93·6	6·4	214·5	++ 7·0	2·7	2·4
3	147·0	138·4	94·1	5·9	217·8	++ 7·1	2·5	2·6
4	148·3	139·5	94·0	6·0	220·5	+ 6·2	2·6	2·3

* Output, Incomes and Employment in the first quarter of 1963 were affected by exceptional weather.

164

The Determinants of Social Action
Michael Polanyi

The essay I am offering here for the celebration of my honored friend Fritz Hayek is on a subject close to his major interest. It bears on the foundations of individualism in economic life and argues that these must be equally respected whether ownership is public or private.

I think I have proved in earlier writings that the production and distribution of modern technological products can be conducted only polycentrically, that is, by essentially independent productive centres distributing their products through a market. From this I concluded that the claim of the Soviets of having a centrally directed production and distribution was essentially fictitious.[1] This opinion conflicted sharply with the views prevailing at the time both among supporters and opponents of the Soviet regime. While the supporters applauded the practice of central direction, the opponents deplored it because it was deemed damaging to liberty.

It seemed pointless at the time to publish a study which elaborated my thesis that central direction was impossible. I set aside therefore the present paper, which I had first presented in the University of Chicago in 1950. Though Arthur Lewis accepted it for the Manchester School, I felt that publication would be useless at that moment. But since the time of Liberman's critique of the economic practices of the Soviet Union, the situation has changed. The existence of central direction in Russia came to be doubted. Besides,

---

1 See Michael Polanyi, *The Logic of Liberty*, London and Chicago, 1951. The semblance of central planning was analysed in *Towards a Theory of Conspicuous Production* (*Survey*, London No. 34, Oct.-Dec. 1960, pp. 90–99) and in *Theory of Conspicuous Production* (*Colloque de Rheinfelden*, Calman Levy, Paris, 1960); more concisely stated in *Quest* (Bombay No. 41 April-June 1964); as broadcast by RIAS Berlin, December 1962. For a further development see P. C. Roberts, 'The Polycentric Soviet Economy', *The Journal of Law and Economics*, XII (April 1969).

during the past ten years or so expectations attached to nationalization in some Western countries have been much reduced. It may be of interest now to develop further the principles of polycentricity, which have proved broadly correct in contradicting the opinions predominantly accepted at the time and during years to follow.

I shall take for granted here the following assumptions which I believe to have established in previously published work.

There are two and only two ways in which the full-time activities of men can be co-ordinated in the achievement of a joint task. One is incorporation in a hierarchy of command, on the lines on which for example an army is organized when it goes into action. The other method is that of self co-ordination. In this case the initiative lies with the individuals (or individual centres) taking part in the joint co-ordinated activity. Each has to adjust himself to the situation created by the others and by doing so he contributes to the adjustment of all to their common task.

It is postulated further that these two distinctive methods of co-ordinating the full-time activities of men are applicable to the performance of different kinds of joint tasks. The performance of an army or a fleet in action must rely for its co-ordination on a hierarchical chain of command. And the same is true of the internal co-ordination of a factory or any business enterprise. But there exist other tasks which involve the mutual adjustment of a much larger number of relations and which cannot be performed by subordinating its participants to a pyramid of corporate order but can be carried out – if at all – only by a suitable process of self co-ordination. It is submitted, in particular, that the allocation of a multitude of resources to a large number of productive centres for the purpose of producing and distributing a great variety of commodities can be carried out in an orderly manner only by a system of mutual adjustments. This is to say that the task of *modern technology is of a polycentric character and that polycentric tasks can be solved only by mutual adjustment.*

I wish to enlarge on these postulates here by showing that *either* method of co-ordination – the authoritarian as well as the self-adjusting or individualistic method – must be implemented by institutions fulfilling a certain set of criteria which I shall call the determinants of social action. I shall argue further that these institutional requirements sharply restrict the scope of social reform and will illustrate this by the example of a universal nationalization

166

of industry. I shall try to show that the State cannot make the managers of nationalized enterprises act in any very different manner from that in which they would act as managers of privately owned companies.

Let me embark now on this programme by defining what are the general conditions for *responsible action* in society – for actions which are *rationally determinate*, as opposed to inconsistent, meaningless actions.

A man can of course act rationally – just as other animals can – in solitary situations, unaffected by social relations. A man living by himself on an island solves all his practical problems for himself. He makes the best use of his resources according to his skill and prudence, without any institutional framework to guide his actions rationally.

The same is still largely true of a self-subsistent farmer cultivating his land within a community of other such farmers. The only institutional element that is indispensable in such a situation is that each member of the group should know what area he is entitled to cultivate. Each must be assigned definite powers over a particular area. These powers must be secure and continuous, so that he who has sown shall also reap. But there must also be established some determinate process by which the powers of landholding are transferred from one person to another, particularly on the death of the landholder. In other words, there must be institutional arrangements in force both (1) for defining current powers and (2) for defining an order of succession by which these powers are reassigned.

This conclusion can be seen to apply over a wide field. Since man almost invariably uses some tools for his work, or at least needs a place of his own where he can work, his rational behaviour in society will always require that he be assigned some definite powers, and that there should exist an order of succession by which these powers are re-assigned.

If we now look at more complex societal situations, we shall readily discover *another three* institutional requirements of rational action in society. Whenever some people are to rely regularly on the services of others, the labours of the latter must be societally determined in three respects. Persons working for other people must rely on these people (1) for *guiding* their labours, (2) *controlling*

167

what they have achieved and (3) providing adequate *rewards* for their efforts. The first two of these determinants will have to be present even when an action is unremunerated and in such cases we can observe them in isolation. Let us take a student in a university pursuing for example a course in medicine. He must both know what he is expected to learn and what kind of examination he is expected to pass. He should not primarily learn in order to pass examinations, for that would replace education by cramming. But while he must apply himself in the first place to the task of his medical studies, he must also learn how to place his knowledge on record by replying to certain questions set to him by examiners. For if the knowledge of candidates for the medical profession could not be tested by examinations, no objective recognition could be granted to medical qualifications; society could not rely on professionally acknowledged medical practitioners and no organized medical service could be sustained.

We have here an illustration for the twin principles of guidance and control, which must operate in every case when individuals are to render regular services to others. The first determines the *task* of a person, the second fixes the *tests* by which the performance of the task will be judged.

Lastly, we have *rewards*. Persons who do not produce anything at primarily satisfies their own needs must produce goods or services for which they will be rewarded by others. In order to act thtionally, they should know what reward to expect for their serraces.

viThis completes our list of the five determinants of societal action, which, for the sake of further discussion, I should prefer to write in the sequence: Powers, Tasks, Tests, Rewards, Accession. For a general theory of rational action in society these determinants would have to be re-formulated so as to include all spheres of intellectual activities, in which case we should have to allow for the fact that intellectually creative people are to some extent judges in their own cause. They have a voice in shaping the standards by which they will be judged, and their creative acts may be important precisely in opening the way for the establishment of new standards. But to begin with, I shall simplify my task by disregarding the special problems of creative intellectual activities and shall be satisfied in formulating the five determinants, as I have just done in the more straightforward manner in which they apply to other than

168

intellectually creative activities and particularly to a modern system of economic life. Even so, we shall have our hands full in tracing the five determinants through the strikingly different forms which they assume for different classes of people who operate in economic life and in evaluating on this basis the scope of state control over industry.

The five determinants are easy to identify within an hierarchical organization, such as a business corporation. Take the familiar chart showing the branching out of authority downward from tier to tier and let us direct our attention on any member of the corporation, except its chief; that is on any single subordinate member of the hierarchy.

(1) It is immediately apparent that every such member must have definite powers. He must know which are his own subordinates, whose performances he is supposed to direct, or – if he is at the bottom of the hierarchy – he must know what are the tools which he may handle, what offices are at his disposal, etc. Any uncertainty in this respect will lead to people receiving contradictory orders from several persons, who believe to be their superiors, and will result similarly in daily conflicts over the use of machinery and offices. A corporation, in which there is general uncertainty as to the powers of each member, will be subjected to chronic unrest. Writers on business administration have often pointed out that such ill-organized corporations will inevitably be 'shot through with politics'. To avoid this, a clear definition of responsibilities, or powers, is indispensable.

(2) Next it is indispensable that each subordinate should know what he is expected to do. Unless his task is laid down clearly he cannot act purposefully. Unless he knows what are his obligations, he cannot act responsibly. The task of a subordinate will be assigned to him by his superior and renewed or shaped in its particulars from time to time by the day-to-day directives given to him by his superior.

(3) In this sense the subordinate must do what he is told, but this does not fully determine his actions. In the performance of his task he must exercise his own judgment. He must take into account for example the particular circumstances in which his job is to be carried out. He must also apply to it his personal skill. In a sense, of course, his is a definite job to start with, but it yet depends on him what job he makes of it. And on this result he will have to

169

report to his superior. The subordinate's report is a summary of what he has achieved, or thinks to have achieved, and also a claim to the recognition of this achievement. If a workman is on piece-work, he will present his score to the foreman and ask for its inclusion in his weekly total. But even when the report made to the superior is not as simple as that, it will always represent a summary of some kind in terms of certain significant features of what has been achieved. In other words, it will be stated in terms of certain data which the superior may be expected to accept as tests of the degree to which the task entrusted to the subordinate has been accomplished.

The problem of providing proper tests for the satisfactory performance of tasks which one person undertakes for another is of great importance for the question which I propose to examine in this essay. We should note in particular that tests must be fair. They must represent a true measure of the achievement of which they form the test, and be definite and objective. For if the tests by which a subordinate can claim to have acquired merit are hazy and based on objectively not controllable data, this offers excessive temptation for specious window dressing, while it penalizes the honest scorer. Nothing is more demoralizing to the conscientious worker than to find his performances classed below those of a colleague who makes up for his lack of true merit by effective talking points which impress his superiors. This must be avoided.

(4) The question of tests is of course closely linked to that of rewards. Rewards are not indispensable as incentives to every human effort. When people write poetry or save a child from drowning, their actions carry much of their rewards in themselves. But this is not so for the production of shoe-laces, toothbrushes, radiators, etc., which is also a satisfying occupation – but not in itself. It satisfies you only if you know that you have provided something that was wanted by others. Therefore the proper measure for your own satisfaction in this case will be whatever your work will fetch from those who buy its products. It follows that a business corporation must pay for the services of its employees and try to pay them fairly, in proportion to their usefulness to the company. In saying this I do not wish to minimize the importance of praise or dispraise; I only affirm that in a business enterprise moral incentives are not enough. Employees must be paid and paid according to their performance. If there had been any doubt about this, the disastrous

170

experience of Russia in trying to dispense with graded material incentives should dispose of these doubts definitively. The proper grading of incentives is indispensable both in order to satisfy a sense of justice within the corporation and thus avoid demoralization, as well as in order to stimulate efforts in the direction in which such exertions are most useful to the company.

(5) Naturally, there must be also an order of succession. People must get their powers assigned to them when they undertake tasks within the corporation, accepting certain tests that are to be fulfilled and the prospect of certain rewards thus to be gained. New powers will have to be assigned and existing powers modified or revoked. This procedure is included among the incentives to the extent as it is covered by promotion or demotion. To this we must add, however, the process of new enrolments. Speaking of corporate bodies in general, new enrolments can be by initiation, as in a monastery, by conscription as in the army, while in the case of business corporations they will be by contract.

Within a corporate body all five determinants are operated by the authority at its head. In the case of business enterprises, they all emanate from proprietary and contractual powers vested in the head of the enterprise. These powers, however, form part of a framework of institutions that lie outside the corporation. Our next task will be to define the nature of this framework from which the corporation as a whole derives its powers and within which its actions are rationally determined.

Business corporations co-operate in the solving of the polycentric task of producing and distributing material goods by modern technical processes. Our task is now to identify in this system of polycentric adjustments the institutions which provide the persons making decisions with the five factors of responsible societal action. In other words, we ask what institutions are required in order to determine the powers, the tasks, the tests, the rewards, and the order of succession, for each individual engaged in adjusting himself to the position of other individuals within a polycentric system of production and consumption?

I shall define firstly the nature of the powers which these individuals must possess. In the economic system there are three kinds of people who have to allocate resources: the W (Workers) allocate their labour, the L (Landowners) dispose of certain plots of land, the I (Investors) assign certain sums of capital.

171

$$\begin{array}{c} W \searrow \\ L \leftrightarrow M \leftrightarrow C \\ I \nearrow \end{array}$$

To be more precise, the W's allocate themselves to jobs offered by M (Managers) while M's give jobs to W's. Similarly the L's assign sites to one of the plants controlled by an M, while an M decides to put his plant on a site placed at his disposal by an L. The I's allocate capital between different M's, while the M's allocate their ideas to one of the I's. On the right of the M's we see them distributing their products between the C's (Consumers) while the C's choose between different M's in allocating their custom. These two-way processes are expressed by the double-headed arrows connecting the symbols in the outline of the economic system.

We have seen that the polycentric nature of the overall task in the solution of which this system is engaged demands it that each W, L, I, M and C, should act on his own initiative. Each must therefore possess personal powers to dispose of the things which it is his function to allocate. In order to define these powers more closely, we have to consider the peculiar two-sidedness of each allocation. It is inherent in the nature of the adjustments occurring within this system that in each adjustment the allocations of two independently acting individuals must exactly coincide. Such coincidence can only be due to agreement between the two individuals in question. In other words, all allocations must be made on a contractual basis. We must have labor-contracts, leases of land, subscription of capital, and on the other side sales to consumers. We may sum up this by saying that from the polycentric nature of the economic system we have derived the necessity that individuals should have powers to make contracts for the allocation of resources and the purchase of products. And we may add that these contracts must be enforceable by a legal order of private law.

Professor Samuel Dobrin of the University of Manchester has shown that even in the Soviet Union the desirability of a reliably operating system of contractual relations has been recognized, and that they have enacted therefore a Civil Code similar to that of capitalist countries, which the Soviet government has tried to enforce by urging its enterprises to go into court against each other for the vindication of their contractual rights.

There is another institution which is a corollary to contractual allocations in a polycentric system, and which is also common both to private capitalism and to a system of universal state ownership. This is the institution of prices expressed in money. In order that a large number of individual allocations may be mutually adjusted, there must be a public indicator of available alternatives and such indicators must make generally known the rates at which alternatives are currently substituted for one another. Such an indicator is a ruling price. Mutual adjustments take place through the fact that all individuals act on the basis of the same price (signifying the availability of alternatives) and that the prices are re-adjusted in response to underbidding sellers or outbidding buyers.

It is also clear that prices must be expressed in *numbers* assigned to each piece that is to be allocated. For this has the decisive advantage that, by adding up such numbers, any combination of things can be recognized as an available alternative of any other combination the numbers of which add up to the same figure. That makes a rapid choice of alternatives possible. Once you have prices fixed in numbers you can use money, provided that the W's, L's, and I's whom the M's would pay in money can become C's and buy from the M's for their money the finished articles that these have produced by aid of the resources purchased from the W's, L's and I's. The M's of course must also be paid in money. They retain some of the money in payment of their own services as the flow passes through their hands from 'west' to 'east'. Each joins then the rank of the C's and makes his purchase from other M's, just as the rest of the C's do.

To complete the picture of the self-co-ordinating economic system we have yet to recall that each of the symbols, W, L, . . . C, stands for a multitude of individuals, whose every self-adjustment competes with that of all the others. It is these myriads of competitive outbiddings that establish jointly a relative economic optimum within the economic system. Soon, however, we shall at last arrive at a point where there is some difference between a privately and a publicly owned industrial system. This will become apparent by setting out explicitly the determinants of societal action that apply to individuals within a competitive system of production and distribution. I have already said something about *powers*. Polycentricity requires that at every centre there should be independent powers for disposing commercially over the things that participate in the economic system at that centre. These powers to sell or hire

173

out for business purposes one's own labour, or certain areas of land, or certain sums of money, we shall call proprietary powers. Such proprietary powers must be present in any polycentric economic system, whether its industries are privately or publicly owned.

Next we come to *tasks*. It follows from the principle of polycentric adjustment that proprietary powers must be used by their holders at their own initiative and (own) discretion. They must set themselves their own tasks: each must allocate, or transform by manufacture, to the best advantage the resources which he controls or the money which he has to spend. Perhaps we may say that self-co-ordination assigns to the individual a general problem within which he has to decide on his own particular task.

Next we come to *tests* and *rewards* which, for the sake of brevity, we shall discuss jointly. For this we must remember that in a polycentric economic system the choice of a task is always bilateral. It is laid down in a contractual agreement of two partners. In fulfilling his contract either partner's position in respect of the other is similar to that of a subordinate carrying out the directions of his superior. His performance must fulfil certain specifiable criteria. By fulfilling the tests of the contract, either partner can claim from the other the compensation agreed upon in the contract. And again, tests must be fair and objectively ascertainable. The old proverb says so: *clara pacta, boni amici*. Obscurity in a contract leads inevitably to conflicting interpretations by both sides and results in quarrels. If tests are inadequate and do not properly define the task to be performed, a partner may be able to claim the agreed payment without performing or fully performing the agreed task. Bad laws and bad contracts will frequently permit this to happen; and it is the principal purpose of good laws and carefully drawn up contracts to prevent such abuses. We have here a contractual framework of *tests* and *rewards* within a polycentric economic system; and there is so far no difference apparent between private and public ownership of industry.

There is one contractual relationship within the economic system in respect to which this identity between capitalism and socialism should be particularly pointed out. Within both systems there are certain people, the I's, whose function it is to allocate money between competing projects represented by their acting or prospective managers, the M's. Under capitalism the I's are private citizens while under socialism they are government officials. (The same

174

holds for the L's who allocate sites for different productive uses; but for the sake of brevity we shall not mention the L's always separately, but concentrate our attention on the I's and speak of them as if they comprised also the L's.) Whether industry is financed by the State or by private capitalists, the subscription of capital must be by contract between the I's and the M's in which the M's agree to use the money remuneratively, and in both cases the test of this will in general consist in making a profit in money. For, other things being equal, profits are the greater the more economically the process of production is conducted and the more closely the distribution of the products conforms to the needs of the consumers.

And here at last our analytical quests are rewarded by a glimpse of our problem in a new setting. Our problem now boils down to this: Are the I's in their contracts with the M's in a better position to include adequate tests for the performance of the M's, in case that they, the I's, are government officials as compared with the case that they are private individuals? But before trying to answer this question let us complete our survey of the determinants by passing on to the order of *accession*.

The power of the W's to allocate their labour is extinguished on their death or retirement and the new generation of W's grows up with powers over their own labour. Similarly, the power of the C's to allocate their custom dies with them and arises naturally in new generations of C's as they reach maturity – these are trivial points which we need not elaborate here any further. The M's will invariably be appointed by those who allocate to them the wealth for the administration of which they are responsible. In other words, the M's receive their *powers* from the I's, whether the latter are private citizens or government officials. The difference between capitalism and socialism lies in the order of accession of the I's. Under socialism these are appointed by the public authorities, while under capitalism they acquire their powers over investable sums of money either by saving up part of their incomes or, perhaps more usually, by inheriting the investments of deceased relatives. The powers of private capitalists are largely hereditary, but the power to invest smaller sums is possessed by every adult citizen under capitalism.

Here is laid bare the only great difference between capitalism and socialism. In the Soviet Union a private citizen may make a lot of money and he may save it. He may buy government bonds on

175

which he will receive good returns, which at times were as high as 7 per cent. But he cannot subscribe any industrial shares. All allocation of capital is in the hands of public officials. All risks of enterprise are pooled in the public treasury. The State bears all the losses and takes all the profits – apart from a relatively small percentage of them which benefits the so-called 'Director's Fund' of the enterprises in which a profit was made.

The doctrine of Keynes that saving and investment are two entirely separate activities is strikingly illustrated by the constitution of the Soviet Union, where all saving is private while all investment is public. The officials acting as investors are, accordingly, devoid of certain powers which their opposite numbers under capitalism possess. They can only choose between different channels of investment and they can presumably also wait and leave some funds uninvested for the time being, but they have no power to spend the funds at their disposal for their own pleasure. They have no right to sell out the factories which they have financed and consume the proceeds. In other words, they have no powers to 'dis-save'.

I shall add the last touches to my distinction between the systems of private and public enterprise, by taking up once more a point hinted at before about the defectiveness of competition between the I's, the investors, if they are not private citizens but employees of the government. If all the financing of industry is done exclusively by public authorities, there cannot be such a large number of independent initiatives among the I's as if anyone can become an investor who has saved or inherited some money. In the competitive order I⟷M, we still have the managers boosting their projects in competition with each other and trying to attract capital in the direction of greatest profitability; but the I's being all officials of the same government cannot possibly pursue as many different and conflicting opinions as private individuals could. It is true that the government is not one person. There are different departments, different branches of the state bank and a multitude of local authorities which will more or less independently seek openings for useful investments. There are also the thousands of individual enterprises re-investing their own profits sometimes on quite new lines. All these modes of investment can be observed for example in the Soviet Union. There is a great multitude of I's, but yet not as many and as varied and independent of each other's policies as in a system of private enterprise. Nor is there an organized capital

176

market available which would allow for rapid mutual adjustments between the actions of the I's. Herein lies a serious imperfection of a system of public enterprise. Its mode of capital allocation is comparatively clumsy, as compared with that of a system of private enterprise. Government investors are not likely to probe as quickly and completely as private investors into all avenues of advantageous investment and to react as sensitively to changing circumstances by an appropriate re-shifting of investments all over the field of enterprises.

This is – rather surprisingly – all the difference there is between a system of private and public enterprise; at any rate so far as public enterprise is conducted in accordance with the polycentric nature of the modern economic task and with due regard to the necessity for providing a complete set of determinants – Powers, Tasks, Tests, Rewards, Accession – for each person participating in the system, so that he may be in a position to act in a definite and responsible manner. Of course, if a socialist government continues to pursue the pretence that it is centrally directing its economic system it will deflect the system from its rational course and cause much confusion, conflict and even violence. Such a government may, moreover, adopt a conception of man and history which leads logically to totalitarianism and it may actually use its power in a totalitarian manner.

In this paper I have tried to purify the concept of state ownership from the illusions of central direction usually attached to it, as well as from the totalitarian political theories which have in fact always been linked in past history to a program of universal nationalization. I can now proceed to answer explicitly the question which I have set myself here, namely, how far the system of state ownership can modify the economic optimum which a system of competitive enterprises is tending to achieve. Or – anticipating my answer to this question – how is it to be explained that even though the public authorities appoint all the managers, as well as the investors, they cannot exercise more – or much more – control over them than if investment were private and managers were appointed by directors elected by shareholders?

In trying to answer this question – or rather to substantiate the assertion implied in it – I must refer briefly to the various imperfections of existing systems of private enterprise. When a manufacturer considers the costs of a project he adds up his accounts in

177

terms of the resources which he would use up. He ignores the wider repercussions which the operation of his proposed factory may spread in various directions. The noise and smoke, the pollution of rivers, the defacing of the landscape and all this kind of nuisance, should be counted among the costs of manufacture, but the manufacturer is not directly affected by them and may leave them entirely out of account. Such costs are social costs and it falls to the public authorities to assess them and to act accordingly, either by making restrictive regulations to which manufacturers have to conform or, in some cases, by imposing special taxes on the production of certain articles which will bring home the social costs to the manufacturer. Similarly, there are enterprises which spread benefits, or supposed benefits, far beyond the range of the primary customers who pay for the products. Universities are sometimes classed in this category; it is assumed that the fees students are prepared to pay do not represent the full value of the universities' services to the community. For a student does not consume the education which he receives as he would consume a slab of ice cream, but embodies some of it in his personality and spreads it around himself throughout his lifetime. Consequently, the public authorities, or public benefactors, consider it proper to make up the difference between the proceeds from students' fees and the costs incurred by universities. And there are many other instances in which the public benefits originating in an enterprise will justify the granting of subsidies to such enterprises. It is in general the proper function of a government to assess all diffuse social costs and social benefits, and to impose restrictive regulations and special taxes in respect to the former and grant subsidies to compensate for the latter.

Compare now the position of the public authorities in carrying out this function in the two systems, that of private and that of public enterprise. In neither case can it deal with every individual enterprise. That in general will exceed its span of control. It must formulate general rules and apply certain definite tests in applying these rules. Every manager must be able to assess in advance how these rules will affect him. The tests should be fair, that is of a definite character, and such as are quickly ascertainable by objective methods. Otherwise the regulations, taxes and subsidies will inevitably result in capricious decisions and corrupt practices.

In this respect there is no difference between a system of private and public enterprise. Regulations, taxes, and subsidies, which can

178

be rationally applied to a few hundred thousand private enterprises, can be equally applied to a similar number of public enterprises, and regulations which would operate capriciously if applied to private enterprises, could not be applied to public enterprises either. The administrative problem of the government in a nationalized system is obviously compounded from its two functions, first as the universal provider of capital and second, as the guardian of the social interest in respect to diffuse costs and diffuse benefits. The first of these functions is vested in the investment departments. As investors, they can rationally control the managers in charge of investments only by the same tests which private investors would use. They must see to it that the enterprises which they finance make profits, and the more the better. This conclusion is clearly borne out by the granting of profit premiums to the 'Directors' Funds' in the Soviet Union. On the other hand, those government departments which are concerned with social costs and social benefits not accounted for in profits, must impose conditions on profit-seeking which will safeguard the general welfare. It appears obvious now that the administrative task facing these welfare departments in trying to control the managers of state-owned enterprises, is exactly the same as if enterprises were owned by individual shareholders.

I need go no further: this conclusion can be readily generalized to cover all other suggested improvements of a marketing system that have been recently advocated, such as the replacement of the profit motive by the equalization of marginal costs and marginal incomes. If these proposals can be formulated in terms of regulations that can be applied to a panel of a few hundred thousand state appointed managers, so that their performances can be fairly assessed and rewarded in the light of the new criteria, then the same rules will operate with equal success in respect to a similar number of privately owned enterprises. For the administrative problem is once more the same in both cases. Public ownership of industry creates no new powers to eliminate the various imperfections of private capitalism.

A Pluralist Approach to the Philosophy of History*
Karl R. Popper

What may be called the philosophy of history persistently turns round three big questions.

(1) What is the plot of history?
(2) What is the use of history?
(3) How are we to write history, or what is the method of history?

Answers have been given to these three questions implicitly and explicitly, from Homer and the Bible down to our own day. And the answers have changed astonishingly little.

The oldest answer to the first question – 'what is the plot of history?' – as given in the Bible and in Homer, is theistic. The plot is only dimly discernible, because it results from the will of God, or of the gods; and though it is perhaps not completely unfathomable, it is not easy to fathom. At any rate, there is a secret hidden behind the surface of events. It has to do with reward and punishment; with a kind of divine balance, a balance of justice; though only by the most discerning can this justice be seen to be done.

This balance which, if upset, swings back like a pendulum, plays its part in Herodotus who sees in the Trojan War a movement of the people of the West to the East which explains the swing back of the Persian Wars with their movement from the East to the West. Twenty-three centuries later we find precisely the same theory in Tolstoy's *War and Peace*: Napoleon's movement to the East into Russia is reciprocated by a movement of the Russian people to the West.

Admittedly, neither Herodotus nor Tolstoy offer what looks at first sight like a theistic theory; but the theistic background –

* Based on a lecture delivered in Oxford on November 3, 1967.

181

a more or less suppressed theory of a divine balance of justice – is unmistakable.

This, after all, is in keeping with the whole structure of European thought, which is fundamentally theological in origin, and which tenaciously clings to its theological ground plan, even in the age of revolutions, and even in these modern times of the rise of science.

For in our own time, the earlier, naturalistic revolution against God replaced the name 'God' by the name 'Nature'. Almost everything else was left unchanged. Theology, the Science of God, was replaced by the Science of Nature; God's laws by the laws of Nature; God's will and power by the will and power of Nature (the natural forces); and later, God's design and God's judgment by Natural Selection. Theological determinism was replaced by a naturalistic determinism; that is, God's omniscience and omnipotence were replaced by the omniscience and omnipotence of the Natural Sciences.

Hegel and Marx replaced the goddess Nature, in her turn, by the goddess History. So we get laws of History; powers, forces, tendencies, designs, and plans, of History; and the omniscience and omnipotence of historical determinism. Sinners against God are replaced by 'criminals who vainly resist the march of History'; and we learn that not God but History will be our judge.

But the sequence *God – Nature – History*, and the sequence of the corresponding secularized religions, does not end here. The Hegelian (alleged) discovery that standards are after all only historical facts (for in God, standards and facts are one) leads to the deification of *Facts* – of existing or actual Facts of human life and behaviour (including, I am afraid, merely alleged Facts) – and thus to the secularized religions of existentialism, positivism, and behaviourism. Since human behaviour includes verbal behaviour, we are led still further to the deification of the Facts of Language. Appeal to the logical and moral authority of these Facts (or alleged Facts) of Language is, it would seem, the ultimate wisdom of philosophy in our time.[1]

The theory that there is a plot in history, whether the plot is theistic or anti-theistic, is what I have called by the name *historicism*. The name has been attacked by people who think that names matter, and who overlooked the fact that I said emphatically that the name does not matter to me; that it is only a label; and that I

1 Compare with the last three paragraphs my *Conjectures and Refutations*, dedicated to F. A. von Hayek, London 1963, p. 346.

182

never quarrel about words: words, in my view, are utterly un-important—mere instruments of what really needs saying.

My criticism of the historicist-plot theories has also been attacked for being out of date. There are no historicists left, it has been said; so why attack them?

Now it is quite true that, especially more recently, there have been few people who have come out into the open in order to defend historicism. Even Marxists, and even followers of Professor Toyn-bee, have become in this respect less vocal, if not subdued. Never-theless, I almost feel as if I were drowning in a historicist flood. I hear constantly that we are living in the atomic age, and in the space age; in the age of television, and in the age of mass com-munication; and I do not doubt that the recent blow to the British Museum is at least partly due to the belief that in our new age of the new means of mass communications and of Xerox and other photocopies, the role of books is to become less and less important. I also hear constantly about the age of specialization in which we live and, at the same time, about the age of the new abstract revolutionary art – which, incidentally, has not changed since I saw, in 1920, forty-seven years ago, practically all its variations exhibited in the *Bauhaus in Weimar*, when it was a revolutionary movement of protest against stagnation and conformity. Ever since it has stagnated and it is still conforming to the pattern of a revolutionary movement of protest against stagnation and conformity. Neverthe-less, as the result of living in an age of both specialization and abstract art, I hear of a specialist who prides himself on specializing exclusively in the history of American abstract art since 1930. Thus the beginnings of the *Bauhaus* fall outside his specialism.

To me it is clear that all these so-called movements and tenden-cies, ages and periods are offsprings of the idea of a historicist plot. However, I am alive to the danger of stagnation, including the danger of letting my own ideas stagnate. I therefore feel I have said and written enough against historicism, and I do not now wish to say more against it.

On the contrary, I will try to look afresh, though only *very* briefly, at our first question – the question of the presence of a plot in human history.

By and large I think the answer to our question is 'yes'. Since the invention of critical discussion and of writing, there has arisen something which may be described as the growth of knowledge, and this knowledge and its growth is becoming more and more pervasive in our life. In other words, there is progress of knowledge, and technological progress, and to this extent there is a plot.

It is only very recently – during the last hundred years or so – that this particular thing, scientific knowledge, has become of obvious importance in human life. But looking back, we can say two very sweeping things. One is that it is in our knowledge that we differ most clearly from all other animals. The other is that we can so look at the evolution of animals that the growth of our knowledge is a kind of continuation of animal evolution, although by entirely new means.

This way of looking at our history is both obvious and extremely one-sided. Four hundred years ago the growth of knowledge was not a fact of history but a programme of a highly dubious prophet, Francis Bacon, which soon turned into a typical intellectual fashion. At any rate, at this moment at least, it looks not only like a plot, but like a kind of universal plot, the main plot of human history, perhaps of the evolution of life.

In this context it is interesting that historians traditionally know extremely little about the history of science. Thus I pointed out in 1945 in my *Open Society* that the history of science was completely ignored in the six huge volumes of Arnold Toynbee's *Study of History*, which had been published at that time. In another famous big book, first published in 1938, by another very famous historian, the following strange sentence can be found: '. . . the study of the material world had been revolutionized by Galileo's assertion that the earth revolved round the sun'.

When I read this sentence I was surprised, for Galileo only re-asserted what, as everybody knows, was the Copernican revolution. I thought, for a moment, that the word 'assertion' might mean here re-assertion. However, the next sentence and some other passages showed me that this famous historian had really mistaken Galileo for Copernicus or the other way round. For the next sentence begins with the unambiguous words *'Before Galileo's discovery'*; words which refer back to the sentence 'Galileo's assertion that the earth revolved round the sun'. Examples like this can be multiplied; but I do not regard it as my present task to complain about the 'two cultures'.

Incidentally, almost all creative scientists know a great deal about the history of their problems, and therefore about history. *They*

184

have to: you cannot really understand a scientific theory without understanding its history.

It is clear that historians in their turn will find out reasonably soon that *they have to* know something about science and its history; they will find out that they cannot possibly understand *any* recent history, and least of all political or diplomatic history, without understanding something about science. For example, in Churchill's *The Second World War* we find an adequate treatment of the development of radar. It just could not have been omitted.

But let us return to our first question, the question of the universal plot.

I suggest that man has created a new kind of product or artifact which promises in time to work changes in our corner of the world as great as those worked by our predecessors, the oxygen-producing plants, or the island-building corals. These new products which are so decidedly of our own making are our myths, our ideas, and especially our scientific theories: theories about the world we live in.

Indeed we may look upon these myths, these ideas and theories as some of the most characteristic products of human activity. Like tools, they are organs evolving outside our skins. They are exosomatic artifacts.

Thus we may count among these characteristic products of man especially what is called 'human knowledge'; where we take the word 'knowledge' in its objective or impersonal sense in which it may be said to be contained in a book; or stored in a library; or taught in a university.

When speaking here of human knowledge, I shall usually have this objective sense of the word 'knowledge' in mind. This allows us to think of knowledge produced by men as analogous to the honey produced by bees: the honey is made by bees, stored by bees, and consumed by bees; and the individual bee which consumes honey will not, in general, consume only the bit it has produced itself: honey is also consumed by the drones which have not produced any at all.

All this holds, by and large, with slight differences, for oxygen-producing plants and for theory-producing men: we, too, are not only producers but consumers of theories; and we have to consume other people's theories, and sometimes perhaps our own, if we are to go on producing.

Thus the growth of human knowledge continues the evolution

185

of other organisms; but in so far as it is almost entirely exosomatic, and transmitted by tradition, it is something new and characteristic of human history.

I have here tried to give a very brief and very sweeping answer to our first question, and this answer may seem to be a monistic rather than a pluralistic one: it may seem as if I would say that the growth of knowledge, and thus the history of science, is the heart of all history.

This is very far from my intention. Admittedly, the life of all men is by now deeply affected by science. But science itself is closely linked with religious myths. I am inclined to suggest that there would be no European science without Hesiod's theogony. And although everybody is affected by the growth of knowledge, there are very few people indeed who contribute to it. On the other hand, we have the new religion of the living gods of the cinema and the gramophone disc. Stars and starlets were gods for the Greeks and for the Polynesians, and stars and starlets have again become gods for many Europeans and Americans. The history of religion – or the histories of religions – is (are) at least as important as the history of science. And so are the histories of literature, and of the visual arts; and, of course, the histories of political and military power; the history of legal institutions, and that of economic change.

In addition you have the interrelations between economic history and the history of architecture, and multiple relations between religious history, the history of literature, and that of art.

All this points to a kind of pluralism: there is a plurality of cultural problems; of interests; and, perhaps most important, of individual characters and of personal fates.

II

I will now proceed to our second question. What is the use of history?

In an excellent paper entitled 'Philosophy of History before Historicism',[2] Professor George H. Nadel traces the history of the answers to this question. Foremost among these answers is what he

2 George H. Nadel, 'Philosophy of History before Historicism', in Mario Bunge (ed.), *The Critical Approach to Science and Philosophy*, Glencoe, Ill., 1964, pp. 445–70.

186

calls the *Exemplar Theory of History*: the theory that history is of educational value, especially for the political education of the statesman or general.

'The Greeks are strong on precepts, the Romans are stronger on examples, which is far the greater thing', Nadel quotes from Quintilian. Polybius, incidentally, agrees, but turns it round: he alludes to Plato's demand that philosophers should become kings and kings philosophers, and he demands that not only should men of action become historians, but also historians men of action, for otherwise they will not know what they are writing about.

Under Stoic influence, history is regarded as a means of moral education, of education in righteousness.

This is a tradition which is still strong with Lord Acton, and whose influence can be clearly felt in Sir Isaiah Berlin's famous lecture 'Historical Inevitability' and, I suppose, also in my *Open Society*. Some of its strongest and wisest recent expressions may be found in the work of Ernst Badian on Roman and Hellenic history.

Professor Nadel gives an outline of related theories – history, says Diodorus Siculus, restores the universal unity of mankind, a unity broken up by time and space. It thus ensures a kind of immortality and preserves the example of good men and good deeds.

Yet the exemplar theory declined. Hegel denied that statesmen actually learned from historical examples. Professor Nadel quotes from Hegel's Philosophy of History:[3]

> It may be allowed that examples of virtue elevate the soul and are applicable in the moral instruction of children for impressing excellence upon their minds. But the destinies of people and states . . . do not belong to this field. Rulers, statesmen, nations, are wont to be emphatically reminded of the teaching which experience offers in history. But what experience and history teach is this – that peoples and governments never learned anything from history, or acted on principles deduced from it.[4]

But the exemplar theory, which was still so powerful with Lord Acton, had actually come to an end, before Acton, with Acton's teacher, Leopold von Ranke. It was replaced, as Professor Nadel points out, by sheer professionalism: the view that history exists

3 *Op. cit.*, p. 469, note 42.
4 G. W. F. Hegel, *The Philosophy of History*; cf. Sibree's translation, 1956, p. 6.

187

for its own sake; which really means that it exists for the sake of the historians. Nadel quotes the famous statement of Ranke which is traditionally regarded as the manifesto of this position:

> To history have been attributed the high offices of judging the past and instructing the present for the sake of the future. These high offices are beyond the aspirations of the present essay: it merely wants to show what actually happened.[5]

This in brief is the story as Nadel tells it. But we need not give in any more than Lord Acton did. Again I propose a pluralistic approach.

History, I assert, can be interesting in itself. But it is interesting to the extent to which it tries to solve *interesting historical problems*. Examples of such problems are: how did the two World Wars break out? Were they avoidable?

The answers to these questions are certainly of great importance for the politician. *Pace* Hegel, a politician cannot be qualified for the Foreign Office unless he knows some of the historical facts and some of the historical conjectures concerning the Second World War. How guilty were 'The Appeasers'? What was the purpose of the Stalin purges? How was the decision to drop the two atom bombs on Japan arrived at? Why was not at least the first dropped on a harbour where Japanese warships were anchored?

These are matters which ought to interest us all, even if we do not aspire to a post in the Foreign Office: these are intrinsically interesting historical problems, and of special interest, if we want *to understand* the world we live in.

But understanding our own world and ourselves is not everything. We also want *to understand* Plato, or David Hume, or Isaac Newton. And a good historian will add new fuel to this curiosity; he will make us wish *to understand* people, and situations, that we did not know about before.

III

With the words 'to understand' I come to my third and, to me, most interesting question: the question of the method of history, and especially the question of historical understanding.

5 Leopold von Ranke, *Geschichte der Romanischen und Germanischen Völker*, (1824) 3rd ed. 1885, p. vii (my translation).

For the last hundred years this question has been discussed very largely in terms of the difference in method between the natural sciences on the one side, and the historical or humanistic sciences on the other. And the opinion is almost unanimous that there is a big gulf between these two.

There have been great quarrels about the details of this big gulf. There are the famous German theorists of the gulf, Windelband and Rickert and Dilthey. There are the English theorists, foremost among them Collingwood. There is Professor Trevor-Roper, who objects to the intrinsic professionalism, and thus to the influence of the natural scientist, and defends the view that history is for the layman; and Sir Isaiah Berlin who warns us not 'to underestimate the differences between the methods of natural science and those of history or common sense'.[6]

I propose now to discuss this question again.

I agree with Sir Isaiah's remark that the methods of history are those of 'common sense', and I always did agree with this view. I agree with Professor Trevor-Roper that nothing can be worse in history than a narrow professionalism; and I always did agree with this view. I do agree with Collingwood and with Dilthey and with Hayek that we must try *to understand* history; and I agree that there is an urgent need for the philosopher of history to analyse, to explain, and indeed to understand, historical understanding.

But my thesis has been for many years: *all those historians and philosophers of history who insist on the gulf between history and the natural sciences have a radically mistaken idea of the natural sciences.* They are not to be blamed for this: it is an idea fostered by the natural scientists themselves; and it is therefore, understandably enough, almost universally accepted. It has been greatly enforced by the spectacular results of applied science. No wonder that almost all philosophers and almost all historians accept it.

It is, of course, undeniable that science has become the basis of technology. But what I regard as the true view of science is expressed on the jacket of a book by the great physicist and Nobel Laureate Sir George Thomson, one of the discoverers of the wave nature of the electron, and son of J. J. Thomson, the discoverer of the electron and its particle nature. Thomson's book is called *The Inspiration of Science* – mark the title! – and the statement on the jacket begins with the words: 'Science is an art'. And it goes on to

6 Isaiah Berlin, *Historical Inevitability*, p. 11, footnote.

189

speak of the 'intrinsic beauty and wonder' of 'the ideas of modern physics'. Other great scientists have spoken in the same humanist vein, but few students of the humanities have taken them seriously. There happen to be some scientists who agree explicitly that the traditionalist and professionalist view of natural science is utterly mistaken. But with two exceptions, I have so far failed to convince any historian, or philosopher of history, that his intuitive idea of science is mistaken, and that science is much more like history than historians think. The two exceptions are Professor Gombrich and Professor Hayek.

Professor Hayek, more especially, has written for years against the emulation of the natural sciences by the social scientists, and especially by historians. He called the tendency to ape the methods of the natural sciences 'scientism'. Now I have been just as opposed to these scientistic tendencies as he; but I pointed out, more than twenty years ago, that these 'scientistic' tendencies are in fact attempts to emulate what most people *mistakenly believe* to be the methods of the natural sciences, rather than the *real* methods of the natural sciences.

I was therefore most gratified and pleased when, quite unexpectedly, I read in Hayek's Preface to his new book, *Studies in Philosophy, Politics and Economics*, 1967, the following most generous remark:

> Readers of some of my earlier writings may notice a slight change in the tone of my discussion of the attitude which I then called 'scientism'. The reason for this is that . . . Karl Popper has taught me that natural scientists did not really do what most of them not only told us that they did but also urged the representatives of other disciplines to imitate. The difference of the two groups of disciplines has thereby been greatly narrowed . . .

Yet almost everybody else believes he knows quite enough about the methods of the natural sciences: is it not notorious that we start from observation and proceed by induction to theory? And is it not obvious that in history we proceed very differently?

Yes, I agree that we proceed very differently. But so we do in the natural sciences.

In both we start from myths – from traditional prejudices, beset with error – and from these we proceed by criticism: by the critical

190

elimination of errors. In both the role of evidence is, in the main, to correct our mistakes, our prejudices, our tentative theories; that is, to play a part in the critical discussion, in the elimination of error. By correcting our mistakes, we raise new problems. And in order to solve these problems, we invent conjectures, that is, tentative theories, which we submit to critical discussion, directed toward the elimination of error.

The whole process can be represented by a simplified schema which I may call the *tetradic schema*:

$$P_1 \rightarrow TT \rightarrow CD \rightarrow P_2$$

We may start from some problem P_1 – whether theoretical or historical – we proceed to a tentative solution – a conjectural or hypothetical solution, a *tentative theory* – which is submitted to critical discussion in the light of evidence, if available, with the result that new problems, P_2, arise.

Of course, this schema is oversimplified: there will be in general more than one problem to start with; and there will be in general a multiplicity of tentative conjectures for every problem, and many criticisms, especially if we can test our conjectures by confronting them with the evidence of observation or, say, of documentation. In other words, our diagram should be fan-shaped: it should fan out towards the right.

Another point of importance is this: since our tetradic schema is, as it were, self-propelling or dynamically self-reproducing, since it begins again with P_2, we can just as well begin the schema from tentative conjectures, (TT), or from critical discussion, (CD), instead of from problems (P_1). Indeed, problems arise, in general, against a background of knowledge: they presuppose what I have called a background of myths, or of tentative conjectures, or of historical traditions; and they presuppose that these are not accepted uncritically, but that some difficulties inherent in them have been noticed; and this means that they presuppose what I have called critical discussion. In fact, I could make out a case for each of the members of the triad, P or TT or CD, that it is a starting point of science or of history. Does not Herodotus begin with a problem? Does not a modern historian like Lord Acton tell us to study problems, not periods; that is, to begin with a problem? And do not our *studies* begin only when we begin to look critically at our surroundings and at views which as children we accepted uncritically?

191

Although I can make out a case for each member of my tetrad, and although there is from a logical point of view little or nothing in choosing one rather than another member of the tetrad as our starting point, I personally have some preference for starting from *problems*. First of all, in saying that we begin with a problem and end with another problem, we point to one very important lesson: the lesson that the more our knowledge grows, the more we realize how little we know. This Socratic lesson is as true in the natural sciences as it is in history: getting educated is getting an inkling of the immensity of our ignorance.

At the same time, if we let our tetradic schema start with P_1, it allows us to say that it is the distance – often the great distance – between P_1 and P_2 which is a kind of measure of our progress in knowledge: the distance between the problem from which we started and the problem with which we are now faced.

A third reason in favour of the choice of P as our starting point is that we are often led to our researches by some practical problem which impressed itself upon us whether we wanted it or not. Thus modern economic theory might be said to start from the currency crisis under William the Third, and from the distress at home and William's urgent need for money which reached its peak in 1696; and from John Locke's co-operation with Newton in supplying Montague with critical arguments which he used in Parliament, in support of the proposed stabilization of the currency, and against the counter proposal of the Secretary of the Treasury to devalue the currency by 25 per cent. As so often, the problem from which the theory first sprang was a practical one. So were at least some of the famous problems of Archimedes. But as soon as a solution is offered, criticism takes over, and criticism is the engine of the growth of knowledge, as indicated by our tetradic schema.

It is of the utmost importance that we realize that a bad problem and an erroneous conjecture are very much better than none. At the same time it is of the utmost importance to realize that this is so because we criticize our conjectures from the point of view of their adequacy; that is to say, of their truth, and of their significance or relevance. That we constantly have their truth and their relevance in mind is perfectly compatible with the fact that many conjectures which may appear to us to be true at one stage may turn out to be erroneous at a later stage. New documents may force us to re-interpret old documents. Or they may raise new problems; and in the light of a new problem an inscription which before appeared insignificant may assume a completely unexpected significance.

This solves a famous but not very serious methodological problem – the problem of historical relativism. Admittedly, our conjectures are relative to our problems, and our problems are relative to the state of our knowledge. And admittedly, there may be much in the momentary situation of our knowledge which is erroneous. Yet this does not mean that truth is relative. It only means that the elimination of our errors and the approach towards truth is hard work. There is no criterion of truth. But there is something like a criterion of error: clashes arising within our knowledge, or between our knowledge and the facts. In this way knowledge can grow, through the critical elimination of error. This is how we get nearer to the truth.

You will see that I can fully agree with Professor Trevor-Roper who in his challenging and controversial inaugural lecture pleads that we should keep the flow of ideas running from all tributaries, and especially from what he calls *lay tributaries*. I will quote from Professor Trevor-Roper's Inaugural Address:

> I myself believe that the historical contributions of both Sombart and Keynes are erroneous. I do not believe in the . . . 'spirit of capitalism', nor do I believe that profit-inflation caused the expansion of sixteenth-century Europe and that we had Shakespeare when we could afford him. But what of that? These great tributaries which we have ignored have caused tremendous historical developments in other countries, and if we exclude them, we impoverish our own studies. They may be erroneous, but the mere correction of error involves first a new study, and then a new interest which that error has created. In humane studies there are times when a new error is *more* life-giving than an old truth, a fertile error than a sterile accuracy.[7]

You will see how great the agreement is between Professor Trevor-Roper and myself – except for one point: his apparent belief that what he says holds only for the humane studies, and not for the natural sciences. I should like to say that although specialists are needed in both, specialization and the professionalist attitude of

7 Hugh R. Trevor-Roper, *History Professional and Lay*, Oxford 1957, pp. 21 f.

193

superiority and exclusiveness towards the outsider or layman must lead to the drying up of both humanist and scientific studies.

Professor Elton in his new book, *The Practice of History*, defends professionalism. But does it need defence? Has Ranke not won this battle a hundred years ago? Has it not by now become necessary to remind the great professionalists, and specialists, whether in history, in science, or in medicine, that they too are liable to make mistakes – that is, professional mistakes? It is regarded as wrong and even humiliating to make mistakes. But who has not made them? The historian may think that a great physicist makes no mistakes in his subject. But were he to study the history of physics he would soon find that even the greatest physicists have made mistakes. Einstein worked from 1905 to 1915 on the problem of gravitation before he arrived at a theory which could replace Newton's, and almost the whole of the last three of these ten years he spent on what he described as a completely mistaken track. And even after he had found his field equation, he was told by Kretschmann in 1917 that what he had proposed as an essential argument was mistaken. Einstein at once admitted the mistake; but what he then said in order to replace his argument (he hinted that Newton's equations could not without undue difficulty be put in a co-variant form) was again mistaken, as has been since shown.[8]

Nobody is exempt from making mistakes. The great thing is to learn from them. And this is done by criticism, and the discovery of the new *problems* brought forth by criticism.

I think that this is implicitly admitted in Professor Elton's book. He distinguishes between historical analysis – the analysis of historical problems – and historical narrative. Yet he argues against Lord Acton's excellent advice to young historians, given in his inaugural lecture of 1895,[9] that they should '*study problems in preference to periods*'.

I think that Lord Acton's views on method, like Collingwood's or Professor Trevor-Roper's, could be shown to be essentially in agreement with those I am defending here. Professor Elton seems to dislike them, however. But a close reading of what he says shows that in the end he seems to agree with Lord Acton. Let me quote Professor Elton:

8 Peter Havas, *Reviews of Modern Physics*, 36 (1964), pp. 958ff.
9 I may perhaps mention here that it was Hayek who, very many years ago, drew my attention to Lord Acton's works.

To study problems not periods was Lord Acton's much-quoted injunction, and those who cite him approvingly fail to note that it is now some seventy years since he uttered those gnomic words, and that in actual fact he proved incapable of studying either problems or periods to a practical conclusion. The historian, working in the records and meeting one unresolved problem after another, quite naturally persuades himself that the real work consists in tackling these dark entities

– that is, the problems. 'But that does not mean that one should pin a special medal on analysis',[10] Professor Elton adds; that is, one should not be specially concerned with problem solving. So far, it will be seen, no argument has been brought forward against Acton except that his words are 'gnomic' and seventy-two years old. Yet Elton's next two sentences are in fact an admission that Acton is right. Elton's first sentence reads: 'Since history is the record of events, and of problems, proceeding through time, narrative must be not only legitimate but also urgently called for.' In this sentence 'problems proceeding through time'[11] are appealed to; this will hardly do as an argument against Acton's stress on problems, for Acton never said that you should not follow your problems through time. The next sentence of Elton's is even clearer: 'Once again, the only point which determines the choice is the historian's purpose, the questions he is asking.'[12] I entirely agree. *The questions* the historian is asking are decisive. But 'the questions the historian is asking' is merely a synonym for the term 'historical problem'. And so we are some seventy-five years back, at Lord Acton's emphasis on problems.

In fact, it is only from problems that our work can possibly start; and this holds not only for what Professor Elton calls 'analysis' but just as much for what he calls 'narrative'.

It may perhaps be useful to point out at this place that Leopold von Ranke's famous professionalist revolution of history has in it more than a streak of what Hayek has called 'scientism'.

The alleged method of the professional scientist is: start from observations; observe and observe. The alleged method of the professional historian is: start from the documents. Read documents and documents.

10 Cp. G. R. Elton, *The Practice of History*, Sydney 1967, p. 127.
11 *Loc. cit.*, pp. 127f.
12 *Loc. cit.*, p. 128.

Both these alleged methods are exactly analogous, and both are precepts which cannot be carried out: they are logically impossible. You cannot start from observation: you have to know first *what* to observe; that is, you have to start from a problem. Moreover, there is no such thing as an uninterpreted observation. All observations are interpreted in the light of theories. Exactly the same holds for documents. Is my return ticket to Paddington a historical document? Yes and no. If I am accused of murder, the ticket may possibly serve to support an alibi, and so become an important historical document. Nevertheless I should not advise a historian to start his work by collecting used railway tickets.

A historical document, like a scientific observation, is a document only relative to a historical problem; and like an observation, it has to be *interpreted*. This is one of the reasons why people may be blind to the significance of a document, and destroy it. Or why they may destroy (as Professor Elton complains) the order of some documents, and with it, one of the clues to their interpretation.

So far I have tried to produce a few arguments to show that there is more in common between the real method of science and the real method of history than most historians realize. With the remarks I just made I have tried to support this by showing that the similarity extends even to the scientistic misinterpretations of the two methods.

But is there not a fundamental difference, connected with *the problem of understanding history*?

I will outline very briefly Collingwood's theory of sympathetic understanding or, as it may be called, empathy, which we find in his posthumous book *The Idea of History* published in 1946. Collingwood's theory may be stated in brief as follows: historical knowledge, or historical understanding, consists in the *re-enactment by the historian of past experience*. Let me quote a passage from Collingwood, a passage with which I agree to a considerable extent.

Suppose, for example, he is reading the Theodosian Code, and has before him a certain edict of an emperor. Merely reading the words and being able to translate them does not amount to knowing their historical significance. In order to do that he must envisage the situation with which the emperor was trying to deal, and he must envisage it as that emperor envisaged it. Then

196

he must see for himself, just as if the emperor's situation were his own, how such a situation might be dealt with; he must see the possible alternatives, and the reasons for choosing one rather than another; and thus he must go through the process which the emperor went through in deciding on this particular course. Thus he is re-enacting in his own mind the experience of the emperor; and only in so far as he does this has he any historical knowledge, as distinct from a merely philological knowledge, of the meaning of the edict.

Or again, suppose he is reading a passage of an ancient philosopher. Once more, he must know the language in a philological sense and be able to construe; but by doing that he has not yet understood the passage as an historian of philosophy must understand it. In order to do that, he must see what the philosophical problem was, of which his author is here stating his solution. He must think that problem out for himself, see what possible solutions of it might be offered, and see why this particular philosopher chose that solution instead of another. This means re-thinking for himself the thought of his author and nothing short of that will make him the historian of that author's philosophy.[13]

What Collingwood here describes I have tried to describe, in my *Poverty of Historicism*, and in my *Open Society*, and in later works, under the name of *situational logic* or *situational analysis*. What we have to do, I said, was to reconstruct the *problem situation* in which the acting person finds himself, and to show how and why his action constituted a solution of the situation.

I have said before that I agree with Collingwood's passage to a considerable extent. Why not entirely?

There *is* a difference between Collingwood's theory and mine. It seems a small difference, but it has far-reaching consequences.

The difference is this. Collingwood makes it clear that the essential thing in understanding history is not so much the analysis of the situation, but the historian's mental process of re-enactment. The analysis of the situation serves only as an indispensible help for this re-enactment. I, on the other hand, suggest that the psychological process of re-enactment is inessential, though I admit that it can be an excellent personal help for the historian, a kind of intuitive check of the success of his situational analysis. What is essential,

13 R. G. Collingwood, *The Idea of History*, London 1946, p. 283.

197

I suggest, is not the re-enactment but the situational analysis: the historian's attempt to analyse and describe the situation is nothing else than his historical conjecture, his historical theory. And the question – 'what were the important or operative elements in the situation?' – is the central problem which the historian tries to solve. To the extent that he solves it, he has *understood* the historical situation, and that piece of history which he tries to recapture.

What he has to do *qua* historian is not to re-enact what has happened, but to give objective arguments in support of his situational analysis. He may well be able to do so, while the re-enactment may or may not work. For the act may be in many ways beyond him. It may be an act of cruelty or an act of heroism which he may be unable to re-enact. Or it may be an achievement in art, or literature, or science, or philosophy, which exceeds his abilities. Yet all this does not prevent him from making interesting historical discoveries – from finding new solutions to old historical problems, or even from finding new historical problems.

The main significance of the difference between Collingwood's re-enactment method and my method of situational analysis is that Collingwood's is a subjectivist method, while the method I advocate is objectivist. Bit this means that, for Collingwood, *a systematic rational criticism of competing solutions to historical problems is impossible;* for we can rationally criticize only conjectures or theories which have not become part of ourselves, but which can be put outside ourselves, and which thus may be inspected by everybody, especially by those who hold different theories. In contradistinction, the objectivist method of situational analysis permits the *critical discussion of our tentative solutions* – of our attempts to reconstruct the situation; and to this extent it is, indeed, much nearer to the true method of the natural sciences.

Let me take a very simple example. It is well known that Galileo was unwilling to accept the lunar theory of the tides, and that he made tremendous efforts trying to explain the tides by a non-lunar theory. It is also known that Galileo did not reciprocate the friendly advances of Kepler. These two facts create two problems; and they may give rise to the following explanatory historical conjecture: Galileo was opposed to astrology; that is to say the theory that the positions of the planets, including the moon, have an influence upon terrestrial events. Documents show that the lunar theory of the tides was indeed part of astrological lore; and the fact that

198

Kepler was a professional astrologist was, of course, known to Galileo.

Now a re-reading of Galileo's *Dialogue Concerning the Two Chief World Systems* actually does produce at once a passage – it is the last passage in which Kepler is mentioned – which seems to me an excellent corroboration of the conjecture. It so happens that when I read the passage for the first time, before I had the two problems and the conjecture, I did not understand it; while afterwards I understood it.

It is clear that this little bit of very simple historical problem solving operates with what I call situational logic or situational analysis: it helps to explain two of Galileo's attitudes – one towards a scientific problem, one towards a person – by way of a conjectural reconstruction of his problem situation, as he saw it. Yet this reconstruction is not a real re-enactment in Collingwood's sense. It is not a re-enactment of Galileo's actions so far as they are of interest here: it is neither a re-invention of Galileo's theory of the tides, an act of which I should be quite incapable; nor is it a re-enactment of his failure to reply to some of Kepler's letters, although failing to reply to a letter or even to two letters is a thing of which I am perfectly capable.

Now Galileo's failure to reply to Kepler is clearly one of those things which simply are not worth re-enacting: in itself it is too trivial an action. But as a symptom, and in connection with another historical problem, it may be interesting; and it is so from the point of view of situational analysis.

I therefore claim for situational analysis that it is a better theory of historical understanding than Collingwood's re-enactment theory. It is less rigid. It is not confined, as is Collingwood's theory, to the re-enactment of conscious thought processes, but makes allowance for the reconstruction of problem situations which were incompletely understood by the agent. It makes, furthermore, room for the construction and analysis of situations which arise as the unintended and unforeseen consequences of our actions – a very important point indeed. It makes room for giving full weight, in the situational analysis, not only to individuals but also to institutions; in other words, it is wider, or, as I may say, far more pluralistic than even that of Collingwood who, by his strong emphasis on problems, approached history in a far more pluralistic spirit than any of his predecessors. For Collingwood, the re-enactment of any thought may become a problem. For situational logic, the reconstruction of any situation, including the reconstruction of the one which brought about another, may become a problem. Moreover, situational logic is as much concerned with the situation as experienced by the acting subject as with the objective situation as it actually was, and thus with the objective errors of the acting subject.

This brings me to the most important difference between my approach and Collingwood's. For Collingwood, as for almost all philosophers, knowledge consists, essentially, in living experiences of the knowing subject; and this, of course, holds for historical knowledge. For me, knowledge consists, essentially, of *exosomatic artifacts*, or products, or institutions. (It is their exosomatic character which makes them rationally criticizable.) There is knowledge without a knowing subject – that knowledge, for example, which is stored in our libraries. Thus there can be growth of knowledge without any growth of awareness in the knower. And the growth of knowledge can even form the main plot of our history, and yet there may be no corresponding increase in either our subjective knowledge, or our abilities. There may even be no change in our interest. Human knowledge may grow outside of human beings. There may be a plot in the history of man, without there being a plot in the history of men.

Thus it is possible to differentiate between the evolution of man, in the singular, with his exosomatic knowledge, and the history of men, in the plural; and there is no doubt in my mind that it is the main value and the main characteristic of the subject which we call history, and of all humanistic subjects, that it has room for interesting itself not only in the evolution of the human race and its institutions, but in the stories of men, in the plural, and their struggles with their institutions, their evolving environment, and with the problems posed by the evolution of man and his knowledge.

Thus history is pluralistic. It deals not only with man but with men. Above all it allows us to raise the problem how much or how little the growth of knowledge, the history of art, and the evolution of man has affected men. This problem, I suggest, is one of the greatest problems of history.

A Behavioral Approach to Monetary Theory
Günter Schmölders

Introduction

More than fifty years after the world left the gold standard, monetary theory has not yet succeeded in developing a generally accepted explanation of money and its functioning in our society, the value and 'image' of world currencies and the factors influencing their price relations, to say nothing of monetary reform, the role of gold in Central Bank Reserves and the conceptual jungle of the so-called need for international liquidity. Four hundred years of metallic currencies, and, in due course, of a purely quantitative approach to the problems of the value of money have left their mark on all theoretical efforts to explain the working of the monetary system both within the national economies and on the international level; even today many authors rely on the metallic or quasi-metallic character of money tokens and/or their quantity and velocity of circulation to explain the value of all other forms of visible and invisible money which have outdone the remaining coins and notes by more than 3:1 in most industrial countries.

It seems rather embarrassing that after centuries of practical experience with and learned deliberations about the subject monetary experts still cannot even supply a precise definition of 'money'.[1] Throughout the long history of monetary theory almost everyone claiming competence in the field has pasted together his own definition to fit his particular monetary '*Weltanschauung*'. Aristotle's commodity interpretation of money ('silver and iron and other such matters') has shown particular longevity and weathered centuries, if superficially updated into the 'convention theory', out

1 For a detailed treatment of historical developments in money use and monetary theory see: G. Schmölders, *Geldpolitik*, 2nd ed. Tübingen and Zürich 1968, Chs. I and II.

201

of which eventually grew the jurisprudential description of money as a 'creation of the legal order'.[2] In the same vein, but asking what money does rather than what it is, functional definitions of money abounded; with the emergence and rapid increase in importance of 'invisible money', monetary theory has amalgamated both viewpoints into a pragmatic, if contested, concept where money is defined 'in the usual way as the sum of demand deposits adjusted at commercial banks and currency outside the banks'.[3]

Common to these attempts of defining money is the tendency by most authors to base their elaborations on particular phenotypes of money, i.e. contemporary and/or previous forms of *currency*. Attacking the question from this angle, however, only led them to lose sight of the nature and the essence of *money*; consequently the somewhat surprising situation ensued that this vital area of monetary theory, the concept of money, is practically still virgin territory.

Even though the idea that 'money in its social sense is a means of communication and social ranking'[4] has been around for some time, monetarians as of yet have not taken advantage of this chance to break through the narrow confines of traditional money theory. Any theoretical concept, however, which purports to be more than just a set of learned teachings for monetary artisans has to deal with the role of money as a communicative symbol in social life, where it is 'indeed one of the most remarkable and important of all human symbolizations'.[5]

I   The Theory of Money*

This idea, of course, imposes upon the theory of money a fundamentally different point of departure while at the same time its

2 G. F. Knapp, *Staatliche Theorie des Geldes*, 3rd ed., Munich and Leipzig 1921.
3 R. L. Teigen, An aggregate quarterly model of the U.S. monetary sector 1953–1964, A paper presented to the *Conference on Targets and Indicators of Monetary Policy*, University of California, April 2, 1966, p. 6.
4 A. Müller, *Versuche einer neuen Theorie des Geldes*, Leipzig and Altenburg 1816; also see W. Andreae, *Geld und Geldschöpfung*, Frankfurt-Main 1952, p. 273.
5 T. Parsons, *The Social System*, New York 1964, p. 12; also T. Parsons, *Essays in Sociological Theory*, New York 1965, *passim;* W. F. Whyte, *Money and Motivation*, New York 1955, Ch. 1.
* The author is indebted to Hartmut Garding for linguistic advice and help with computer technique.

direction and final destination also change. It implies a breaking away from the glitter of gold and silver, or any other current and awe-inspiring physiognomy which monetary tokens and symbols may have or have had, and calls for the humble chore of observing people in their actual day-to-day dealings with whatever means of payment they may use. If indeed, as we hypothesized, money's role is that of a communication symbol, then we must watch its actual performance in its natural environment and not be satisfied with speculations about its maximum performance in an ideal monetary system; we must try to understand how millions of individual decisions cause the figures of our bank statistics to swell or dwindle.

What we are suggesting in effect here is to ban the chimera 'velocity of circulation' from monetary theory and substitute habitualized cash holding patterns, the income-expenditure rhythm of households, and the popularity of cash versus bank accounts in its stead. While, as Heinrich Rittershausen[6] observes, no country has ever been successful in producing reliable data about the velocity of circulation of money, the concepts mentioned above can all be operationalized and documented without great theoretical pains.

But also the motives for changes in spending- and saving-habits must become targets of inquiry so that the causes for monetary fluctuation may become clearer. This demand follows the lead taken by the income theory of money, which started from the laudable premise that causal relationships are not to be sought between money volume and price level, but rather between the motives and reactions of people who either do or do not spend, save or borrow money. Unfortunately, though, income theory will remain trivial as long as it does not contain information about the process by which habitualized behavior is formed in the first place and by which such behavior changes quite drastically at times.

No justification whatsoever remains to the widespread argument that an admission of psychology, social psychology and sociology into the realm of monetary theory is illegitimate.[7] The consequences of such an admission are clear: Up to now, the principle of construction and instruction in monetary theory was to begin by building highly abstract, over-simplified models and to relax the theoretical assumptions step by step in order to adapt the model to the reality of a given currency- and credit-system. The result was a neatly boxed-in

6 H. Rittershausen, *Bankpolitik*, Frankfurt-Main 1956, p. 104.
7 G. Schmölders, *Gutes und schlechtes Geld*, Frankfurt-Main 1968, p. 11.

scheme with the banking sector on the one and the private and public sector on the other side. Communications between and within sectors were very rigidly defined and concerned the creation and the disappearance of means of payment. In these sterile surroundings, monetary theory deteriorated into a description of national variations on the basic scheme and taught the skills of how to operate within various national banking systems.

This needs to be amended and the most fundamental change is implied in regarding the monetary scene as an event that is carried by a population of actors, each one acting his part as it is defined by his individual psychological make-up, by his intents, and by the prescriptions of his social role. Attitudes, motives and group behavior certainly must concern and interest the monetary economist – unless, of course, he chooses to regard his work as artistic rather than scientific.

'Science', Skinner says, 'is first of all a set of attitudes. It is a disposition to deal with the facts rather than with what someone has said about them.'[8] This is not enough, though, because the attempt to turn to the facts holds the potential danger of operating the already proverbial 'data-collecting vacuum cleaner' while trying to gather facts; a phenomenon not at all unfamiliar in the social sciences. The disposition, then, to 'deal with the facts' must include a basic hypothesis about their nature, or as Skinner put it:

> If we are to use the methods of science in the field of human affairs, we must assume that behavior is lawful and determined. We must expect to discover that what a man does is the result of specifiable conditions and that once these conditions have been discovered, we can anticipate and to some extent determine his actions.[9]

If monetary theory is to be put on a true scientific footing, any 'specifiable conditions' of the monetary communication system as well as the resulting human behavior must be extracted from the stream of social activities and, subsequently, fitted into an explanatory theoretical framework. A prerequisite for this undertaking, of course, is a definition of money which is both operational and practical, i.e. which has room not only for coins and notes, checks,

8 B. F. Skinner, *Science and Human Behavior*, New York 1965, p. 12.
9 B. F. Skinner, *loc. cit.*, p. 6.

204

credit cards or, to go to the extreme, magnetized spots on a tape reel, but also for ancient currencies, like cowrie, or not so ancient ones, like unopened packs of American cigarettes.[10]

Departing from this stage of explanation, the further development of monetary theory is aimed at the goal of prediction. Here we must go beyond the stimulus-response relation of our descriptive stage and search for the reasons behind monetary dispositions. These include decisions about income allocation (spending or saving), about the timing of purchases (save now, buy later, or vice-versa), decisions about the ways of saving and means of capital accumulation and, last but not least, the specific techniques employed in implementing such decisions (cash, check, credit, etc.).[11]

In such analysis of motivated behavior, which it all boils down to, we cannot possibly overlook the key role of attitudes as the long-term organizers and stabilizers of human action.[12] It is through attitudes and their future-oriented counterpart, expectations, that we can find a way to make the transition from individual behavior to group phenomena within a society. Attitudes toward money and its part as a symbol are the 'Sesame' which opens the road to an understanding of inflation or stagnation; by virtue of their relative stability they also permit prediction, so they can be used as tools of prognosis.

From here on, the further direction and final destination of monetary theory is quite obvious; after discovering the 'specifiable conditions' of behavior and after being able to anticipate it, only the control of human actions is left. In the realm of money this is probably the most serious and difficult task. Restraining or inducing people to spend, save or borrow is never an isolated affair of the money market but has repercussions throughout the entire economy. Measures of the above kind quickly go beyond the cool atmosphere of monetary policy decisions into the heated climate of political and economic goals, interests, and pressures. Monetary policy can ill afford to remain uncommitted in such value-laden controversies. Since the preservation of the essential role of money is, almost by definition, its prime objective, the long-term defense of that role over short-sighted attacks can come from its quarters only.

10 see G. Schmölders, *Die Zigarettenwährung*, Kölner Universitätszeitung 1947.
11 see G. Schmölders, *Geldpolitik*, p. 45.
12 T. Newcomb, R. Turner, Ph. Converse, *Social Psychology*, New York and London 1965, Chs. 3 and 5.

If based on a thorough insight into the ways people handle money and the extent to which they trust the monetary system, monetary policy becomes a most effective *'defensor fidei'*.

II Monetary Theory and Empirical Research

Fortunately we do possess the tools needed to deal with the task laid out here; the days when social scientists had to direct much of their energy towards seeking recognition and acceptance for their newly developed methods of empirical research may safely be considered as bygone. The technique of conducting large field surveys addressed to thousands of respondents in an attempt to uncover meaningful relationships between opinions, knowledge, attitudinal preferences and overt behavior has proved its viability and is here to stay.

To an economist who has directed much of his interest towards survey research this is a most gratifying observation. The reception of surveys as a valuable research tool now permits scholars to focus attention on the very essential problem of trying to consolidate the many divergent theoretical concepts about origins and types of human behavior.

The need for such consolidation and integration is widely recognized and, characteristically, being dealt with interdisciplinarily: K. Boulding, K. Deutsch, P. G. Herbst, Th. Newcomb and T. Parsons may be named as examples.[13] Whereas these efforts, originating in history, political science or sociology, are concerned mostly with concepts that would eventually be applicable to human behavior as a whole, our interest here is with economic behavior primarily, more precisely with questions relating to monetary behavior. Here the theoretical gaps separating contenders of various schools seem almost unbridgeable, even though the near-irrepressible doggedness with which inflation continues to creep up on national economies all over the globe makes it imperative to search for

13 K. Boulding, *The Image*, Ann Arbor 1961; K. Boulding, *The Meaning of the 20th Century*, New York 1967; K. Deutsch, *The Nerves of Government*, New York 1967; P. G. Herbst, 'A Theory of Simple Behavior Systems', I and II, *Human Relations*, 14 (1961); T. Newcomb, Turner, Converse, *op. cit.*; T. Parsons, E. Shils (eds.), *Toward a General Theory of Action*, New York 1962.

common theoretical grounds, on which combined efforts to combat the deterioration of currencies may be based.

It is in this light that the argument for a consolidation of theories should be evaluated. The unfortunate state of affairs as revealed in almost any volume of any economic periodical is that authors not only waste much time and energy on such irrelevant considerations as the formalization of money demand, velocity of circulation, income-expenditure formulas and the like, but also block publication space by splashing their petty squabbles about importance of quite insignificant parameters or impractical variable definitions all over the pages of renowned journals. Not even the claim that the monetary fate of the nation is at stake can serve as an excuse for these academic exercises, because in the last analysis it is still presidential or prime-ministerial authority and/or the diligence, swiftness and intuitive judgment on the part of central banks which decide whether a currency is traded higher or lower on the world market.

There can hardly be any doubt that the recent availability of high-speed digital computers has revolutionized, or rather is still revolutionizing, the social sciences. After a mere twelve years of development the fourth computer generation has emerged and the enormous storage capacities combined with a wide versatility in programming allow for relatively easy handling of the large bulks of data typical in survey research.

As increasing interest in economic behavior meets with expanding facilities of electronic data processing the stage is set for a confrontation between the various factions of monetary theory. The heart of the question seems to be whether the general concept of economic processes should orient itself along the lines of stringently defined abstract models, apt to be expressed in mathematical terms but rather removed from real life, or whether it should rely on the more cumbersome and voluminous results of survey series, which are, however, immediate reflections of reality.

The model approach certainly may be expected to bridge some theoretical gaps rather quickly, revealing certain interaction patterns among socio-economic aggregates, as simultaneous processing of far greater numbers of relevant variables than ever before has become possible through computers. On the debit side of the model approach the substantial loss of information alongside with the necessity to make all sorts of untested, untestable and sometimes outright unrealistic assumptions in creating models weighs heavy.

A few other aspects of mathematical economics need to be listed here, even though this author rather uneasily recognizes the fact that such critique must, in the light of the nature of this contribution, be made rather summarily and without due reference to specific models. Nevertheless some of these remarks might prove general enough to apply to at least a large number of specimens of the model family.

A basic shortcoming of such constructs is the lack of a provision which would allow the model to undergo the same type of blow-up and shrinkage that continuously occurs in an economy. By virtue of its contribution the model economy merely spins in its mathematically described orbit, unable to simulate the gyrations along an expanding and contracting spiral of its real-life counterpart. A behaviorally-oriented system, on the other hand, can easily provide this essential, by simply introducing changing moods, waves of optimism and pessimism, or other attitudinal variables into the scheme. Given the possibility to locate and measure such variables accurately, this procedure hardly leaves any ground for misreading the actual stage of the business cycle. Where mere extrapolations of statistical series fail to indicate a turning point in advance, our 'gyroscope' of attitudes rather reliably does just that.[14]

As a further consequence of mathematically confining reality, technical considerations necessitate the distillation of 'chemically pure' and 'autonomous' variables which no longer possess even remote resemblance to factors in real life and only serve to complicate the model construction. This method therefore is not only highly inflexible, but also most unrealistic as the essence of any real life economy, namely the feedbacks and interdependencies, are defined away and excluded from the model.

It is not by chance that in many so-called empirical tests made with aggregate time series, years with extraordinary characteristics like World War II or the Korean War are frequently left out. There is no conceivable reason why a theoretical model should back away

14 E. Mueller, 'Effects of Consumer Attitudes on Purchases', *American Economic Review*, 47 (1957); E. Mueller, 'Consumer Attitudes: Their Influence and Forecasting Value', in National Bureau of Economic Research (ed.), *The Quality and Economic Significance of Anticipations Data*, Princeton 1960; E. Mueller, 'Ten Years of Consumer Attitude Surveys: Their Forecasting Record', *Journal of the American Statistical Association*, 58 (1963).

from such periods of 'special circumstances', unless, of course, by its very construction it is not equipped to deal with them. In such cases, however, the question arises whether the goodness of the fit for 'normal' periods truly represents an heuristic advance or whether it does not simply mean that these times are normal, something we knew before; the fact that in times without internal or external disturbances any social subsystem is upheld and aided in its smooth functioning by any number of psychological and sociological factors based on authority or habitualization, is common knowledge to sociologists. Only in times of crisis and severe stress, the essential structure of a subsystem as well as its viability become apparent; but in such periods the model regressions fit badly.

Even in 'normal' times subsystems undergo fluctuations by which they are altered. Authorities and institutions suffer from wear and tear, losing in influence by abrasion and erosion; others move in to fill the void. Changes in institutions provoke changes in behavior; another commonplace which model economics do not provide for. Nor can they recognize the influence of changing preferences, moods and fashions, where habitual behavior (which suits the model) is discarded in favour of 'problem-solving behavior'[15] (which breaks it wide open).

In summary, there is no reason to accept the underlying assumption of any model construction that extrapolation even from extended time series *eo ipso* solves the problem of prediction. Neither institutional structures nor attitudinal preferences typical of the past can be assumed to be necessarily relevant for the future. The use of surveys as a base for developing notions about the functioning of a monetary system may, in contrast, involve a much more prolonged and painstaking search for behavior patterns; once known, however, these ultimately will allow both for prediction and control. Most of the relevant information about types and causes of economic activities can be retained using this approach; the theoretical edifice can be built on the firm ground of empirically verifiable theses.

Oddly enough the advent of computers in the social sciences, which made large scale survey research feasible in the first place, has also tipped the scales in favour of a more mathematical approach. This may well be due to the relative ease with which rigorously

15 As for the concepts 'habitual behavior' and 'problem-solving behavior' see: G. Katona, *Psychological Analysis of Economic Behavior*, New York 1951, Part I.

defined data-set properties and relationships can be described to and processed by the machine. None the less, this author would like to make a case for the survey approach not only because he considers the development of a theoretical scheme based upon a wealth of factual information drawn from surveys more adequate to the nature of live behavior, but also because he believes that the application of electronic information processors to survey-data analysis imposes the necessity to adapt research methods and analysis techniques to the flexibility and potential of these machines.

a. *Psychological Variables in Economic Behavior*

As to the necessity of incorporating psychological findings into economic research, Katona has delivered a most convincing argument in his *Survey of Consumer Finances* series.[16] This record of successful research as well as the results of our own studies at the 'Forschungsstelle für empirische Sozialökonomik' in Cologne demonstrate convincingly that consumption, public finance and monetary theory may well profit from widening their horizon by employing survey research.

To provide some evidence for this claim, mention may be made of a study conducted by our Cologne Research Center several years ago. It dealt with monetary dispositions in both senses of the word, i.e. with attitudes *vis-à-vis* saving, spending, and money borrowing and with the actual saving and spending decisions. Of particular interest was the question whether demographic and attitudinal variables could be ranked according to their strength of influence upon monetary decisions. Traditional thinking usually favored demographic variables (like income, age, education, profession, etc.) over psychological factors, like optimism or pessimism regarding the current business situation, and trust or distrust in the monetary system and its institutions. Our basic assumption was that such attitudinal preferences would influence people's decisions about spending and saving quite noticeably; a conviction which was supported by the performance of a Consumer Sentiment Index,[17] where consumer optimism or the lack thereof has proven most powerful

16 G. Katona *et al.*, *Survey of Consumer Finances*, Ann Arbor, available for 1960 through 1967.
17 G. Katona, *op. cit.*, and Eva Mueller, *op. cit.*

in predicting consumer behavior. On the other hand, it was quite clear that demographic variables in some form or other would duly display an influence of their own; so the question arose: Which ones and in what strength? Our quota sample was representative of private households in the Federal Republic; it comprised 1,050 family units in which a total of 2,435 persons were interviewed. In order to find out whether every individual in an economic community can, except for income difference, be assumed to act in the same way – as traditional thinking will have it – we planned to test various kinds of monetary decisions against a number of different character types. In other words, we are now dealing with the specifiable conditions of the monetary system, i.e. the question is: who does the spending, saving and borrowing? An added feature of particular interest is the question whether demographic or psychological variables are more powerful in determining the 'who'.

Rather than trying to construct psychological homunculi we asked our respondents to classify themselves with respect to a list of 17 'good' and 19 'bad' character traits. As might be expected, socially acceptable qualities like: 'I can't keep grudges against people'; 'I get along with anyone' or 'I make friends easily' were checked rather frequently (by 46 per cent, 42 per cent and 34 per cent of all respondents respectively). Approximately a third confirmed to be industrious, thorough and exact in their work. Roughly 25 per cent enjoyed solitude, tended towards moodiness, were punctual or felt they could keep a secret. Traditional virtues like moral strictness and austerity, self-discipline, the ready acceptance of social responsibility, firm principles, emotional balance and energetic conduct were claimed by a fifth to a sixth. With approximately the same frequency of 15 to 20 per cent people confessed, on the other hand, to be just a bit on the extravagant, easy-going, inconsistent, talkative, irascible, indecisive, ruthless, vindictive or penny-pinching side.[18]

It soon became apparent that certain clusters of traits recurred rather frequently across individuals, as could actually be expected since these qualities reflect a basic psychological make-up that manifests itself with considerable internal consistency. We therefore combined repeatedly coinciding traits into personality syndromes in order to be able to test the emerging psychological types for differences in their attitudes toward money as well as their spending

18 G. Schmölders, *Psychologie des Geldes*, p. 37–42.

211

and saving habits. Technically this was done by registering for any one individual four to five traits of one type and allowing only one or two mentions of qualities of its antipode type.

So, for example, respondents who named four or more qualities of the left column below, but only one or two of the right column were categorized as 'punctilious' (which was possible in 10 per cent of all cases), whereas naming three or more of the right and one or two of the left column would put that person on to the category 'easy-going' (9 per cent).

Punctilious	*Easy-going*
resentful	extravagant
meticulous	inconstant
avaricious	untidy
thorough	light-minded
austere	erratic
punctual	

In the same fashion the following other dichotomies could be constructed:

	%			%
Orderly	9		Desultory	15
Vigorous	12		Weakly	15
Introverted	11		Extraverted	11

b. *The Psychology of Saving*

For our particular purposes it seemed even more important to have some indications as to the attitudes held towards thrift and extravagance; the answers to the following questions gave us some clues.

Question 1

When it comes to spending money, would you say you can keep your pennies together, you carefully budget your expenses, or do you rather like to spend freely?

Question 2

Would you think that thriftiness is an essential and desirable quality of character?

Question 3

Suppose you'd like to see a particular movie. But as you get to the theater all except the expensive balcony seats are sold out. Would you still see the film or would you rather return some other night?

Question 4

Suppose you've just been to visit someone and as you want to return home you miss the bus. Your alternatives are to wait two hours for the next bus or to take a cab and pay about two pounds. What would you do?

Question 5

An old proverb says: 'Save in time to have in need!' Do you think that this is true for our present time or do you feel that it doesn't make much sense nowadays to save and prepare for bad times?

Question 6

Here are three opinions about saving. With which one would you agree?

Left: Saving? I think one should enjoy life now with the money one has. Who knows whether the money in the banks won't be devalued and lost again?

Middle: In my opinion one should think twice before spending a penny, one should save as much as possible and if necessary give up a thing or two in life.

Right: I feel it makes a lot of sense to save some money, but within limits. I wouldn't want to forego every little wish one may have.

Upon the reactions to these questions we were able to categorize as 'very thrifty' 12 per cent, as 'thrifty' 19 per cent, as 'extravagant' 5 per cent and as 'extremely extravagant' 6 per cent. In order to add still a further dimension, the classification of tempers rendered as 'very conscientious' 10 per cent, as 'conscientious' 20 per cent, as 'carefree' 8 per cent and as 'very carefree' 7 per cent.[19]

Even though a large part of the sample remained outside the taxonomy in each case, the various types were represented in large enough numbers to allow for some checks against demographic variables in order to exclude misinterpretations later. In most of our contrast pairs, men and women were found in near equal proportions; the fact that male respondents had a slight edge over the

19 G. Schmölders, *ibid.*, p. 47–49.

213

'weaker sex' in the vigorous-category does not surprise at all. Women on the other hand were generally somewhat thriftier than men.

Another matter is age, which did influence the classification to some extent. People under 30 were found three times as often in the easy-going-group than were their elders, who in turn dominated among the punctilious. Similarily extravertedness was much more prominent among young people; those over 60 seemed more introverted. The 30- to 40-year-olds are markedly more vigorous than either the younger or the older age groups. But most interesting was the fact that thrift was not only considerably more widespread among the older people than among the younger, but that equally distinct differences appeared between the orderly, the punctilious and the introverts and their respective antipodes; the differences here lie between 1:2 to 1:3.

Switching from saving to spending, it is quite clear that income expectations play a certain role in purchasing decisions. An increase in income over the next twelve months was expected by the easy-going, desultory, carefree and young unless they evaded the point by arguing their income would remain the same. A cut-back in income was thought possible by the introverts, the older and the orderly groups. These examples indicate that psychological dispositions do have an influence of their own right in certain areas of economic behavior; after all, it is not money that 'rules the world' but rather people who shape the monetary events according to their own peculiar whims.[20]

But not only age and sex are among those variables which, it is claimed at least, influence human behavior. A number of social constraints and group norms are thought to wield their weight. We wanted to know: which ones?

Neither religion (Catholic-Protestant) nor residence (urban-rural) had any significant impact on our classification. Education did show a slight influence as respondents tended to be less punctilious and less weakly with increasing levels of schooling. This was confirmed by a check against social strata, where vigor and extravertedness increased with higher rungs on the social ladder and, of course, with age. The same trend again appeared with income groups where vigor, and, due to age, punctiliousness tended to register more often in the higher income brackets.

Marked differences, however, occurred within the life cycle,

20 G. Schmölders, *ibid.*, p. 41–53.

where marital status combined with age to produce an effect which justifies the claim that this variable should be considered the most important among the sociological and demographic ones.[21]

Table 1

Marital status of respondents

	single %	married %	widowed %	all groups %
punctilious	5	11	14	10
easy-going	21	5	3	9
total	100	100	100	100
cases	648	1500	229	2377
thrifty	38	56	68	52
extravagant	19	7	5	10
total	100	100	100	100
cases	647	1499	229	2375
conscientious	16	35	36	31
carefree	30	9	7	14
total	100	100	100	100
cases	647	1499	229	2375

Several annotations should be made at this point.

First, it is indeed possible to extract specific personality types from a number of survey questions. The *Q.E.D.* that still remains open now is a display of the explanatory power of such types in the prediction of behavior.

Second, social and demographic influences do not differentiate impressively our dependent variables, i.e. character traits and savings attitudes.

Third, these observations represent two important pointers for us in our search for the 'specifiable conditions' of the monetary system.

We shall consequently continue to maintain that the disposition *towards* money shapes the disposition *of* money. Our next task then is to search actual monetary decisions for differences between the psychological types. As we shall see presently, this job will have to

21 G. Schmölders, *ibid.*, p. 54–56.

215

be shelved for a while, because another consideration enters into our line of thought.

The ways in which attitudinal differences might bear upon monetary decisions had been indicated by J. M. Keynes with his concept of liquidity preference, though his interpretation of the phenomenon as a function of the interest rate and the income, business, precautionary and speculative motives[22] deserves further investigation. While referring monetary behavior into the realm of motives and psychology, these hypothetical categories assume a completely rational decision process and do not explain the causes for changes in monetary behavior. But it is precisely these reasons that we need to know about. We also must realize that in a modern economy account money and its symbols increasingly displace traditional forms of cash. Consequently the Keynesian concept of liquidity preference must be extended to cover bank deposits,[23] but the question, of course, is: what qualitative changes do we encounter in the liquidity preference as the quantity of liquid means to which it refers is increased?

The question of whether people prefer to carry cash rather than check-books in their pockets, or the question of how much money settles at the bottom of a check account over time and remains there unused, and the question of how both these facts vary with age or income and with economic optimism and pessimism are not at all academic. No more academic anyhow than the discussion about the maximum credit capacity of the money market. For if the limit of credit extension indeed is:

$$\triangle K_r = \frac{1}{r + c\,(1-r)}\,\triangle Z,^{24}$$

22 J. M. Keynes, *The General Theory of Employment, Interest and Money*, London 1936, Chs. 13 and 15.
23 V. F. Wagner, *Geschichte der Kredittheorien*, Vienna 1937, p. 460.
24 E. Schneider, *Einführung in die Wirtschaftstheorie*, part III, Tübingen 1967, pp. 47–67.

$\triangle K_r$ = the limit of any additional credit expansion by credit institutions based on their surplus reserves ($\triangle Z$).

$\triangle Z$ = the surplus reserves in the credit institutions comprising cash and accounts with the central bank.

r = the rate of minimum reserves the credit institutions are held to maintain is fixed by the central bank.

c = the amount of central bank money that is transferred to and retained in the non-banking sector at each stage of the credit expansion process.

216

then we do need some information about the coefficient c. It represents the amount of central bank money that is withdrawn from the banking sector during each phase of the credit expansion process. We also want to have some idea about the residuals in check accounts that remain untouched, for they represent the amount of surplus reserves upon which further credit extension by the banks is based. In other words, we are now turning to some specific manifestations of monetary behavior as they appear in the banking sector.

c. *Monetary Transactions Habitualized*

The principal question we raised concerned the extent to which various types of payment techniques enjoyed popularity among users. We expected differences simply on the grounds that patterns of money handling would vary with the degree of familiarity with the various forms of account money. Since check payments and credit cards are nowhere nearly as widely used in Germany as they are in the U.S., the distribution of account types is quite indicative of the payment habits.

We found that some type of pass book or checking account was reported by 66 per cent of all households, which means that still one third of the households in Germany handle money in the form of cash only. But even the two-thirds figure is not quite accurate, because only half of all respondents kept any sizeable amount in their accounts.

Among the savings accounts the savings bank pass was the most popular (40 per cent of all households), followed by the postal savings book (20 per cent),[25] and the commercial bank savings accounts (7 per cent). Savings banks also lead in the area of check accounts which were found in 17 per cent of the households, check accounts in commercial banks ranked second with 10 per cent and postal accounts last with 8 per cent. These figures add up to more than 100 per cent, because households may have several account types.

Of those families who do possess accounts, 20 per cent have a savings book, 45 per cent a check account and 26 per cent own both

25 The German postal system offers a low-interest savings account as well as low-fee check service.

types. It soon became clear that each account type had its own 'profile' and so we tried to find out: Who held how much in what type of an account?

As for the amounts, the picture looked like this:

29 per cent of all households with accounts reported no substantial deposits;

23 per cent had up to DM 500;

33 per cent held more than DM 1.000;

8 per cent had more than DM 5.000; and

2 per cent held more than DM 10.000 in their accounts.

These amounts are distributed quite differently among account types; the postal savings book is left with minimal sums only, check accounts generally contain small to medium sums and the amounts in savings accounts range small to large. Also, bank saving usually registered higher amounts than savings bank passes and check accounts in commercial banks top the postal accounts.

As far as the people who have accounts are concerned, we found that accounts are more frequent among older people than among the young. But within this distribution we made an interesting observation: whereas savings pass books can be found in all age groups, the check account dominates among the 30 to 50-year-olds and the postal check account in the young age group. This we took as an indication for a learning process whereby familiarity with the more mobile account types is inversely related to age. The influence of education would point in the same direction: savings accounts were frequent in households with medium-level education ('*Mittlere Reife*') and the more mobile check account in families with college education ('*Abitur*', university). Since the types of occupation or profession showed similar differentials, we are quite safe in assuming that age, education and professional exposure determine the degree of familiarity with various account types, and familiarity in turn shapes the paying habits.

To demonstrate the profile of the three account types a bit more clearly, we grouped the reasons for saving into three categories: consumptive saving (money to be spent shortly), precautionary saving (reserves for cases of illness, accidents, repairs, etc.), and capital accumulation. The following distribution resulted:

218

Table 2

The account is for:	Postal savings account %	Savings bank account %	Bank account %
consumptive saving	65	45	41
precautionary saving	18	39	41
capital accumulation	16	37	33

Quite clearly consumption motivates deposits in postal accounts. This is quite often, though not always, due to the fact that postal accounts are being used as traveller check substitutes, since even in the most remote part of the country there is always a post office which will service the account. Interestingly enough the differences between savings and commercial banks are not large at all, which would seem to indicate that deposits in postal accounts represent an entirely different, i.e. more liquid type of 'money' and one closer to consumption. To probe deeper into this relationship we offered a list of purposes for saving to our respondents with the following results:

Table 3

The account is for:	Postal savings account %	Bank savings account %	Savings bank account %	Bank check account %	Savings bank check account %
current household expenditure	9	13	9	35	51
consumptive saving	65	41	45	60	63
precautionary saving	18	41	39	41	31
capital accumulation	16	33	37	30	14
Total	108	128	130	166	159
Households having accounts	100	100	100	100	100

Again the consumptive character of the postal accounts is confirmed and it is also apparent that savings bank check accounts are even more mobile than commercial bank accounts.

Precisely to this point, i.e. mobility of account types, we asked the owners of check accounts whether they usually paid by transfer orders (account to account transfer, no cash), by check or in cash.

Table 4

Payment	Postal check account %	Savings bank check account %	Bank check account %
by transfer order only	64	42	36
by transfer and check	19	28	36
by check only	8	14	19
in cash only	9	16	9

Another interesting aspect in this area of account money is the barrier that still exists in Germany against pay-checks instead of wages being paid in cash.

	Households with family members in labor force %
Receive wage in cash	78
	%
and keep money at home	68
and put money temporarily in bank	10
Receive pay-checks	22
	——
	100

Civil servants, about half of the people in administrative jobs and about a fifth of the blue-collar workers receive monthly pay-checks rather than cash. Of those who are being paid in cash a considerable proportion objected to the idea of paychecks, i.e. 35 per cent of the white-collar and 53 per cent of the blue-collar

220

workers. The reasons for this resistance which we subsequently uncovered turned out to be typical ex-post rationalizations and confirmed to us that the key element is simply the degree of familiarity with the 'cashless' forms of payment.

d. *Purchasing Power versus Value of Money*

If attitudes toward money do, as we were able to show, influence monetary behavior, we can safely assume that similar relationships exist between people's opinions about the value of money and their reactions to value changes. As usual our first objective was to identify the possible attitude objects,[26] i.e. we wondered whether the development of prices or the image of the currency would serve as focal points for the attitudes toward the money value and possibly, too, for ensuing reactions to value deterioration.

The DIVO-Institute (Frankfurt) helped to solve this puzzle by showing that there are, in fact, two distinctly different objects of cognition and attitude formation. DIVO asked its respondents each year:

A: 'What would you think: in two years will the Mark still have the same, a higher or a lower value?'

B: 'How do you expect prices to develop in the next twelve months? Would you say that they will in general rise or fall, or what?'

In April 1961, for example, the reactions to those questions were as follows:

The value of the Mark will			Prices will
	%	%	
fall	40	70	rise
rise	7	4	fall
stay the same	38	24	stay the same
do not know	15	2	do not know
	——	——	
	100%	100%	

26 Newcomb, Turner, Converse, *op. cit.*, Ch. 3.

Seventy per cent of the population felt that prices would rise, but only 40 per cent drew from that the logical conclusion that the value of the Mark would consequently have to fall. This means that we are confronted with two separate phenomena, price development and currency image. The opinion about prices is reflected as an attitude of confidence (or distrust) in the continuity of purchasing power and relies for its information on the development of prices, which can be experienced directly. The confidence in the stability of the monetary system, on the other hand, cannot possibly be based on personal experience, but rather represents an unreflected stereotype incorporating different attitudes towards the economic and political development.

In our 1959 survey we had tried to tap the price attitude with the following question:

Suppose someone misplaces DM 20 and finds them again in ten years. Would you think he can buy as much with that money as he can buy today, or more, or less?

We then compared our results to those of DIVO in 1959:

September 1959	June 1959
In ten years 20 Marks will buy	Over the next 12 months prices will
55% less	52% rise
45% just as much, more, no answer	48% stay the same, fall, don't know
100%	100%

The answers are almost identical and both apparently reflect an attitude that is based on considerations of purchasing power and price development, though in this context it was quite significant to note that heads of households have a much keener eye on such developments than the average person.

That the monetary value would fall was expected by:

55% of all respondents	64% of heads of households
61% of all men	64% of all male heads of households
51% of all women	62% of all female heads of households.

Yet another interesting observation was that, contrary to common

222

belief, the actual experience with inflation does not influence the overall monetary scene in Germany to any noticeable degree. This rather surprising result may, however, be explained by the consideration that only people with savings had really been hurt by the inflation. Today only 20 per cent of all households in Germany have savings of more than DM 1.000 and only of those we may expect, if they had been savers before the currency reform in 1948, that the experience has made them cautious and distrustful.

A certain influence on the confidence in the monetary system could be discerned by looking at the psychological disposition. People with a pessimistic tendency generally expected a deterioration of the currency. Extraverted persons were more often sceptical about the development of purchasing power than were the introverts, who in turn reacted much more sensitively to changes in interest rates. The trust in money is also influenced by education and profession; college and business people are more apt to be suspicious about price and currency developments.

We may now return to the original point, from which we deviated a while ago. To recall the problem at hand: our task was to demonstrate that psychological types as extracted from the survey indeed display different forms of monetary behavior and therefore constitute explanatory and predictive tools. At the same time we may tie the results just discussed into the following considerations, since the choice of account type as well as the amounts held there are reflections of the liquidity preference. The precise question then is: how is this liquidity preference shaped?

Our assumption was that, in addition to individual psychological dispositions, monetary decisions are influenced both by expectations about the general economic climate and the stability of the currency as well as by attitudes toward the institutions of the given currency system. As these economic, institutional and psychological factors combine to produce a stream of decisions about amounts to be spent and saved, each economic unit (an individual, a household or a firm) is left with a certain amount of resources, the total sum of which constitutes his objective liquidity. Beyond this, though, units tend to develop a subjective notion about the limit to which they feel they could make additional means available, should the need for them arise (e.g. through credits or sales).[27]

27 G. Schmölders, *Psychologie des Geldes*, p. 64–68.

It is the whole liquidity position that is relevant to spending decisions, and our interest in the supply of money is due to its significance in the whole liquidity-picture. A decision to spend depends not simply on whether the would-be spender has cash or 'money in the bank', although the maximum liquidity is obviously the most favorable springboard. There is the alternative of raising funds whether by selling an asset or borrowing.[28]

The extent to which the conversion of subjective into objective liquidity is both possible and controlled represents the degree of effectiveness of any monetary authority.

First, by bringing about a change in interest rates, the monetary authorities can induce a change in the incentive or purchase of capital goods and so cause a change in actual spending on labour and other means of production of those goods . . . Secondly, the monetary authorities can bring about a change in the liquidity condition of financial institutions and of business firms and people generally, so that those wanting money to spend find it more (or less) difficult to get than it was before.[29]

The subjective notion of one's own financial mobility, naturally, is quite open to influences of optimism or pessimism, and is by this virtue a crucial link between economic decisions of individuals and economic mass phenomena. The concept of subjective liquidity thus represents an important juncture between psychology and economics.

For the individual, the notion of liquidity, subjective or objective, is in the majority of cases condensed into the simple problem of budgeting income and expenditures in response to Question 1. Twice as many people in our survey claimed to be very careful and economical in allocating their money than admitted to being rather casual in handling money matters.

Generosity went with extravagance, light-mindedness and untidyness; meticulous, consistent, thorough and austere people also stuck to careful planning of expenditures. Such differences between character traits became even more pronounced in the answers to

28 *Report of the Committee on the Working of the Monetary System*, London 1959, p. 132.
29 *ibid.*, p. 130.

224

Question 2 about the importance of saving. Only a sixth of all respondents professed to the carefree attitude of regarding thrift as non-essential. The majority, and here most prominently the thorough, the austere and the consistent, but also those who had admitted to be indecisive, easy-going and soft, opted for thrift as an essential quality.

The proverb drew twice as many 'ayes' than 'nays', but also thoughtful, responsible and punctual people joined the slight and untidy in arguing that safeguarding against bad times made little sense nowadays.[30]

To pinpoint the genuine savers still more precisely, the projection test (Question 6) was analyzed in greater detail. Very thrifty ('think twice before spending a penny') were less than 10 per cent of all respondents, mostly those tending towards avarice, austerity and meticulousness. Five times as many men than women took the moderate position ('save within limits') and a substantial proportion refused to see any sense in the idea of saving. The latter answer, which incidentally was only slightly more frequent among men than women, was given predominantly by extravagant, easy-going and carefree characters but also by those who had confessed to be a bit vain, inconsistent and lazy or claimed to be efficient on their job. It would seem that the more the idea of thrift is translated into concrete terms of saving, the smaller will the number of its supporters get. To stress this point, our respondents were confronted with three hypothetical situations:

The first two (Question 3 and 4) have already been reported; the third ran as follows:

> Suppose you watch a woman giving a boy from the neighborhood two sh. because he helped her carry a heavy shopping bag up several flights of stairs. Would you think that that is too much money or not too much?

As could be expected, the penny-pinchers kept the purse strings tight in all three cases, while the extravagant were true to their type with equal consistency. But the more interesting observation are the coalitions which form around the extremes.

Thorough, austere and punctual people would also forego the movie. Loners and shy types would wait two hours for the next bus,

30 G. Schmölders, *op. cit.*, p. 70–71.

225

while the efficient, easy-going, the vain and the social types would call a cab. The majority feels that two sh. is too much for carrying the shopping bag and only the extravagant, erratic, shallow and vain opposed. Combining these single traits to psychological types again, the impression we had gained earlier about preference for or aversion to saving is confirmed. Twice as many of the easy-going than the punctilious type would see the movie despite the price of the balcony seats; the case is similar for the extraverted and the desultory versus the introverts and the orderly. This difference is even more pronounced in the conscientious-carefree dichotomy. Only a third of the conscientious type would see the film and a mere fifth would call the cab, while the carefree reacted in the exactly opposite manner.

Differences of this magnitude were not found in any of the other variables; neither income, nor age, nor sex showed comparable variances. Occasionally income and age even collide as, for example, in the movie-case, where higher income makes it easier to afford the expensive seats but higher age makes it easier to resist. Consequently these factors tend to neutralize each other in part; the differences in the psychological make-up, though, remain.

One might, however, argue that hypothetical situations, precisely formulated as they may be, nevertheless are still another matter than actual, real-life decisions; only in those the influence of demographic variables really comes through. So we asked our respondents about their saving habits, starting with the question whether they had been able to put aside a little money during the last few months. The loophole-answer 'That was impossible' was chosen by about half of those whose income was less than DM 500 per month. From the DM 800 a month bracket upwards this answer was given by 25 per cent only, which would indicate a clear influence of income. However, these differentials increased considerably when the psychological types were tested. Twice as many of the extravagant than of the thrifty type 'were not able' to save any money. Punctual, austere and efficient people also were among the savers, while the shallow, untidy and the inconsistent formed the majority among those who did not save.

Another question dealing with the regularity of savings deposits brought similar results. The efficient, consistent, punctual, self-disciplined and the responsible are overwhelmingly regular savers whereas occasional saving occurs in the other groups.

All in all, neither age nor income could outdo the personal traits and psychological types in predicting saving behavior. A breakdown into income groups and types showed that the conscientious in the lower (DM 300 to DM 500 per month) as well as in the higher (DM 500 and over) income-bracket saved twice as much than the carefree of the same income brackets, i.e. 10–12 per cent against 5–7 per cent of their respective incomes. Savings of DM 2000 and more occur twice as often among the conscientious than among the carefree; almost half of the latter possess no savings at all.[31]

These and other results of the study indicate quite forcefully that the knowledge of 'objective' income data is by no means sufficient to evaluate the savings potential; only after ascertaining specific attitudes and expectations of individuals any projection and forecast becomes feasible.

Feasibility given, the achievement of accuracy in predicting is yet another and quite complicated problem. When it comes to forecasting economic behavior, the complex interaction patterns of socio-economic variables emerge as the main obstacle. We therefore decided to subject data on saving behavior to a tree-analysis, which has been developed as one methodological tool for ranking predictive factors according to their ability to reduce the variance in the dependent variable. Thus interdependencies among factors influencing economic behavior can be traced.[32]

Our Cologne data not being in a processible form we fell back on SCF data[33] and ran a tree-analysis on amounts saved as the dependent variable. The resulting tree has been trimmed slightly so as to improve readability; only those branches containing attitudinal variables have been retained. Consequently, interpretation has to be rather conservative and it should also be kept in mind that the data used reflect a particular point in time. Any generalization for the United States would require more data points and a generalization beyond the U.S. economy extensive international comparisons.

31 G. Schmölders, op. cit., p. 70–76.
32 For a short description of tree-analysis see page 242.
33 The data deck contained multiple-punched columns, the conversion of which into machine-readable form proved too thorny a problem to be achieved in time. The data used stem from the 1965 Survey of Consumer Finances, Project 741. The particular tree-program used is an adaptation of ISR'S Automatic Interaction Detector. For a description see: B. Biervert, M. Dierkes, A. Walzel; Automatischer Split zur optimalen Kombination erklärender Faktoren, Köln 1968.

GÜNTER SCHMÖLDERS

Factors Influencing Saving Behavior
('Tree-Analysis')

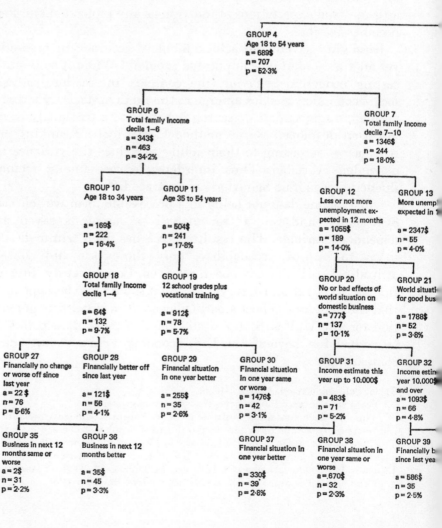

GROUP 4
Age 18 to 54 years
a = 689$
n = 707
p = 52·3%

GROUP 6
Total family income
decile 1—6
a = 343$
n = 463
p = 34·2%

GROUP 7
Total family income
decile 7—10
a = 1346$
n = 244
p = 18·0%

GROUP 10
Age 18 to 34 years

a = 169$
n = 222
p = 16·4%

GROUP 11
Age 35 to 54 years

a = 504$
n = 241
p = 17·8%

GROUP 12
Less or not more
unemployment ex-
pected in 12 months
a = 1055$
n = 189
p = 14·0%

GROUP 13
More unemp
expected in 1

a = 2347$
n = 55
p = 4·0%

GROUP 18
Total family income
decile 1—4

a = 64$
n = 132
p = 9·7%

GROUP 19
12 school grades plus
vocational training

a = 912$
n = 78
p = 5·7%

GROUP 20
No or bad effects of
world situation on
domestic business
a = 777$
n = 137
p = 10·1%

GROUP 21
World situati
for good bus

a = 1788$
n = 52
p = 3·8%

GROUP 27
Financially no change
or worse off since
last year
a = 22 $
n = 76
p = 5·6%

GROUP 28
Financially better off
since last year

a = 121$
n = 56
p = 4·1%

GROUP 29
Financial situation
in one year better

a = 255$
n = 35
p = 2·6%

GROUP 30
Financial situation
in one year same
or worse
a = 1476$
n = 42
p = 3·1%

GROUP 31
Income estimate this
year up to 10.000$

a = 483$
n = 71
p = 5·2%

GROUP 32
Income estin
year 10.000$
and over
a = 1093$
n = 66
p = 4·8%

GROUP 35
Business in next 12
months same or
worse
a = 2$
n = 31
p = 2·2%

GROUP 36
Business in next 12
months better

a = 35$
n = 45
p = 3·3%

GROUP 37
Financial situation in
one year better

a = 330$
n = 39
p = 2·8%

GROUP 38
Financial situation in
one year same or
worse
a = 670$
n = 32
p = 2·3%

GROUP 39
Financially b
since last yea

a = 586$
n = 35
p = 2·5%

228

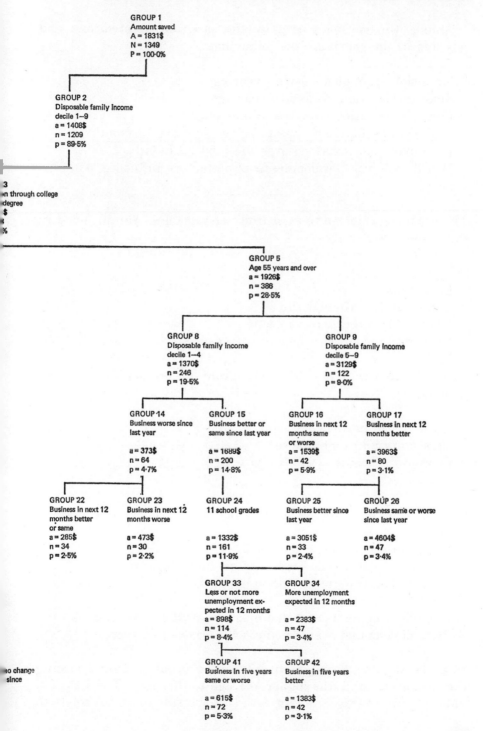

GROUP 1
Amount saved
A = 1831$
N = 1349
P = 100·0%

GROUP 2
Disposable family income
decile 1—9
a = 1408$
n = 1209
p = 89·5%

3
n through college
degree
$

%

GROUP 5
Age 55 years and over
a = 1926$
n = 386
p = 28·5%

GROUP 8
Disposable family income
decile 1—4
a = 1370$
n = 246
p = 19·5%

GROUP 9
Disposable family income
decile 5—9
a = 3129$
n = 122
p = 9·0%

GROUP 14
Business worse since
last year

a = 373$
n = 64
p = 4·7%

GROUP 15
Business better or
same since last year

a = 1689$
n = 200
p = 14·8%

GROUP 16
Business in next 12
months same
or worse
a = 1539$
n = 42
p = 5·9%

GROUP 17
Business in next 12
months better

a = 3963$
n = 80
p = 3·1%

GROUP 22
Business in next 12
months better
or same
a = 285$
n = 34
p = 2·5%

GROUP 23
Business in next 12
months worse

a = 473$
n = 30
p = 2·2%

GROUP 24
11 school grades

a = 1332$
n = 161
p = 11·9%

GROUP 25
Business better since
last year

a = 3051$
n = 33
p = 2·4%

GROUP 26
Business same or worse
since last year

a = 4604$
n = 47
p = 3·4%

GROUP 33
Less or not more
unemployment ex-
pected in 12 months
a = 898$
n = 114
p = 8·4%

GROUP 34
More unemployment
expected in 12 months

a = 2383$
n = 47
p = 3·4%

o change
since

GROUP 41
Business in five years
same or worse

a = 615$
n = 72
p = 5·3%

GROUP 42
Business in five years
better

a = 1383$
n = 42
p = 3·1%

229

Among the variables used by the program as predictors and reported in the graph are the following:

Financial situation vis-à-vis a year ago
Business situation vis-à-vis a year ago
Financial situation expected in one year
Business development expected over the next 12 months
Unemployment expected over the next 12 months
World political developments expected to influence domestic business

These will be referred to as attitudinal variables. Also included in the graph are:

Age
Education
Total family income decile
Disposable family income decile
Estimated income for the current year

Predictors that were used by the program but are not reported here include:

Good or bad news heard about business
Total family income bracket
Change in income *vis-à-vis* a year ago
Life cycle

On the other hand those variables not used at all by the program were:
Rising prices to the good or bad
Business situation expected as of one year from now
Good or bad time to buy household goods
Sex
Price developments expected over the next twelve months
Price developments expected over the next five years

In its arrangement the graph follows the usual procedure placing the split group with the higher average to the right. The letter 'a' indicates the average amount saved in the subgroup, 'n' refers to

230

the number of cases in that group, and 'p' gives the percentage of the total sample that fell into the subgroup.

Upon first glance three interesting features emerge from the display. First, the education-income-age syndrome does indeed exert its influence as could be expected. Second, the attitudinal variables, whenever they enter, quite consistently split their parent group into people with optimistic attitudes and expectations versus those with indifferent or pessimistic points of view. Only in some of the splits optimists and neutralists are set off against pessimists. The point to be made here is that attitudinal variables apparently do exert a consistent influence upon saving behavior so they could indeed contribute as predictors to accurate forecasting. The third feature is that the splits occurring in the attitudinal variables do not always tend into the same direction when the group averages are taken into account. Offhand one would expect the people tending towards optimism to be, on the average, better savers, as is the case in the groups (14/15); (16/17); (20/21); (27/28); (35/36); and (41/42). In several of the other groups, however, people with indifferent and pessimistic views appear as saving more.

Whether this is due to statistical reasons, i.e. the end groups having rather small numbers of cases, or whether it does reflect a systematic influence caused by the combination of different variables as the splitting progresses through the tree, we could not determine at this point. Though in some of these cases an explanation could be construed, the evidence is too scarce to volunteer any *ad hoc* hypothesis about the reasons for the directional differences.

The strong impression, however, remains that the knowledge about interaction patterns and the stability of their occurrence could well improve our ability to forecast saving behavior, and this could easily be extended into other areas of economic behavior. And, secondly, it seems that the particular technique of tree-analysis is quite well suited to give better insights into the form of such interdependencies.

e. *'Borrowing' versus 'Schuldenmachen'*

In our attempt to get, amongst others, at the temporal sequence of money dispositions our interest was not only in the save-first-buy-later scheme but also in the range of money borrowing. Especially we wondered whether it would be possible to get at the roots of the rather widespread resistance against borrowing money.

Even though it might be considered a task for a linguist to investigate into the origins of certain 'loaded terms' used in economic life, the economist, if interested in behavior and perceptive, may certainly take a first clue about specific attitudes from language, folk lore or literature.[34] In this context we cannot bypass the fact that 'Schuldenmachen' is by no means as neutral as the English term 'to take out a loan' or 'contracting a debt'. 'Schuld' is both 'debt' and 'guilt', and this moralistic undertone is not lost in the economic context of 'Schuldenmachen'.

It therefore came as no surprise that in a situation of monetary illiquidity no less than 80 per cent of our respondents preferred to 'cut down expenditure' to 'borrowing money from a friend'. Particularly the introverts and the punctilious virtually shied away from the idea, whereas a third of the extraverted and the easy-going had no objection to borrowing the money. The case was similar for the conscientious-carefree pair: ten times as many of the very conscientious type objected to the idea of a loan than accepted it, while 'to borrow or not to borrow' split the carefree-group in two halves.

This strong aversion to the idea of 'Schuldenmachen' apparently is carried over undiminished into practical life. Instalment purchases, in Germany much less widespread than in the United States, were reported by no more than 20 per cent of all households. Again, the very conscientious resisted the most whereas the carefree had contracted considerably more instalment debts than the conscientious.

In this case, however, demographic variables intervened to a more noticeable degree besides the psychological factors. While in the lower income brackets, i.e. among the younger people, the readiness to buy on instalment plans correlated significantly and in the expected fashion with the psychological types, the exact opposite was true for the income groups of DM 500 a month and more. Three times as many of the conscientious than of the carefree type dodged the prevailing taboo against instalments; a result

34 G. Schmölders, op. cit., p. 113; also K. Boulding, The Meaning . . ., op. cit., p. 58–60, especially p. 59: 'Similarly the wise social scientist will not neglect the rich insights which are derived from the poets, and will use them in the formulation of theoretical models.'

232

which may well be due to the increasing tendency in the urban middle class to follow the American lead and accept instalment buying as a legitimate form of quasi-saving which allows to overcome existing divergencies between rising consumption standards and present income.

With all due caution, if for purposes of record only, the results of a recent *Survey of Consumer Finances* about instalment buying and attitudes towards it may be quoted here. In 1965,

> the ratio of debt payments to income . . . was highest among those with $3000 to $5000 income . . . Moreover, the overwhelming proportion of high debtors in this income group were young (under 35 years of age) and in a period of their life cycle when income rises . . . people with a rising income trend borrow more often than people with stable or declining income . . . among those who early in 1965 said they were making more money than a year ago, 60 per cent had instalment debts (against 38 per cent for those with no change and 45 per cent for those with declining incomes, G.S.), as against 49 per cent among all families. Among those who expected income increases, the incidence of debt was 63 per cent (against 42 per cent for those who expected no change and 32 per cent for those who expected a decline, G.S.).[35]

Over and beyond all the differences between the two respective countries the interesting fact remains that young people (the carefree) are in the forefront of instalment buyers and that, partly because of age differential, income expectations worked in the same direction in Germany and in the United States.

The same is true for attitudes toward instalments because 80 per cent of the 60 years and over group would rather cut down their purchasing than borrow money and 93 per cent reported no current instalment debt. The corresponding figures for the 16–29 years olds are 59 per cent and 40 per cent.

In the Unites States 'negative opinions about instalment buying were most frequent among older people and among those having no debt. The users of instalment credit were overwhelmingly in favor of what they were doing . . . The primary explanation for

35 G. Katona *et al.*, *1965 SCF*, Ann Arbor 1966, p. 29–32.

233

satisfaction with instalment buying continued to be that it is the "right thing" to pay for large items while using them.'[36]

These results may well be an indication that attitudes toward 'Schuldenmachen' are presently undergoing a change in Germany and may increasingly resemble those in the United States. Even though these figures by themselves may be considered insufficient to speak of a trend, we cannot overlook the existence of similar indications of learning processes in regard to paying habits.

III. Consequences for Monetary Theory and Policy

It is obvious and inevitable that there will be far-reaching consequences for monetary theory developing from empirical research. In part, these have already been implied above inasmuch as the theoretical background for various parts of our survey was mentioned. Specific consequences, however, arise in three respects:

(a) A revision and gradual re-writing of monetary theory can hardly be avoided.

(b) Intensified research into attitudes and motives guiding monetary behavior is called for.

(c) Appropriate research and analysis techniques must be developed.

Since the listing above is obviously reversed with respect to what comes first, let us give some consideration to the last two points: where to do research, and how to do research. It will be extremely difficult always to distinguish clearly between these two aspects, because quite naturally each subject of research at hand will usually require its specific research technique. The optimum, therefore, that we have to look for is the combination of a maximum number of meaningful hypotheses with a minimum number of analytical tools. As far as the first part of this combination is concerned we may be sure that considerable effort will have to be spent on further exploration of the 'specifiable condition'. While attitudinal influences – as we found – constitute the main influence, the part of demographic factors as limiting conditions of behavior

36 G. Katona et al., op. cit., p. 31; see also Table 2–10, p. 44.

should not be overlooked. As long as, for example, neither education nor professional experience have exposed a person to the various forms of bank accounts he cannot be expected to utilize such facilities. But this statement is not reversible; knowledge does not automatically lead people to avail themselves of accounts.

It is vital for monetary theory to know exactly in what way and to what extent those limiting conditions constrain monetary behavior. If certain age-income combinations correlate highly with varying rates of saving, it is pointless to assume a constant savings rate for the entire population. Nor can the law of large numbers be adduced as an excuse here, because none of these variables need to be distributed normally. Monetary theory therefore must integrate both the attitudinal and demographic determinants of monetary decisions into a scheme of behavior patterns. And it must at the same time contain information about the range of decisions that are primarily affected by attitudes, establishing those areas in which demographic circumstances intervene and modify the relevant behavior.

Another group of the 'specifiable conditions' is best described as institutional constraints. These comprise construction, constitution, as well as incentives and sanctions of the monetary sector. Apparently no one seems to have noticed that a haughty bank palace elicits a different kind of behaviour from a corner savings bank. Nor do theoretical treatises indicate the fact that interest rates simply are not perceived by bank customers until they have a certain amount (in our case DM 2.000) in their account. A similar result may be quoted from the 1966 *Survey of Consumer Finance*, where the knowledge about rising interest rates increased with rising income (see Table 5).

As all good theory leads to the formulation of executable policy statements, the consequences of our approach for monetary policy need to be mentioned in this context also. Obviously with the change in the theoretical framework that we have advocated here a change in monetary policy is also required. As one example for the shift in emphasis that should come about, the point of residual amounts in check accounts may be mentioned here in connection with pay-checks. If it is desirable as a policy aim to increase the efficiency of the monetary sector and/or to enlarge its credit issuing capacity, the encouragement of pay-checks instead of cash payments would be the obvious answer. Empirical research can contribute a

235

Table 5

People's Information about Changes in Interest Rates by Income (Percentage distribution)

Have heard of higher interest rates	Family income Less than $3,000	$3,000–$4,999	$5,000–$7,499	$7,500–$9,999	$10,000–or more	All families
On mortgages	4	6	7	11	14	8
On other consumer borrowing	10	17	24	26	31	22
On savings accounts	18	28	26	27	30	26
On bonds	2	2	2	2	2	2
On business borrowing	3	2	(†)	2	3	2
Uncertain on what	8	10	14	17	17	14
Have not heard of higher interest rates	63	50	44	38	28	44
Total	(a)	(a)	(a)	(a)	(a)	(a)
Number of cases	207	207	324	249	422	1,434

(†) Less than 0·5 per cent.
(a) Adds to more than 100 because respondents were allowed two mentions.

The question was: 'Do you happen to know whether there have been any *changes* during the last few months in the interest rate paid on savings, or in the interest paid by individuals or businesses when they borrow money? What kinds of changes?'[37]

37 G. Katona *et. al.*, *Survey of Consumer Finances*, Ann Arbor 1967, p. 197, table 9–3.

precise statement about the factors that will determine success or failure of the measure:

> to the degree that blue-collar workers can be induced to hold money in the form of check books rather than cash, and
> to the extent that they can be induced to participate in the cash-less money traffic, the policy aim will be reached.[38]

Since we know that the readiness for both of these forms of behavior depends on the exposure to check payments and on the familiarity with banking procedures, a corresponding educational campaign could guarantee success. We are, in other words, utilizing our knowledge about the learning process involved in this type of behavior; a knowledge gained by observing the performance of money in its natural environment. To put it in a nutshell: monetary theory must be asked to describe monetary behavior as it is, not as it should or could be under ideal circumstances.

There is, however, another group of consequences that follow from our study in particular and from empirical research in this area in general. Such research enables the policymakers to investigate into the reasons for changes in monetary behavior, i.e. into the motives that guide the actions. As we have seen, survey research not only reveals in detail how people act and who follows particular behavior patterns, but also permits to get at the causes of such behavior.

We cannot accept the philosophy that:

> even if consumer surveys are able to provide an accurate measure of the current state of consumer anticipations, it does not necessarily follow that they will also be able to explain the way in which anticipations are formed. But for making predictions it is unnecessary to decide whether anticipatory variables are in some sense basic determinants of consumer behavior, or whether they are themselves wholly predictable from purely objective (i.e. historical) factors like income levels, or past income change, and so on.[39]

38 G. Schmölders, 'Umgang mit Geld als Forschungsaufgabe', in H. E. Büschgen (ed.), *Geld, Kapital und Kredit*, Stuttgart 1968, p. 36–37.
39 F. T. Juster, *Anticipations and Purchases: An Analysis of Consumer Behavior*. Princeton 1964, p. 3.

237

The objections that we would raise are these:

(a) If surveys are capable of detecting anticipatory variables, i.e. expectations and intentions, that can be shown to correlate with subsequent behavior, there is basically no reason to believe that factors explaining the formation of such variables cannot be found at the same time and by the same instrument. The question, however, is: should we look for them?

(b) Indeed, we should. It seems pointless to disregard the causes that lead to the formation of anticipatory variables on the grounds that the latter suffice to predict subsequent behavior. We know in fact too little about this area of human behavior to be sure that any expectations and intentions we are using will always reliably foreshadow an imminent change in behavior. In order to test, in other words, the dependence of our anticipatory indicators we must extend our research into the area of attitude formation. It would be of little advantage if prediction could only indicate small deviations from a general and stable trend, but would fail completely in signalling an impending break in the development. This is especially important in economic behavior where we are up against various forms of threshold phenomena; so far, we do not have sufficient information about their functioning. Where should we look, though? Can we indeed assume that anticipatory variables are themselves predictable from 'purely objective factors, like income levels or past rates of income change'?

(c) No. It would seem much more consistent with what we know about attitude formation to assume that 'subjective' factors have their share in shaping anticipatory variables. Not income change *per se*, but income changes in combination with certain psychological make-ups will result in optimistic or pessimistic expectations and/or an increase or cut-back in purchasing intentions. It would seem more likely that here, too, attitudes other than, but related to, those under study influence the formation of anticipations.

This field, however, probably represents, up to now, the largest number of unknowns in monetary theory, even though certain features have emerged. One of these revolves around the essential role of confidence in the monetary system, in monetary symbols, and in the stability of money value. It is often referred to simply as the attitude towards money, though this name is merely a proxy for a bundle of interdependent attitudes with different but closely related attitude objects. This subject is by no means new, the 'integrating quality of faith, without which hardly a coin, regardless of its precise standard weight and alloy, can perform its function'[40] has been debated for quite a while.

It is about time to make some precise statements about it, and preferably more constructive ones than Irving Fisher's irate tirades against the 'money illusion'.[41]

Again, we cannot expect to find answers easily, but a few indications we have. Part of this belief, that we circumscribe as confidence in the monetary system, certainly affects the reputation of a currency. We have seen examples of this in the reactions to the DIVO-question (see page 221). Surely this attitude also includes a goodly portion of confidence and trust in the given political system into which the monetary system is intricately woven.

People are indeed willing to accept some rise in prices without transforming this expectation into an immediate repudiation of the currency. This, of course, is money illusion *par excellence*; an empirical document confirming Mr. Fisher's hypothesis about the existence of such a phenomenon. And, to continue hypothesizing, let me suggest that money illusion acts as a vital safety mechanism for any monetary system and its currency. What might happen, we may ask, if everybody were to repudiate the current currency to the degree at which he expected prices to rise? In our study, for example, more than half of our respondents expected an increase in the price level; the SCF-studies have rarely found less than 70 per cent of their interviewees expecting continued price rises in recent years.[42] Further research might well discover that the reputation of a currency furnishes, at least temporarily, a buffer against the impact that rising prices would otherwise have on monetary behavior. This would mean, though, that the money illusion is not at all 'god-given ignorance' and 'primitive superstition' but an indispensable component of our monetary system.

40 G. Simmel, *Philosophie des Geldes*, Munich 1930, p. 164f.
41 I. Fisher, *The Money Illusion*, New York 1928.
42 G. Katona *et al.*, *op. cit.*, p. 248.

This confidence in the monetary system could easily become a rather important variable, permitting us to explain wide areas of monetary behavior, especially such perplexing phenomena as the rapid increase in savings deposits in a period of rather stiff price rises.[43]

We know further that the money illusion cannot be stretched indefinitely. At a certain point, the buffer of trust in the political and monetary system ceases to be effective; the repudiation of the established monetary symbol begins and other forms of money (cigarettes, carpets, jewels, paintings, etc.) appear. What we do not know is when and how this threshold is reached. This question was never put before us more clearly and urgently than during the Great German Inflation in which the principle 'A Mark is a Mark' was upheld despite fast rising prices until the very turbulent, final phase of depreciation in 1923.[44] It was precisely this principle that caused Mr. Fisher's ill-tempered remark about 'a brain lodged behind the ear in which as a deeply-rooted ingredient of the mental equipment the near ineradicable money illusion is anchored'.[45] But have not the rather questionable maneuvers on international money markets in recent years shown quite convincingly what happens to a currency if the 'integrating quality of faith' is absent?

There is in fact hardly an area of monetary behavior where the existence of faith is more essential and obvious than in international money transactions. No matter for what reasons, aesthetic, religious, or psychological, gold became the prime money metal, the 'gold illusion' has been and still is very much alive. Even though domestic money traffic has been separated from gold in almost all countries, and has been thriving ever since, international money markets are still based on it. No exercise in rationalization, clever as it may be, can disguise the fact that the 'gilded edge' of international finance is not only anachronistic, but also purely irrational. The illusion is so strong that in recent years the demand for a 'return to gold' was voiced, and not from French quarters alone. The world monetary system and world trade were pushed to the brink of collapse in pursuit of this demand. It took domestic upheavals of revolutionary measure finally to puncture the gold illusion.

43 - - -, 'Das Ausmaß der Geldentwertung seit 1950 und die weitere Entwicklung des Geldwertes', *Monatsberichte der Deutschen Bundesbank*, March 1968, p. 13.
44 See G. Schmölders, *Geldpolitik, loc. cit.*, p. 71.
45 I. Fisher, *Feste Währungen*, Heidelberg 1948, p. 24.

It is certainly a task of international monetary theory to dispel the myth of gold quickly and radically. But the necessary condition for this task is the acceptance of the fact that monetary behavior, domestic or international, is based on beliefs, on attitudes and on motives. This condition is yet to be realized. Part of the problem in achieving this is the fact that research techniques are clearly still in an experimental stage. Great progress has undoubtedly been made by the works of G. Katona, Eva Mueller, J. Morgan, J. Tobin, Th. Juster, A. Okun and others. Yet the reproach that the computer is nothing but a giant-size desk calculator for social scientists is certainly not wholly unjustified. Many statistical concepts used today in survey analysis are hold-overs from the days when small group behavior and small samples were the order of the day. Survey research operates in totally different dimensions as far as volume of data is concerned. First, the number of interviews lies between 2,000 and 3,000 per survey. Second, the amount of individual characteristics per interviewee is usually extensive. Third, a frequency of semi-annual to quarterly surveys is highly desirable. This is necessary in order to avoid the interpretation of cross-sectional data as a time-series study, as, *faute de mieux*, we have to do more often at present than we would like to. Besides, while cross-sectional data give us 'an almost complete spectrum of possible differences in household circumstances as well as potentially unlimited numbers of observations',[46] they indicate nothing about changes over time. For a demonstration of the efficiency of time series based on survey data we recall Eva Mueller's articles. It would follow from this that we have to strive for a combination of time series and cross section data, and that means semi-annual to quarterly surveys.

The complexity of analysis due to the mere size of the data is further increased in Europe by considerations about the comparability and compatibility of various national survey series, for example within the Common Market or within EFTA.

The need for new analysis techniques is obvious and we may hope that it will force methodological problems into the focus of attention within the social sciences. The pattern to follow would seem to be this:

The detection of interaction terms among both demographic and psychological variables through multi-variate analysis is a first item

46 See F. T. Juster, *op. cit.*, p. 3.

on the list. Though already rather complex, this is by no means insurmountable nor is it more than a beginning. A second phase, then, is the interface of demographic and psychological variables plus their respective and mutual interaction in our attempt to explain and predict behavior. This could well strain the capacity of our current statistical concepts to the limit of their applicability, which is set by their underlying mathematical assumptions. At the end of the process there will consequently have to be a number of demographic/psychological 'types' or 'groups' which adequately represent a given population at a given time.

The third stage then is simulation. The resulting types will have to be tested, on the basis of the information we have gained about them with respect to their past behavior for their reactions *vis-à-vis* hypothetical future events. This phase, of course, already represents the transition from pure economic behavior research to practical policy making, reducing to an extent heretofore unknown the ambiguity and uncertainty about the outcome and side effects of policy measures; an ambiguity which up to now still allows room for much emotional debate unduly delaying any necessary steps to be taken. Fortunately, some successful steps have already been taken in this direction. A notable example is the Automatic Interaction Detector, developed by J. Morgan and J. Sonquist of the ISR, which utilizes the capacity of electronic data processing to make decisions according to given criteria.[47] Their method is to reduce stepwise the total variance of a dependent variable by such an independent predictor as can do this maximally at any given step. Additivity is relaxed by permitting any one predictor to perform more than once. The result is a consecutive splitting of the original parent group into sub-groups each of which may again be split until either one of two criteria is reached, namely either a lower limit of cases per split group or a lower bound for the test value F which puts the quotient of explained/unexplained sum of squares within the area of statistical chance difference. The graphic presentation of the Automatic Interaction Detector resembles a tree with a trunk and branches; accordingly, the method is often referred to as tree-analysis.

The final aim, at least for the time being, is certainly simulation. Already there are computer facilities available that allow processing

---

47 J. Sonquist and J. N. Morgan, *The Detection of Interaction Effects*, Ann Arbor 1964.

simulation;[48] their basic concept would have to be adapted to social simulation problems, i.e. to be programmed to handle a vast amount of interdependent decision criteria. Though this task seems herculean, it is not at all impossible; monetary policy, thereby, could be put on much firmer ground than it rests on today.

48 *General Purpose Systems Simulator III*, White Plains, N.Y. 1965.

Hayek On Growth: A Reconsideration of his Early Theoretical Work
Erich Streissler

I

In reading present-day textbooks or monographs, one gets the feeling that the monetary theory of the trade cycle or the so called Austrian theory of the crisis has justly been relegated to the limbo of forgotten causes; that F. A. v. Hayek's writings stretching over the whole thirties and into the early forties only led into a gigantic intellectual blind alley; and that in the struggle for the survival of the fittest in economic doctrines Keynesian macro-economic thought has totally eliminated and replaced the reptilian monsters sprung from the pen of the jubilar here to be honoured. Hayek's defeat appears to have been so complete that even among his friends he is mainly honoured as the author of the *Road to Serfdom* and *The Constitution of Liberty* and little mention is made of his earlier work.

I believe, however, that this view is both unjust and wrong. I shall therefore try to reconsider our jubilar's essays and books on the trade cycle and on capital theory. I thus intend to honour the young Hayek, the teacher of economic theory of the inter-war years.

It can easily be shown that Hayek's ideas on the above-mentioned subjects just now are cropping up again. Sir John Hicks has only lately published his 'Hayek Story'[1] (the discussion of which with Hayek has, in fact, given me the idea for this paper). Paul Samuelson, without mentioning Hayek at all, has recently revived Hayek's central idea that – technical progress and changes in consumer tastes apart – variations in the rate of return on capital are

1 Sir John Hicks, 'The Hayek Story' in: the same, *Critical Essays in Monetary Theory*, Oxford 1967, p. 202–215.

245

the *sole* cause of changes in technique.[2] Former pupils of Hayek's have shown that they have not completely forgotten the teachings of the master; though, in the years which have passed, these ideas have – to the regret and now to the acute discomfort of many – undergone in their mind a not inconsiderable mutation: what, e.g. is N. Kaldor's Selective Employment Tax other than warped or misplaced Hayekianism?

Above all, the three dominant strains of growth theory – originating respectively from John von Neumann, from Joan Robinson and from Robert Solow – all show a marked resemblance to Hayek's thought. It was under the impact of Hayek that Austrian economic theory, which was just then teetering on the brink of dynamic analysis (without, however, successfully reaching it) turned to the rate of interest as *the* strategic variable; and it is just this variable which is the central key to the above-named growth theories.

This close link is neither imaginary nor must it surprise us. It has to be remembered that John von Neumann developed his now famous model in Vienna very shortly after Hayek had brought out the first versions of his ideas; that he developed his model among Austrian economists and in close contact with some of them in the seminar of the son of Carl Menger, the founder of the Austrian school, a mathematician, well versed in Austrian economics[3] via the writings of his father, in the republication of whose works he had been instrumental. In fact the link between some of Hayek's and some of von Neumann's thoughts are so close that we shall find occasion in this paper to interpret Hayek's ideas in terms of the von Neumann model. Joan Robinson, too, is influenced to a not inconsiderable extent by Hayek's ideas. Here the influence has come, as she herself states,[4] more indirectly via discussions with Hayek's pupil, Nicholas Kaldor. Between Hayek and Solow finally (or rather his pupil Edmund S. Phelps) there is, to my knowledge, no direct doctrinal link. They arrived independently at stressing the same

2 P. A. Samuelson, 'A New Theorem on Nonsubstitution', in: *Money, Growth and Methodology and other Essays in Economics (in Honour of Johan Åkerman)*, Lund 1961, p. 407 ff., esp. p. 419 f.
3 J. V. Neumann, 'A Model of General Economic Growth', Review of Economic Studies, 13 (1945), p. 1 ff., is the English version – as the author points out in footnote 1 – of an essay published in the volume K. Menger, *Ergebnisse eines Mathematischen Seminars*, Vienna 1938.
4 See p. VII of Joan Robinson, *The Accumulation of Capital*, London 1956.

variables – but by the same road: the introduction of production functions (of different appearances, it is true) into models of economic growth.

In the title of my paper and in my last remarks, I have already sketched the approach which will here be followed: Hayek's monetary theory of the trade cycle has not only and not even mainly to do with the trade cycle proper – be it the Great Depression of the thirties or even our present mild and short growth cycles; it has also relatively little to do with money; it must rather be interpreted as a theory of growth.[5] This is not at all an absurd claim. In the twenties, when Hayek's ideas arose, growth theory lay in the air. It must be remembered that Gustav Cassel had explicitly stated the 'Domar' model and introduced his concept of the 'gleichmässig fortschreitende Wirtschaft' (smoothly-progressing economy) in 1918 in his Theoretische Sozialökonomie,[6] one of the then major German textbooks which everybody had read at Vienna; and that Sir Dennis Robertson has claimed[7] to have been a precursor of Domar in his Banking Policy and the Price Level,[8] a book which Hayek knew intimately. The twenties were groping towards growth theory, calling it 'dynamic theory', the title which even in the early fifties was still retained by Baumol.[9] But just because of this name it was a mistake to think that as both the trade cycle and economic growth were in a sense dynamic phenomena, that, as both described processes over time, they were the same.

Hayek's analysis of the 'trade cycle' was the description of a quasi-equilibrium process with a sudden break, a point of

5 In this respect, I follow closely Sir John Hicks, 'The Hayek Story', loc. cit., p. 210 f.: 'The Hayek theory is not a theory of the credit cycle, the Konjunktur, which need not work in the way he describes, nor is it, in fact, at all likely to do so. It is an analysis – a very interesting analysis – of the adjustment of an economy to changes in the rate of genuine saving. In that direction it does make a real contribution. But it is a contribution which, when it was made, was out of due time. It does not belong to the theory of fluctuations, which was the centre of economists' attention in 1930; it is a fore-runner of the growth theory of more recent years. In that application we can still make something out of it'.
6 C. Gassel, Theoretische Sozialökonomie, Leipzig 1918, 5th ed. 1932, p. 28 ff. brings the 'Gleichmässig fortschreitende Wirtschaft'; p. 54 ff., in § 8 brings the 'Domar' model.
7 Dennis Robertson, 'Thoughts on Meeting some Important Persons', Quarterly Journal of Economics, 68 (1954), p. 181 ff.
8 Dennis Robertson, Banking Policy and the Price Level – An Essay in the Theory of the Trade Cycle, London 1926.
9 W. J. Baumol, Economic Dynamics – An Introduction, New York 1951.

247

discontinuity; and it was the description of the cycle in the view of prosperity. It was thus by its very nature the description of a relatively long-term and of a relatively tame phenomenon; and it was the recipe of how to get into a mess more than one for getting out of it. This is quite understandable when one remembers the timing of its conception: it was first stated explicitly in 1928, i.e. *before* the great crash of late 1929; and even at that date it looked back towards the late nineteenth and early twentieth century, the time before the First World War – understandably so, for the twenties were a time of economic chaos in central Europe, which the economist could not take as representative. It was Hayek's tragic mistake that he thought his theory applicable to the much more violent disequilibrium of the thirties and as an indication of how to get out of depression. No wonder that Keynes won the day with his very short-term analysis and his focus on depression economics, both born out of considerable hindsight. In justice, it should be stated that for the purpose of policy for the thirties *both* Hayek and Keynes were useless: Hayek because he formed his thoughts too early and Keynes because he wrote – on the whole – too late. Nevertheless Keynes gained an intellectual victory among economists of a completeness rare in our discipline; a victory which was, in fact, as Sir John Hicks has pointed out,[10] partly due to luck and thus partly undeserved.

Keynesian doctrine will long be relied upon, whenever a depression threatens and, I think, rightly so; though, as I shall briefly argue, it can be supplemented to its own advantage by Hayekian prescriptions. But it is quite unjustified to see in Keynes the best source of growth theory, too. It is a curious repetition of the history of economic doctrines that the first decade after the Second World War made essentially the same mistake as the twenties: While the twenties thought trade-cycle theory had to be growth theory slightly touched up, the decade of 1945–55 thought growth theory had to be Keynesian trade-cycle theory slightly remodelled. The next decade, it is true, shed many of the Keynesian shackles. But to

10 John Hicks 'Methods of Dynamic Analysis' in: 25 *Economic Essays in Honour of Erik Lindahl*, Stockholm 1956, p. 139 ff., points out on p. 150: 'The Keynes theory was not only the child of genius, it was also the heir of luck. The world of the thirties, which was Keynesian for one reason – because the working of the price-mechanism was largely suspended by Depression – was succeeded by the world of the forties which was Keynesian for quite another reason – because the price-mechanism was superseded by controls'.

my mind there are still far too many Keynesian relicts left in the present theory of growth.[11]

The purpose of this article is, therefore, not only to point out, for many concepts of growth theory: Hayek was here before. This would be a well-deserved, but relatively arid tribute to our jubilar. As there is mainly a family resemblance between Hayek's thought and present growth theory, I shall much rather try to ask which of Hayek's ideas can be fruitfully reintroduced into present growth theory and developed further there. For Hayek had a rather different growth theory from the present: it was a strategically disaggregated growth theory and it was – up to a point – disequilibrium growth theory. Hayek presented something in between trade-cycle theory and present over-secular growth theory. He furthermore presented something in between the perhaps too much disaggregated growth theory of von Neumann (an idea taken over by this mathematician from Walras) and the too much aggregated growth theory stemming from Keynes. And it is my contention that we have an urgent need for both these kinds of intermediate positions.

The remainder of my paper will therefore first re-state Hayek's ideas in two different formal ways in order further to substantiate my claim that they were growth theoretical. Next I shall try to examine the underlying factual assumptions on behaviour and institutions and contrast them with those of the General Theory. From this re-statement I shall try to develop a re-application: In the fifth part of my paper in the form of a short-term growth theory of the sixties in Central Europe; and in the final section by applying Hayek's ideas to a very long-term problem of development, the economics of education.

II

In order to make Hayek's argument more easily understandable and to make it fit in better with present growth models, I shall in

11 The only Keynesian idea I would retain – in contrast to Hayek's set up – is the most controversial, the one which Joan Robinson considers the distinguishing mark of Keynesian growth theory, the Keynesian investment function: investments cause savings within the saving-investment identity, not the other way round.

249

re-stating it change its terminology in two respects. Firstly, wherever Hayek speaks of the rate of savings, I shall put the rate of *investment*. When speaking of saving, Hayek implies the neo-classical idea that inside the saving-investment identity the (dominant) cause of the level achieved is saving and not investment; and that if investment plans are not fulfilled, they adjust placidly to savings without starting a disequilibrium adjustment process. Following Keynes, I use the other terminology which implicitly assumes that in modern developed economies investment decisions are the (dominant) cause of the saving-investment level; and that (if such a thing as ex-ante saving plans exists at all!) positive or negative deviations in ex-post from ex-ante savings create no further reactions. To use the term investment instead of saving is not only preferable because of the wrong causation the word 'saving' implies; but also because in speaking of the importance of saving one tends to stress that *consumers* have to alter their plans when, in fact, most saving is done *pari passu* with their investment decisions by entrepreneurs. These and other implications have frequently tripped up readers of Hayek in the thirties. It is, therefore, better to avoid the term 'saving' in spite of the fact that present-day readers are much less likely to get confused by it than their predecessors: we are perfectly used to the term 'saving' for the saving-investment identity by our training in neoclassical growth theory. Here, as in many other respects, it is not only the thought, but also the language which shows the affinity of Hayek's writings in the thirties to today's models of economic growth.

The second point where I shall deviate from Hayek is in the use of the word 'interest'. It is well known that Hayek uses Wicksell's distinction between a natural and a market rate of interest. In order not to confuse the two (which again many readers of Hayek have done) I think it preferable to speak – instead of the natural rate of interest – of the *rate of profit*, or more explicitly of the rate of return on capital invested in the production process (to distinguish it from the rate of return on financial investment). Thus the term 'interest' can be limited to the market rate, i.e., in the case of Hayek, the rate of interest on commercial credit. Here again, this terminological precaution is perhaps unnecessary as the modern reader is less likely to confuse the two rates of interest: he has been conditioned in the ways of thought of Hayek by growth theory, which uses, both in its linear variety derived from von Neumann

250

(classical growth theory in the sense of Joan Robinson[12]) and in its neoclassical variety, the word interest for the rate of return, exactly as Hayek has done.

The essential point in Hayek's theory now is that, because of some 'autonomous' change (relative to the rates of interest), the two rates of interest, the rate of profit and the rate of interest, suddenly diverge, or better, diverge by more than the usual differential of risk premiums.[13] Though this divergence could be due to a change in the rate of interest,[14] e.g. because of a change in the degree of monopoly of the banks,[15] it is more likely that the rate of profit will show short-run fluctuations of a marked degree. Such fluctuations of the rate of profit can come about in many ways and have all been examined by Hayek; to the great confusion of economists who thought that Hayek was constantly changing his argument[16] in spite of the fact that anybody looking only a little closer could have seen that he was merely giving different examples of causes of the same phenomenon. Such causes of a divergence between profit and interest rates from the profit side could be: improved profit expectations due perhaps to an improvement in export chances or even due to no tangible economic causes at all, or improved profit expectations due to a lowering of the saving propensity of consumers;[17] they could be increases in the rate of profit because of the introduction of new production processes or new commodities or because of a better use of existing factors of production in existing processes (an approach towards the maxima of the production functions hitherto not generally reached); and

12 J. Robinson 'A Model of Models' in: the same, *Essays in The Theory of Economic Growth*, London 1962, p. 78 ff.

13 N. Kaldor has most explicitly stressed the necessary differential in risk premiums between rate of profit and interest in 'Economic Growth and the Problem of Inflation', Pt. I, *Economica*, N.S. 26 (1959), p. 212 ff., Pt. II p. 287 ff., here p. 217, p. 287 ff.

14 To consider such a change in interest rates as the reason for the divergence of profit and interest rates was Hayek's first approach. See F. A. von Hayek, *Geldtheorie und Konjunkturtheorie*, Vienna and Leipzig 1929, p. 69 and *passim*.

15 The degree of monopoly of the banks is very strong in many countries, e.g. in Austria. It can easily be changed, e.g. by policy measures allowing a more internationally integrated market for credits.

16 For this – and many other misunderstandings – see N. Kaldor, 'Professor Hayek and the Concertina Effect,' *Economica*, N.S. 9 (1942), p. 359 ff., *passim* and: 'Professor Hayek . . . later produced a new version of his theory which in many ways radically departed from, and contradicted, the first'. (p. 359)

17 Considered in Hayek, *Geldtheorie und Konjunkturtheorie, loc. cit.*, p. 80 f.

they could finally be variations of the rate of wages per efficiency unit of labour relative to the prices of consumption goods.[18] Though the rate of profit exhibits an astonishing degree of secular stability in its very long-run average,[19] it does most certainly show both short-run variations during the business cycle and relatively long-run variations during what one might term growth cycles. The rate of interest, on the other hand, in most economies fluctuates much less. *Thus Hayek focuses on a point of indubitable empirical existence and relevance: the stronger fluctuation of the average rate of profit than of the average (long-term) interest rate.*

Hayek then considers the effect of the divergence in these two rates of interest on the rate of capital formation. In this respect his model progressed during its development – and in the same direction present growth theory has gone in the last five or six years.

Hayek's model started out as a two-sector model with one consumption good and one capital good; it became in the later phases a multisector model with still essentially only one consumption good, but many capital goods. Hayek could thus not only examine the effects of the divergence between profit and interest rate on the *rate* or average of accumulation, but also on its *structure* or direction. *The fully developed Hayek model is thus a multi-sector disequilibrium growth model showing two different, and therefore disequilibrium, interest prices:* the demand price for capital (the rate of profit) and its supply price (the rate of interest). For even if the equilibrium rate of profit has risen for some autonomous reason, and we could thus couch our whole argument in terms of the change of this equilibrium price – as Hayek mostly does – it is perhaps preferable to recognize at the outset that the *actual* rate of profit is just as much a disequilibrium price as the actual rate of interest: if, because of some price rigidity, the rate of interest is held *below* its equilibrium level, the actual rate of profit for just this reason lies *above* it.

It is interesting that Hayek, the liberal, essentially constructed a theory of the *misallocation of resources due to the working of the price mechanism.* He did not hesitate to do so, because he thought

18 This is the approach followed by Hayek e.g. in 'The Ricardo Effect', *Economica*, N.S. 9 (1942), p. 127 ff.
19 I have built a thesis on the long-term trends in the structure of incomes around this fact in E. Streissler, 'Long Term Structural Changes in the Distribution of Income', *Zeitschrift für National ökonomie*, 29 (1969), p. 39 ff.

bank credit a distorting effect on 'natural' market forces. The problem, however, persists. And we know now that, even in general, the price mechanism may not be a good guide to the *dynamic change of production conditions*. A good deal of the stability of present market economies is, in fact, due to the reliance of modern enterprises on quantity adjustments as a first step.

Hayek's contention is that a rate of interest (more than normally) below the rate of profit will increase 'the degree of roundaboutness of methods of production'. What modern concept corresponds to this archaic term? For Hayek the answer is completely clear: An increase in 'the degree of roundaboutness of methods of production' is nothing but *an increase in the capital-output ratio or in the capital-coefficient*! To any modern reader of lecture II in *Prices and Production* this interpretation is evident.[20] Hayek was, in fact, the first author to use the concept of the capital-coefficient extensively.[21] It should be noticed that, in taking the capital coefficient as equivalent to 'the degree of roundaboutness of methods of production', Hayek made a fruitful innovation in the Austrian argument on the theory of capital. He was replacing a clumsy measure, Böhm-Bawerk's 'average production period',[22] a concept to which nothing empirically observable exactly corresponds, by a handier and more easily calculable measure. The two measures do *not* coincide, though they will point in the same direction in many, if not most, meaningful economic cases.[23]

---

20 To quote only one sentence: 'The proportion of the demand for consumers goods to the demand for intermediate products will then ultimately be changed from 40:80 to 30:90, or 1:2 to 1:3'. F. A. Hayek, *Prices and Production*, London 1931, p. 46. Intermediate products are the only capital considered by Hayek and consumer goods the only output in the stationary equilibria he compares.

21 Without, however, giving it a name. The term 'capital coefficient' is due to Sir Roy Harrod, *Towards a Dynamic Economics*, London 1948, p. 22. Early use of this concept, though not as extensively, had been made by G. Cassel and D. H. Robertson.

22 See E. v. Böhm-Bawerk *Capital and Interest*, Vol. II *Positive Theory of Capital*, South Holland, Ill. 1959, p. 87.

23 Call $g(t)$ the amount of inputs invested in the production of a capital good at time t when time runs from the first appearance of man (to be called $t = -\infty$) to the present moment ($t = o$). Take r to be the rate of interest at which inputs increase in value. Call the inputs of time t in their present moment valuation $f(t) = g(t)e^{rt}$. Set the value of the product produced each period by the capital good when completed at unity. Then the capital coefficient κ equals:

$$(1) \qquad \kappa = \int_{-\infty}^{o} g(t)e^{rt}dt = \int_{-\infty}^{o} f(t)dt = F(g,r)$$

253

Böhm-Bawerk's germinal idea of the 'round-aboutness of production processes', which in his more precise statements was given by him one interpretation, the average production period, was thus given by Hayek another, that of the capital coefficient. I sometimes wonder, whether both writers did not have at the back of their mind still a third interpretation. Böhm-Bawerk stresses as inputs not only labour, but perhaps even more the 'useful manifestations of nature', the 'natural endowment'.[24] Might he not be understood to have meant that during economic growth on the average the *value of commodities rises relative to the value of their content of raw materials* and that *that* is the expression of the increase in roundaboutness? After all he stressed that through roundaboutness we produce not only more, but *better* goods, we are 'obtaining *comfortable* houses, *safe* ships, *precision* timepieces'.[25]

The increase in the value of commodities relative to their raw material content is a much more marked and much more con-

24 See E. v. Böhm-Bawerk, *loc. cit.*, p. 80.
25 E. v. Böhm-Bawerk, *loc. cit.*, p. 94 (italics by Böhm-Bawerk).

The average period of production of the capital good, τ, on the other hand is:

$$(2) \quad \tau = -\frac{1}{\kappa}\int_{-\infty}^{o} tg(t)e^{rt}dt = -\frac{1}{\kappa}\int_{-\infty}^{o} tf(t)dt = \frac{1}{\kappa}\int_{-\infty}^{o}\int_{-\infty}^{o} f(t)dt = \frac{1}{\kappa}\int_{-\infty}^{o} F(t)dt$$

(In computing (2) we have assumed that both the integrals (1) and (2) converge, which alone makes them economically meaningful. In this case $t\int_{-\infty}^{o} f(t)\, dt$ must be zero at both limits of the integration. Furthermore, the weight function $\int f(t)dt$, in order to sum to unity, has to be divided by κ.) If both the integrals converge, the capital coefficient and the average period of production stand to each other in the relation of derivative and integral divided by that derivative.

If, e.g., the input function $g(t)$ were to increase monotonically over time, the closer our capital good approaches completion, in the manner $g(t) = e^{at}$, then κ, the capital coefficient, would be $\frac{1}{a+r}$, while τ, the average period of production also would equal $\frac{1}{a+r}$. Even taking account of the fact that we must have $r \geqslant O$ and all $g(t) \geqslant O$, a change in the input structure will in general, however, not necessarily change κ and τ in the same direction. This will only be the case whenever we increase or keep constant all 'early' inputs before a certain date and decrease or keep constant all 'late' inputs after that date; e.g. if the input functions $g(t)$ and/or $f(t)$ are monotonically increasing the closer we approach the present and this increase is made more 'rapid' (larger a or r in the example above). Bohm-Bawerk's examples suggest that he had only this possibility in mind so that in the Austrian tradition, although not necessarily in general, the two measures are synonymous.

254

tinuous change during growth than the increase in the capital coefficient, which seems to have been present in Böhm-Bawerk's late nineteenth century, but is absent today. More precisely speaking, the former is due to the greater degree of economic progress in the production of raw materials than in later stages of production, a fact to which the proneness of raw materials to over-production bears eloquent witness; to the greater degree of substitutability of raw material inputs for other inputs, for instance synthetics, while the degree of substitutability between later inputs seems to be smaller (e.g. that between the large groups capital and labour appearing to be below unity); and finally to the fact that we seem to need more and more highly-qualified labour to develop raw materials into final products (especially complicated machines), relative to the qualification of the labour required for the production of raw materials themselves.

A rise in what we might call the average raw-material-output-ratio has a very important consequence for trade cycle theory: it means that on the average capital goods are likely to become more *specific*. In a primitive society if one activity, e.g. war, becomes less profitable, and another, e.g. agriculture, more so, it is easy to 'beat swords into ploughshares'. As the raw material content relative to the total value is high both in the capital goods for the production of war, swords, and in those for agriculture, ploughshares, the two production goods can be transformed into each other with a relatively modest loss. Try on the other hand to change electronic computers into something else, e.g. speed boats, and you will find that you have first to suffer a total loss of the value installed. If the increase in roundaboutness during growth via its raw material-output effect also means greater specificity of capital, it becomes more and more dangerous to choose a degree of roundaboutness not appropriate in the light of further developments. Böhm-Bawerk's capital theory thus attains overtones of a theory of the trade cycle, overtones which Hayek tried to bring out. And, indeed, he laid great stress on the dangers of the specificity of producers' goods,[26] a stress which perhaps caused him to overestimate the dangers of a capital structure out of equilibrium.

After this brief detour into the overtones of certain central ideas of the Austrian school let us return to Hayek's main argument. Hayek states that a relative increase in the rate of profit over the

26 See Hayek, *Prices and Production, loc. cit.,* p. 67 ff.

255

rate of interest will increase the capital coefficient. This increase will be above the new equilibrium level, on the one hand because actual profits are above equilibrium profits and – even more importantly – because, on the other hand, actual interest is below equilibrium interest. This development towards a disequilibrium level of the capital coefficient is all the more dangerous, he implies, because *pari passu* the specificity of capital goods is also increased.

Let us first show that the Hayek process – a rise of the rate of profit above the rate of interest – will under his assumptions bring about a rise in the *investment ratio*. This may be argued in two complementary ways: a rise in the rate of actual profits implies in the short run an unambiguous increase in the profit share. With constant saving propensities – and Hayek does assume them constant, his whole argument centering on the fact that *if* they remain constant a crisis ensues – a higher profit share implies a higher investment share. This is the first chain of argument to which a second might be added. The higher than equilibrium actual rate of profit and the lower than equilibrium rate of interest imply a relative redistribution of the total profit share in favour of productive entrepreneurs and against banks or savers in banks. Hayek now probably assumes – without saying so explicitly – that entrepreneurs in production have a higher propensity to invest (or save) than financial intermediaries or private lenders to or stock owners of these. Thus, because of the redistribution of the profit share towards those types of entrepreneurs with a higher propensity to save, the investment share is likely to rise even more than the profit share.

Let us call the social product at current prices X and consumption at current prices C. The rise in the investment share then implies (writing ↑ for an increasing function over time):

$$(1) \quad \frac{X}{C} \ (\uparrow) \ \text{or} \ \frac{d\left(\frac{X}{C}\right)}{dt} > 0$$

Hayek furthermore implies that not only does the investment ratio increase but that, because of the lowering of the rate of interest relative to the rate of profit, the capital coefficient increases also. This can again be argued in two ways. One is to say that Hayek is more an adherent of neoclassical growth theory (in which

256

an increase in the investment ratio in long-run equilibrium increases the capital coefficient and not the rate of growth) than a follower of the Domar model or the classical growth theory of the von Neumann type (in which the same increase only works on the growth rate, but not upon the capital coefficient). And indeed Hayek's argument fits the neoclassical frame better. For the difference between these two types of growth models is whether they consider technical progress as autonomous in its *production* relative to investment[27] (the neo-classical case) or as endogenous, i.e. created by research and development investment (the Domar case). Hayek treats technical progress as exogenous, which was indeed sensible in a small country like Austria, and thus comes down on the neoclassical side; in fact it would be enough for his argument if technical progress were *partly* exogenous. Qualitatively speaking, he is thus certainly on safe ground; though much more so in a long-term than in a short-term analysis, one more reason for treating his ideas as long-run arguments. For we know that short-term growth processes are much closer to the Domar case, in which the capital-coefficient does *not* rise with the investment rate, than to the long-term equilibrium of neoclassical growth.[28]

We can, however, construct a more cogent second reason for the increase of the capital coefficient in the Hayek process. The rate of interest falls, relative to the new equilibrium rate of profit (e.g. by remaining constant while the equilibrium rate of profit rises). This low supply price of capital induces more highly mechanized methods of production. As Joan Robinson has aptly argued, a higher degree of mechanization at a lower rate of interest does, however, not imply a higher capital-output-ratio: The fall in the rate of interest with which quantities of inputs are weighted to arrive at the relative value of capital may overcompensate the increase in these quantities of inputs themselves.[29] Not so, however, in the Hayek process: While the inducement to mechanization is given by the relatively *lower* rate of interest, the inputs themselves must be valued at the *higher* rate of profit! In this case, because both a more

---

27 As everybody knows nowadays from the study of vintage models, autonomy in production does not imply that in *application*, too, technical progress has to be independent of investment.

28 See R. Sato, 'The Harrod-Domar Model vs. the Neoclassical Growth Model', *Economic Journal*, 74 (1964), p. 380 ff.; W. Krelle, 'Investition und Wachstum', *Jahrbücher für Nationalökonomie und Statistik*, 176 (1964) p. 1 ff.

29 See J. Robinson *The Accumulation of Capital*, London 1956, p. 127.

highly mechanized technique is used *and* it is reckoned at a higher notional rate of profit, we certainly get a higher capital coefficient. It is true that this is mainly a nominal capital coefficient and one valued at prices that cannot be sustained. But we have to reckon the magnitudes in the Hayek process in the values of these 'unreal' prices. For it is just his argument that this valuation cannot be sustained.

If we call K the capital valued at the prices corresponding to actual (disequilibrium) profits we can state the rise in the capital coefficient by writing:

$$(2) \quad \frac{K}{X} \; (\uparrow) \; \text{or} \; \frac{d\left(\frac{K}{X}\right)}{dt} > 0$$

Hayek's next argument, which was only developed fully some ten years after the first publication of his ideas, is most ingenious. Though the capital coefficient increases, it is perfectly possible that *at the same time and for the same reasons the capital intensity falls*! The capital coefficient and the capital intensity are, of course, two quite distinct concepts; and it is a curious reflection on the lack of training in precision of economic thought in the thirties that a scholar of the calibre of Nicholas Kaldor could not distinguish between the two, thinking Hayek contradicted himself by assuming a fall in the capital intensity at the same time as a rise in the capital coefficient.[30]

Hayek states that a rise of the rate of profit *relative to sales or output* (and this is primarily implied in a rise in the profit share) will increase the profitability of those capital goods most, which can produce the desired commodity *and are also the least durable*. Or, to put it in another way, if the rate of profit is equal per turnover and increases, the demand price of those capital goods with the highest rate of turnover increases most. The idea can also be expressed differently: if the rate of profit increases, entrepreneurs will try to expand production in a crash program as quickly as possible at the least investment cost: and this will drive them towards capital goods with a high capacity effect. Thus, as far as any substitution between means of production is possible, entre-

30 See Kaldor 'Professor Hayek and the Concertina-Effect', *loc. cit.*, p. 360 ff., repeatedly, in fact in most arguments.

preneurs will try to change the mixture of capital goods towards the less durable types: a typical example would be the introduction of shift work, which uses larger stocks of materials (capital of lowest durability) with the same amount of durable plant, incidentally decreasing the durability of this plant at the same time, as it is used more intensively. Furthermore, the same effect may also be achieved by switching production as far as possible – without changing prices too much – to commodities which are produced at a low degree of capital intensity and thus at particularly high rates of profit *per unit of capital invested*.

We can thus summarize Hayek's double argument in two ways: On the one hand, he says that a sufficiently high positive divergence of the rate of profit from the rate of interest will make the desired capital stock rise so far above the old levels that, in spite of a higher production of investment goods, one will have to try to economize the still insufficient means of production by *decreasing* capital intensity. On the other hand, he points out that an increase of the rate of profit *on sales* will create a divergence of the rates of profit *on capital invested*, the least mechanized technique becoming the most attractive; a point which has, of course, become completely evident to any present day student who has ever pondered Joan Robinson's reading mark.

It is worth noting that in his argument on the durability of capital chosen – to my mind Hayek's most important and permanent contribution among his capital theoretical arguments – Hayek has again innovated upon Böhm-Bawerk, and this time very considerably. Böhm-Bawerk believed that *in general* the degree of durability of capital will tend to move in the *same* direction as the degree of roundaboutness of production (or approximately that capital coefficient and capital intensity will move together).[31] There is, however, no necessary argument why the gestation period of capital before its 'birth' should in any way correspond to its 'life expectancy' *after* 'birth', particularly in Hayek's disequilibrium process.

In my argument I have taken Hayek's concept of durability to be equivalent to that of capital intensity, though in general the two need not be quite the same. This is, however, the case in Hayek's argument. He assumes higher employment with a

31 See E. v. Böhm-Bawerk, *loc. cit.*, p. 89 ff. However, he stated explicitly on p. 90 that this does not *necessarily* obtain in every case.

relatively small increase in capital and in this case the two concepts will coincide. Let us call L the number of labour hours employed. Capital intensity is then K/L. If it falls we get for its reciprocal value:

$$(3) \quad \frac{L}{K} \, (\uparrow) \text{ or } \frac{d\left(\frac{L}{K}\right)}{dt} > 0$$

Finally we have to turn to Hayek's argument on the relative movement of wages and commodity prices. Here he presents many variants. Prices of capital goods are considered constant in the short run in spite of an increase in demand due to a higher rate of profit (at the old prices); but rising in the long run. Prices of consumption goods are generally considered as constant or sometimes as rising. And wages can be constant, rising, or falling. One of his arguments, that in 'The Ricardo Effect', could, if we call wages w and prices of consumption goods p_c, be rendered by:

$$(4a) \quad \frac{w}{p_c} \, (\downarrow) \text{ or } \frac{d\left(\frac{w}{p_c}\right)}{dt} < 0$$

But Hayek's argument is brought out even more cogently – and with more justice to certain phases of present trade cycles – by assuming the following: Wages *per efficiency unit of labour*, to be called w', fall; i.e. technical progress (relative to labour inputs) is *larger* than wage increases. Profitability is therefore increased, so that we get the Hayek process. On the other hand, as technical progress is substantial, wages still *rise* relative to the prices of consumer goods. We then get

$$(4b) \quad \frac{w'}{p_c} \, (\uparrow) \text{ or } \frac{d\left(\frac{w'}{p_c}\right)}{dt} > 0$$

From the four movements described, all of Hayek's conclusions follow identically in a way evident to any modern reader. Combine (2) and (3) and you get:

$$(5) \quad \frac{K}{X} \, (\uparrow) \cdot \frac{L}{K} \, (\uparrow) \equiv \frac{L}{X} \, (\uparrow \uparrow)$$

Labour input relative to the value of the product rises.[32] Combine (1), (2) and (3) to deduce:

$$(6) \quad \frac{X}{C} (\uparrow) \cdot \frac{K}{X} (\uparrow) \cdot \frac{L}{K} (\uparrow) \equiv \frac{L}{C} (\uparrow \uparrow \uparrow)$$

Labour input relative to the amount of consumption in real terms rises even more. Finally combine (1), (2), (3) and (4b)[33] in order to conclude (L': labour measured in efficiency units):

$$(7) \quad \frac{X}{C} (\uparrow) \cdot \frac{K}{X} (\uparrow) \cdot \frac{L'}{K} (\uparrow) \cdot \frac{w'}{p_c} (\uparrow) \equiv \frac{w'L'}{p_cC} (\uparrow \uparrow \uparrow \uparrow)$$

The wage bill relative to the present value of consumption goods will rise most of all. And here we immediately come up against Hayek's inherent contradiction. Wage earners consume practically their whole income and are responsible for most of total consumption; or at the least they are thought to have a constant saving propensity. Wages thus *cannot* rise relative to the value of consumption goods at current prices *unless* the saving propensity of wage earners is *increased*. (7), though here written as an identity, in reality is an ex-ante equation which is difficult to fulfil. Therefore Hayek's statement: As long as (1) to (4b) hold, the upward spiral of production can only go on *if savings are increased.* (1) to (4) are plans, resulting from economic data, which can, however, not be fulfilled for long.

Of course the contradiction implied by (7) can also be resolved in quite a few other ways; the most evident being that the *prices of consumption goods are increased.* But even then there is still some likelihood for the truth of a wider thesis of Hayek: the growth process is only likely to continue at an increased pace if *someone* saves more, in this case the entrepreneurs. This means that Hayek is, in fact, stating nothing but the now familiar dictum: If higher growth is to be more than a short-run approach towards the ceiling *it has to be sustained by a higher rate of investment.* Though in saying this we find that, in contrast to the first possible argument on

32 See Hayek 'The Ricardo Effect', *loc. cit.*, p. 149: '*In the short run* the more capitalistic methods will require *more* labour for any given increase of output'.
33 Using (4a) instead of (4b) might make this deduction ambiguous.

261

the capital coefficient (that of its relation to technical progress), Hayek is here closer to Domar than to neoclassical growth models.[34]

We must not forget Sir Roy Harrod's interpretation of the Hayek identity either. He focuses attention on relation (2). Entrepreneurs *try* to increase the capital coefficient for the reasons given by Hayek; but they find they cannot do so. In fact they find they *decrease* it.[35] Harrod's process is thus also a disequilibrium process, but in the result perhaps somewhat less so than Hayek's: if expectations falter, inflation stops without too much disequilibrium having been caused in the structure of capital goods.

III

We have now presented an elaborate reformulation of Hayek's disequilibrium process in terms of modern growth identities, in terms of an inherent contradiction between ex-ante and ex-post magnitudes, between plans and achievements. A more sophisticated reformulation in terms of a multi-sector linear growth model, as set out by Morishima[36] or Mathur[37] in the vein of von Neumann, is, however, also possible, a reformulation which sheds a special light on certain of Hayek's ideas and which therefore merits attention. I shall attempt such a reformulation if only to substantiate the claim presented earlier that Hayek's thought is very closely akin to von Neumann.

Let us take a von Neumann production possibility set with m possible processes and $n-1$ commodities, the commodities of material and immaterial production apart from finance. Let us take the saving propensity of workers and of entrepreneurs as given, the latter being larger than the former. In this case the equilibrium rate of profit will stand in fixed proportion to the equilibrium rate of growth, a proportion determined solely by the propensities to

34 By choosing an intermediate position on technical progress, which makes the first argument on the capital coefficient hold true, Hayek can, of course, also assume this second point, though more strongly in the short, than in the long run.

35 Harrod, *Dynamic Economics*, loc. cit., p. 85 f. See especially also Baumol's interpretation in his *Economic Dynamics*, loc. cit., p. 45 ff.

36 M. Morishima, *Equilibrium, Stability and Growth*, Oxford 1964.

37 G. Mathur, *Planning for Steady Growth*, Oxford 1965.

save and the relative factor shares in the distribution of income.[38]

We have now to introduce the last commodity and the last sector in efficient production: *the production of credit by banks*. Indeed it is the essential feature of Hayek's model that such a sector and such a commodity exist and are just as real as all the other sectors and all the other commodities: this is the central thesis of the non-neutrality of money. It is one of the most fruitful features of Hayek's argument, but has not yet been rediscovered in recent growth literature, in spite of the fact that monetary theory has been rapidly working towards it.[39]

Why should money not be considered as a real commodity produced and needed? What, after all, is its difference relative to real stocks, which we always include in input-output analysis? Only a minute fraction of stocks are used to bridge the inevitable gap between the time point of production and the time point of consumption, a fraction constantly dwindling with the decline of agriculture with its point output function at long intervals. Most stocks are held for probabilistic reasons, to forego the loss of customers, who have to be sent away unsatisfied because of a chance lack of the exact commodity they desire, to forego the dangers of an unforeseeable time schedule of supply and to forego losses due to unforeseeable needs during the production process itself. There is thus no *technical* relationship between real stocks as inputs and production as output; but much rather a kind of 'liquidity' relationship governed by the probabilities of chance divergences between inflow and outflow of commodities and the estimated losses of non-deliverance. Exactly the same considerations hold true for money, a fact recognized by its modern inventory-theoretic analysis: it is held because of the danger of the divergence of payments and receipts, considered as stochastic magnitudes, and weighed in its use against its interest costs on the one hand and the prevention of possible losses due to insolvency or the application for credit in panic situations on the other. Thus money has a utility of

38 See John Hicks, *Capital and Growth*, Oxford 1965, p. 176. Call the rate of profit r, the rate of growth of product g, s_1 and s_2 the saving propensities of entrepreneurs and wage earners respectively and f the share of profit in income, then:

$$r = \frac{g}{s_1 + s_2\left(\frac{1}{f}-1\right)}$$

39 See especially J. G. Gurley and E. S. Shaw, *Money in a Theory of Finance*, Washington 1960.

263

its own apart from the utility of the goods to be bought by it, a fact stressed perhaps by no one as much as by Keynes with his battle cry of 'money as an asset'. Hayek has not raised this battle cry which is of little practical consequence in Keynes' own work. But he has fully brought out its consequences by embodying the 'production' of money in a multi-sectoral model of growth.

The easiest way to embody the 'production' of money in a von Neumann growth model – and one which brings out all the essential features – is to think of credit entering the production of all commodities in all processes. The banking sector, on the other hand, shall have only two inputs: labour and credit itself. Why does credit enter into its own production? For the reasons usually presented in the theory of the money multiplier: dependent upon the degree of integration of the banking system and the relative use of cash and credit, a part of the credit expanded flows back to the banks and enables a further expansion of credit. (We might elaborate this model by considering two kinds of money, cash or the 'monetary base' and bank credit, cash also entering all production processes including that of credit.)

Once we have added the banking sector to the von Neumann model, we have to consider two possible cases. On the one hand, the 'technical input coefficient' in the production of credit is so low, relative to the output coefficient, and the need for credit in the other sectors is so small that credit becomes a free good. This is the case considered in neoclassical economics and even that generally considered by economists in the fifties: it is the case of the infinite elasticity of the banking system (one asks oneself, however, why people should pay any interest at all if this case holds true). But this is certainly not the Hayek case. Here credit is among the scarce commodities.

In this second model let the 'technique' for producing credit change. The own input coefficient of credit into credit falls (or, in the model incorporating also cash, the cash input coefficient alone or in conjunction with the credit input coefficient falls). This may basically have two causes. Either the credit system becomes more or better integrated so that it can *permanently* get along with a smaller reserve ratio. In this case we get a long-term equilibrium Hayek process. Or there might merely occur a change in the degree of confidence of bankers and in the degree of credit-worthiness of customers: prosperity starts. In this case bankers will, by a revaluation of the state of the economy, *consider* their reserves to be excessive and expand credit. This, too, in the language of growth theory is 'technical progress', though one which is – by the way, in common with most kinds of technical progress – of a very economic nature.

What happens in a von Neumann system if there is one technical progress (the lowering of one input coefficient) in the efficient technique of an economic good? In this case the growth possibility increases, i.e. we can have either higher wages or higher growth or both. In the Hayek case, wages are held constant at first and this is still realistic for present booms (they have only to be held constant relative to the efficiency units of labour applied, i.e. relative to productivity). In this case, at given saving propensities, the rate of growth will rise and with it – and, in fact, even more – the rate of profit and the profit share.[40] On the other hand, the price of credit will certainly fall relative to other prices, as one of its input coefficients has been decreased and none increased. Hayek's upward movement of the rate of profit relative to the rate of interest immediately follows; this time, however, essentially as an equilibrium process.

The higher profit share at given saving propensities immediately brings about a higher investment ratio and possibly, though not at all necessarily, an increase in the capital coefficient,[41] as Hayek concludes (note that this time no one has to increase his saving propensity because we have a new equilibrium process; entrepreneurs automatically provide the higher savings). Furthermore, as we have an increase in the rate of profit we get – on certain plausible assumptions, to which we have to return – a lowering of the capital intensity. Finally those sectors of production will be most expanded where credit is most needed.

As Hayek explicitly states, everything can go on beautifully, as long as the 'technical innovation' in the production of credit lasts. But it is the essential feature in the short-term Hayek process that

40 From $r = \dfrac{g}{s_1 + s_2\left(\dfrac{1}{f} - 1\right)}$ in footnote 38 we get $\dfrac{dr}{dg} \cdot \dfrac{g}{r} = \dfrac{dg}{df} > 0$

and $\dfrac{dr}{df} \cdot \dfrac{f}{r} = \dfrac{dg}{df} \cdot \dfrac{f}{g} + \dfrac{s_2}{s_1 f + s_2(1-f)} > 0$

Thus due to a change in the profit share, the rate of profit rises even more than the rate of growth.

41 See Hicks, *Capital and Growth*, loc. cit., p. 169.

265

it cannot do so, if wages start rising.[42] This will by itself bring about a slower growth path, a lower equilibrium rate of profit and therefore a higher lender's risk for the banks. But if, in addition, wage earners transact their purchases mainly in cash, banks will find they do not only have higher risks but also dwindling reserves. Thus the input coefficient of credit for the production of credit starts edging up again, and with it the rate of growth and the rate of profit falls. *It is the essential feature of the Hayek model that there exists (at least) one sector in the economy, here the banking sector, with a cyclically varying technology.* It can vary because it is not technically fixed. And this cyclical variation in 'technology' can be said to cause the cycle.[43] The moment we drop the concept that all 'technical' coefficients' in growth models are technically fixed, we get highly interesting disequilibrium processes.

Furthermore, we have so far glossed over the fact that the input coefficients of credit in the production processes are not related to real, but rather to *nominal*, production. We have assumed – and I think with Hayek – an extreme kind of money illusion in the first stages of expansion; credit demands relative to real output remain constant as long as prices are *thought* to be constant. Once the rise in prices is perceived they, too, start to change; they edge upwards. We get another kind of fluctuating coefficients. The process can now only be continued at *increasing* rates of credit creation, while, in fact, they are already *falling*.

There is one further feature in Hayek's growth model which should be stressed. The variations in the growth and profit rates cause *capital losses;* and Hayek's entrepreneurs are highly sensitive to these. Now it is well known that we can prove adjustment processes in linear growth models with changing techniques to be stable only when we ignore capital losses.[44] In fact, even without changes in technique multi-sectoral growth models, which allow

42 See already his earliest full scale statement of his theory, *Geldtheorie und Konjunkturtheorie, loc. cit.*, p. 101: Für die Krise '*genügt* es vollständig, daß, wie es früher oder später geschehen *muß*, die Banken *aufhören*, den Umfang ihrer Kredite *weiter auszudehnen*'. See also *Prices and Production, loc. cit.*, p. 80.

43 See *Geldtheorie u. Konjunkturtheorie, loc. cit.*, p. 103: 'Die entscheidende Ursache der Konjunkturschwankungen ist also, daß infolge der Veränderlichkeit der Umlaufsmittelmenge der Zins, den die Banken fordern, nicht notwendig immer gleich dem Gleichgewichtszins ist, sondern in der Bewegung über kurze Frist tatsächlich von den Liquiditätserwägungen der Banken bestimmt wird.'

44 See Morishima, *loc. cit.*, e.g. p. 105.

266

for capital gains and losses, can become highly unstable.[45] It is one of the main reasons of the high degree of instability of the Hayek process that it explains how capital losses are caused and that it takes them seriously.

IV

We have seen that the essential point in generalized models of the Hayek type is the demonstration – easy in practice – that there exist efficient technologies with fluctuating production coefficients, fluctuating, because they are not merely technical. The specific Hayek model, on the other hand, points to credit as the commodity produced in this way. This specific model therefore is relevant only, but also always, when *credit creation is an important limiting factor of expansion*.[46] By stressing this particular restraint, Hayek in the last resort revives Mercantilist modes of argument to the same measure as Keynes did. But while Keynes stressed the trends of thought in Mercantilism which emphasized the importance of creating effective demand and of creating employment, if need be by interventionist methods, Hayek turned to another strain in the

45 F. H. Hahn, 'On Warranted Growth Paths', *Review of Economic Studies*, 35 (April 1968), p. 175 ff.

46 We can sharpen the von Neumann model of the Hayek process even further and at once make the idea of a limiting factor clearer by stating with Mathur, *Steady Growth, loc. cit.*, p. 94 that credit is *both the upper and lower restraining good* of the whole development process. It is upper restraining *if* we assume that it is 'the good which is the least self-reproductive among all goods in their most self-reproductive processes' (for credit there exists, in fact, *at any one moment* only one process of production). Furthermore credit exactly reproduces itself in all other processes but the production of credit: unless we have a Gesell-type economy money remains the same in amount in the next period. In each process the least self-ratio is therefore either 1 (credit) or lower. In the production process of credit itself, its self-ratio is higher; and this, therefore, is the maximum for all the minima in the process rows. Credit is therefore *always* the lower restraining good.

When credit is, by assumption, the upper restraint and, as always, the lower, the increase in the rate of production of credit is, in fact, *exactly* the increase in the equilibrium growth rate of the economy as a whole.

In the *cashless* pure credit model we can prove this result also in another way: credit in this case is exactly the *investment good of the highest order* as it enters into all processes and nothing but labour enters into its own production. As it still is also the lower restraining good it follows immediately that the rate of growth is equal to its self-ratio of expansion (Mathur, *Steady Growth, loc. cit.*, p. 351).

267

Mercantilists' credo: the all pervading importance of money; though with Hayek, in contrast to the Mercantilists, money, much rather than being the root of all good, is the root of all evil.

The similarities between Keynes and Hayek go much further:[47] they can be shown to have presented in many respects mirror images. What, e.g., is the market structure of Hayekian relative to Keynesian markets? As Sir John Hicks has shown,[48] Keynesian entrepreneurs in the production sector use the 'Fixprice' adjustment mechanism, i.e., use a strategy of quantity variation in disequilibrium. Keynesian money markets, on the other hand, are 'Flexprice', i.e., their prices change easily and quickly to adjust for disequilibrium. One can combine these statements by saying Keynesian entrepreneurs show a much higher degree of monopoly or oligopoly in the production sector than in the financial sector. This assumption mirrors the structure of modern large, often international, enterprises on the one hand and the great degree of competition on the then most developed money market of the world, the London market. In contrast, Hayekian entrepreneurs, at least in the consumption sector, show a very high degree of price flexibility (the producers of investment goods take much longer to adjust their prices); while, on the other hand, banks change the credit conditions very little, merely adjusting the amount of loans according to demand. Thus we get exactly the opposite hierarchy in the market structure: Banks show the highest degree of monopoly or oligopoly, followed by producers of investment goods, while producers of consumption goods are in strict competition. This picture was very realistic for late nineteenth-century or early twentieth-century Austria: Large banks, medium-scale producers of investment goods (or imports from abroad!) and tiny and utterly dependent entrepreneurs in final production. The trouble is that present-day Austria (or even Germany) now fits none of these descriptions exactly: there is little price flexibility both in the financial *and* in the production sector; but the opening of financial

47 Hayek and Keynes, e.g., are also both in strict opposition to Say's law. See *Geldtheorie und Konjunkturtheorie, loc. cit.* p. 50: 'Allein das Eintreten des Geldes (vermag) die automatische Anpassung von Angebot und Nachfrage zu stören, die nach den am klarsten in der Say'schen Theorie der Absatzwege zum Ausdruck kommenden Gedankengängen in der Naturalwirtschaft immer bestehend angesehen werden muß.'
48 Hicks, *Methods of Dynamic Analysis, loc. cit.*, 1956, p. 149; more muted Hicks, *Capital and Growth, loc. cit.*, p. 77.

markets to foreign competition brings them closer all the time to the Keynesian description.

Due to their high degree of competition, Hayekian entrepreneurs have no price-fixing power. Thus, they cannot satisfy their investment desires by mulcting the consumer: therefore investments depend upon voluntary savings of consumers, who might even receive higher incomes than entrepreneurs (e.g. landowners or high civil servants). Hayekian entrepreneurs are not only weak and small, they are also poor: they absolutely depend upon credit for financing any extension in plant. They are starved for capital. They always have unfulfilled investment desires. Therefore, whenever new credit becomes available, they eagerly lap it up. There may even be an unsatiated demand to become an entrepreneur so that cheap credit causes the creation of new enterprises.[49] Development thus proceeds in a bumpy way, in leaps and lulls, as it still does in many relatively underdeveloped countries and for exactly the Hayekian reason. Keynesian entrepreneurs, on the other hand, have long lost any desires for new investments, for new horizons (were they, too, painted from life?). No mere credit expansion could force these animals to drink.

Apart from relatively underdeveloped economies, such an extreme degree of dependence on credit will nowadays be rare. But this does not mean that even today the influence of finance on the real production process has to be negligible. It is true, in great depressions, as in the thirties, credit is of marginal importance relative to the cataclysmic changes in demand;[50] it is true that in war economies, as in the forties, credit is supplied practically free; it is true that in phases of very rapid growth, as they have been witnessed by Germany or Austria in the fifties (5·5 per cent average *per capita* growth) or are experienced today in Japan, credit seems to be of little importance, finance accumulating by itself. But in a

49 See *Prices and Production, loc. cit.*, p. 76 f. Also J. A. Schumpeter, *Business Cycles*, New York and London 1939, p. 110 f.

50 One should, however, even for the thirties not play down the applicability of Hayekian thought too much. Keynes himself has, in fact, applied it. See J. M. Keynes, *The General Theory of Employment, Interest and Money*, London 1936, p. 219: 'The post-war experiences of Great Britain and the United States are, indeed, actual examples of how an accumulation of wealth, so large that its *marginal efficiency has fallen more rapidly than the rate of interest can fall in the face of the prevailing institutional and psychological factors*, can interfere . . . with a reasonable level of employment' (italics mine, E.S.). This is exactly the Hayek process, appropriately put into reverse!

269

period of relatively sluggish growth both entrepreneurs stress and governments suspect that credit gains in importance as a limiting factor. And it is therefore not at all surprising that the specific Hayekian analysis stressing the importance of credit achieves new interest and new actuality in the sluggish growth of today.

This is so because the Hayekian importance of finance is not only relevant when entrepreneurs on the average are in a weak strategic position in the market i.e. when they stand in severe competition with each other. This was the case in the eighteenth and nineteenth century,[51] the situation Hayek essentially described, but is no longer the case today. Finance also becomes a limit when the pressure of final demand on supply slackens in a longer term sense (which of course, causes a lowering of the average degree of monopoly); a situation characteristic of the last quarter of the nineteenth century in Austria, as in many other European countries, i.e., the time when the Austrian theory of value was born; a situation next typical in Hayek's inter-war Austria (which actually had *on the average* a *declining* real national product!); and a situation which has finally again become typical over most of Europe since the beginning of the sixties. In the relatively mild decline of the pressure of final demand on supplies characteristic of the sixties, a decline due to a large extent to an increase in foreign competition, one has, however, to add a further reinforcement to get a bottleneck in finance: a great pressure of investment opportunities. If both technical progress and wage increases are particularly rapid, as they were in the sixties, even monopoloid or oligopoloid firms will be forced to supplement their possibilities of self-finance by resorting to some extent to credit, unless the demand for their products is quite unusually buoyant.

The original Hayekian entrepreneurs, on the other hand, being poor and small and in severe competition, show a more short-term oriented investment behaviour than modern large scale enterprises in a long-term need for credit. Whenever they have a sudden spate of demand they let their prices edge up on the one hand (otherwise profitability would not increase); on the other hand, they start a crash program of investment. Like the alpine flora they have to

51 N. Kaldor, 'The Economic Aspects of Advertising', *Review of Economic Studies*, 18 (1950), p. 1 ff., has, I think rightly, argued that the real situation corresponding to our concept of competition of manufactures in the nineteenth century was 'wholesalers domination' of the markets: manufacturers essentially had to produce at prices and standards wholesalers made them offer. See p. 15 ff.

blossom quickly in order to catch the brief rays of the sun of buoyant demand. Their investment program in turn at first does not affect prices of investment goods (probably producers of investment goods have free capacities; they are chronically depressed – as they were, in fact, in Austria during the inter-war period). Finally, however, investment drives prices up, too.[52] Though there is, therefore, some expansion of production and investment in real terms, a large part of the process is channeled into cumulative price increases, the larger, the higher the stages of production. Hayek thus strongly mixes *the usual quantitative accelerator process with a heavy seasoning of its price dual:* If investment demand rises, prices of investment goods are thought to spread out like a fan, the higher the stages of production. We get a cumulative build-up of prices and, even more so, of capital values, the more basic investment goods become.[53] Hayekian entrepreneurs thus have an inordinate urge to revalue their capital, a sort of stock-market mentality. It is quite likely that this behaviour was indeed to a certain extent a feature of the highly unstable Austrian economy in the inter-war period. Is it possible that, on the other hand, the apparently much more sales-maximizing bent of mind of American entrepreneurs has made the United States economists, from J. B. Clark to R. Eisner and D. Jorgenson,[54] the great adherents of the mere quantitative accelerator proper?

Hayekian entrepreneurs thus try to adjust their capital extremely quickly because apparently they calculate with the new rate of profitability while, at the same time, at the back of their mind they fear that the prosperity will be of short duration. On the other hand, the gestation period of capital goods seems to be very long: for if savings dry up, great losses occur due to the impossibility to

---

52 Sir John Hicks, 'The Hayek Story', *loc. cit.*, p. 206, is, I think, wrong, when he concludes from Wicksell that Hayek cannot let prices of investment goods move differently from consumption goods. Hayek on the one hand frequently considers the situation where investment goods have not yet found their new equilibrium price level (he is more 'Fixprice' on investment than on consumption goods). Hayek here presents short term disequilibrium analysis. But even more importantly, Sir John has missed the point that in Hayek money is *not* neutral: money creation *changes* the rate of profit and thus the price structure.

53 See *Prices and Production, loc. cit.*, p. 70 ff.

54 See D. W. Jorgenson and J. A. Stephenson, 'Investment Behaviour in U.S. Manufacturing, 1947–1960', *Econometrica*, 35 (1967), p. 169 ff. as one of the latest contributions. This article is particularly interesting to us as it starts mixing the purely quantitative accelerator with price considerations.

complete capital structures. This friction between stable expectations, rapid adaption of investment plans and long gestation periods will frequently appear to be an implausible cumulation of circumstances. Thus the more violent consequences of the Hayek process will be rare; which does not mean that it will not frequently appear in a less virulent form, as a cold instead of as pneumonia.

There is, however, one sector of the economy in which the Hayek process can exist even today in its purest form: that is *building*. In fact the whole theory was probably started by Böhm-Bawerk in the light of the building recession which struck Vienna, then just building the Ringstrasse, during the 'great depression' of the 1870s. In building it may be quite usual to plan at current prices; and to initiate new ventures when credit is cheap and plentiful.[55] Because of the length of the producton period one can, if funds dry up, observe 'uncompleted capital structures' in the most literal sense of the term. And such a thing, due to an over-optimistic extrapolation of current growth rates (!) of income – e.g. by all the ministries of education and of finance of the 'Länder' of Germany at the same time – can still occur today, as everybody knows who has been a member of a German University in 1967. If the building recession is sufficiently severe it can draw down the whole economy with it; as again in Germany in 1967.

Let us next turn to Hayek's assumptions on the effect of a change in the rate of profit on the value of capital. Hayek assumed that a rise in the rate of profit (or a lowering of wages) would unambiguously make capital goods – by and by – more valuable relative to consumption goods. This assumption, is, of course, innocent of the arguments brought out in the reswitching controversy.[56] But they are probably not of too great an empirical significance. Hayek furthermore assumed that the Wicksell structure of production would be negative (in the terminology of Mathur), i.e. roughly that productivity becomes lower and lower, the higher we go in the order of production. Mathur himself thinks[57] that this is the normal

55 See the concept of credit dependent (i.e. long-term) investment in W. Ehrlicher, *Geldkapitalbildung und Realkapitalbildung*, Tübingen 1956. See also J. S. Duesenberry, *Business Cycles and Economic Growth*, New York, Toronto, London 1958.
56 See especially M. Bruno, E. Burmeister and E. Sheshinsky, 'Nature and Implications of the Reswitching of Techniques', *Quarterly Journal of Economics*, 80 (1966), p. 526 ff. and other articles in that issue of the *QJE*.
57 Mathur, *Steady Growth*, loc. cit. p. 162.

272

case in developed economies and I have recently enlarged on his argument.[58] Thus Hayek's assumptions are probably of wide applicability.

There is another stimulating feature in Hayek's argument about the dangers of capital 'shallowing', the lowering of capital intensity when production is speeded up. According to him, too many capital goods of lowest durability are built, i.e. especially stocks; and, of course, an undue build-up of stocks, which have then to be sold at a loss, is a feature of strong business cycles: Hayek here has made an important contribution to the understanding of the stock cycle. But does not the disequilibrium prevalence of stocks also explain part of the Hayek problem that finance for expansion might run out? Fixed capital, after all, when gainfully employed, provides amortization funds applicable in the medium run to further investment. Stocks, on the other hand, as long as they are not liquidated, do *not* provide such a source of finance for further expansion!

We have seen that, from a growth-theoretical point of view, it is better to call Hayek's demand for higher savings a demand for higher investment. It is evident that there is a considerable difference between investment and consumption demand for purposes of growth. But, after all, Hayek tried to write a theory of the trade cycle. Is there perhaps even in a short-run sense a difference in consumption and investment demand which made him favour the latter over the former?

It can very well be that, quite apart from any capacity or learning effect, which investment produces, Hayek thought that consumption also had both a lower employment and a lower income multiplier than investment. Much additional consumption in a relatively underdeveloped economy, as Austria then was, might go into the products of artisans, especially in the form of services, and into the products of agriculture; and the increased income of artisans and farmers might be partly hoarded (or used for paying back heavy agricultural mortgages) and partly again spent on the products of artisans and farmers; but very rarely invested. Thus, an increase in consumption might just mean that artisans and farmers lived more opulently without creating any more employment outside their own – chronically underemployed – circle. In the terminology of growth models, consumption is thus only too likely to land in

58 E. Streissler, *Long Term Structural Changes in the Distribution of Income*, loc. cit., Ch. V.

273

a closed sub-economy without any backward or forward linkages.

Another part of additional consumption would probably seep out of the country altogether in the form of foreign travel and imports. This again causes no additional income or employment at home and brings the headache of a deficit in the balance of payments. By now, even the most inveterate English or American Keynesian has learned to distinguish between different kinds of aggregate effective demand, if only for the last named reason. Because of high imports and foreign travel expenses, balance of payments deficits were a real problem in Hayek's Austria of the inter-war years. As Austria, in contrast to the past, is now so nicely placed at the receiving end, it has for once become somewhat less fashionable than in Hayek's day to deplore the fact that consumption might seep out of the country, especially the fact that *other* people's consumption might seep out of *their* countries.

The special features of the multiplier effect of credit may also have contributed to Hayek's strictures on this instrument of expansion. It is true that he nowhere explicitly mentions the fact that credits have to be *repaid*, thereby eventually setting off a demand contracting multiplier. But was he not thinking of this aspect too? It is not sufficient that *gross* credit creation would have to proceed at a new rate in order that investment expansion continues, *net* credit creation, the expansion of new credits minus repayments has to do so; and Hayek evidently doubted that the banks would be willing to let this happen. To understand Hayek's doubt one has to consider the peculiar features of the Austrian banking system – or, indeed, many other banking systems. Banks are unwilling to transform the maturities between their deposits and their loans, wish to grant only relatively *short-term* credits, at least legally if not actually. In prosperity they may wink at a customer who wishes to use funds for longer-term investments. To reduce the risk thereby incurred they frequently insist, however, upon a speedy repayment plan. When business gets worse the particular danger of bank credit is therefore that, on the one hand, it may not be continued at all and, on the other hand, the large repayment sums (relative to the size of the original loan) can easily choke off any expenditures of an enterprise outside those for current production and repayment. All this would not have happened if enterprises had incurred long-term funded debts, if they had issued bonds. And it was exactly this *tendency towards short-term instead of long-term debts*, not only

274

among Austrian banks, but also among Austrian entrepreneurs, which was the main cause of Austria's particularly heavy financial crisis in the Great Depression, a crash occurring in 1931, the year of *Prices and Production*. Hayek's strictures on credit have, therefore, largely to be read as *strictures on unsound habits of investment finance*! Bonds would not and did not fall under his ban, because they were thought to embody 'genuine savings'; when, in fact, it would have been enough to say that they just showed the right maturity structure.

V

Let us now turn to a reapplication of Hayek's ideas to present situations. We have seen that the major weakness of his argument on the business cycle is his assumption of too rapid reactions to price changes by entrepreneurs, too rapid achievement of new equilibrium levels, which in the light of further development then appear as disastrously wrong levels. For this reason, we have to apply his analysis to relatively long-term processes,[59] disequilibrium processes to be sure, but disequilibrium in growth, disequilibrium of a long-term nature. We have to apply it e.g. to the analysis of the disequilibrating effects which the development during one decade leaves as a heritage to the next.

Such an analysis in the light of Hayek has recently been attempted for the case of Great Britain in the sixties by Sir John Hicks;[60] he did not, however, take the specific Hayek process but a close relative, a general type Hayek process, as his point of departure. As I have already pointed out, the Hayek process can be applied to *any* limiting factor of production with a cyclically varying 'technology'.

Hicks took *labour* as such a factor. Labour, just the same as credit, has a cyclical variation in its supply relative to its price: *labour-productivity increases vary over the cycle relative to wages*. When labour-productivity increases are large relative to wage increases, entrepreneurs invest and expand their production because it has become more profitable. The reason is essentially the divergence

59 It has to be remembered that when Hayek produced his theory of the trade cycle this was thought to be a relatively long term phenomenon, a nine- to eleven-year cycle, in contrast to our present (much weaker) four- to five-year cycles.
60 Hicks, 'The Hayek Story', *loc. cit.*, p. 213 ff.

between two 'rates of interest' at the core of Hayek: the rate of profit rises while there is a fall in the rate of wage increase over productivity increase (also a price with a time dimension, an 'interest' rate).[61] We might also say that, while Wicksell analyzes a divergence between the natural and the market rate of interest, Hicks gets concerned over a discrepancy between the 'natural' and the market rate of *wages*.

English trade unions, however, quickly catch up: they push up wages because of the higher profits of entrepreneurs. This, by itself, would not necessarily choke off the new expansion: an increase in prices remains to the entrepreneurs as a way out. The higher rate of inflation, however, is by itself a political headache; and it is vastly complicated by an ensuing balance of payments problem. Thus the government steps in to restrict demand and the new rate of expansion drops to its old dismal level. The stop-go policy, which in the Hayek process proper is quasi-automatically exercised by the banks – the sector which produces the limiting factor, credit – is here exercised in a very similar quasi-automatic way by the government, i.e. by another sector than that producing the limiting factor, labour, but reacting to the changes in the relative price of the limiting sector and its macro-economic consequences. The remedy which Hicks suggests is the same as that of Hayek: increased savings, so that the attempt to increase investments does not always run into the barrier of restrictive government policy, but can run its course.

I myself wish to describe another Hayek process, one closer to the original. It is meant to explain the development during the sixties relative to the fifties in Germany and Austria, but particularly in Austria. The fifties compared with the sixties stand in the relation of boom and (mild) recession, though the swing in growth rates was not very large: some 5·5 per cent average per capital growth during the fifties in both countries and some 4 per cent during the sixties, Germany having had a boom, as compared with Austria, a shade stronger – 0·1 per cent additional average growth rate – but also a markedly stronger recession – probably at least a 0·25 per cent smaller average growth rate.

61 W. Stützel has only recently stressed the importance of prices with a time dimension, generalized interest rates, in all aspects of economic analysis, in his case particularly Balance of Payments problems. Such an analysis was, of course, started by Hayek. See W. Stützel, 'Währungskrisen vermeiden lernen', *Der Volkswirt*, 22/50 (Dec. 13, 1968), p. 48 ff.

What was the limiting factor during this development? In this case there was no specific limit during the boom, certainly neither labour nor finance. These two factors became limits of expansion only during the sixties and thus provided major causes for the decline of the growth rate. In the sense of a von Neumann growth model we have therefore to say that *all sectors* were mutually limiting each other (in this system it is, of course, always difficult to point to any one sector as *the* limit).

Where were the cyclical fluctuations of production coefficients, which lie at the core of the Hayek process? Again there were many: above all there were *fluctuations in the rate of fall* of input coefficients which, in conjunction with a less varying rate of increase of wages,[62] act in the same way as fluctuating coefficients themselves. The most important feature of technology in the fifties in Germany, and especially in Austria, where due to a lack of growth in the inter-war period hardly any investments had then been made, was the introduction of radically new machines, of machines embodying from two to five decades of technical progress, a 'great leap forweard'. Evidently such a leap could not be repeated in the sixties. Wages, on the other hand, edged up relatively slowly during the fifties and only accelerated in the sixties. Rapid technical progress with slow wage increases was thus followed by slower technical progress and larger wage increases, the whole process presenting the picture of fluctuating cost coefficients.

But there were also subsidiary fluctuations in coefficients on the demand side (also 'production' coefficients in an integrated production model), e.g. (compared with the sixties) probably lower price elasticities of final demand while the restocking of households after the war lasted and also probably lower price elasticities in export demand (less competition by other exporting nations). Add to this the peculiar profitability of a system approaching sectoral equilibrium after the disequilibrium of the haphazard destruction of certain sectors during the war or the incompleted start of other sectors (the new industries partly built up by the Nazi government in Austria), a temporary movement which itself can be interpreted as a fluctuation of production coefficients (at least as far as it entailed economies of scale), add this to all the other increases in the efficiency

62 It is well known that in growth-theoretical models which allow a variation in wage levels wage increases act as negative technical progress. See e.g. Mathur, *Steady Growth, loc. cit.*, p. 266 ff.

of production, and the fact of a high rate of profit, but at a level not permanently to be held, is explained for the fifties.

What was finally the divergence in 'interest rates'? It was exactly this high rate of profit rising relative to the price of finance in general. In explaining the relative stickiness of the average price of finance we again cannot point at one sector, e.g. Hayek's banks. True, the bank rate did not rise much; but bank credit was not the most important part of finance. More important were government credits (often through the Marshall Plan), credits outside the market at low and inflexible rates of interest.[63] Most important, finally, was self-finance. And we can probably state correctly that the notional interest rate on self-finance, the rate which was considered necessary as a recompense in order not to withdraw funds, remained relatively sticky. In Austria, this was reinforced by one of the most successful investment-stimulating tax-schemes ever, Professor Kamitz' tax write-offs, which in effect gave anyone investing a large *interest free* and relatively long-term public loan, amounting, e.g., for machines to some 50 per cent of the sum invested for a period of upwards of five years.

Thus, the Hayek process could start. The investment rate rose, though probably not the capital coefficient (or the latter only on a notional basis taking account of the fact that capital is thought to be more valuable relative to production, if production is very profitable). But investment was planned relative to a very high rate of profit, which could not be maintained.

When the break came somewhere around 1961 or 1962, it was a very mild break and a very gradual break, a break due to labour bottlenecks and more rapidly rising wages, credit bottlenecks and stiffening domestic and foreign demand conditions. It therefore did not have the dramatic effect of uncompleted capital structures and business failures. It did not even have the milder consequence of unemployment – quite on the contrary. It had the mildest effect possible; but still one of greater and greater concern the more time goes on: It had the effect of a *very marked reduction in the degree of profitability* from one decade to the next. Just *because* the rate of profit was so high in the fifties and investment had been adjusted

63 In Austria government credit had, by the way, a peculiar Hayekian flavor: it was largely placed in the highest departments of production in the hope that price effects might filter down. It thus made highest order investment particularly profitable.

278

to it, this 'malinvestment' caused a *much* lower rate of profit in the sixties. Certain unused investment capacities showed up where investment – in the light of later developments – had been over-expanded particularly heavily. Furthermore, it became difficult to alter the situation: the lower levels of profits made necessary a longer use of machines, which meant a smaller rate of cost reduction and a rate of profit once again lower: what Meyer and Kuh call the 'senility effect'[64] made itself felt. In Austria the profit share in industry according to some (probably exaggerated) statistics fell on the average to hardly more than half its former level. Low profits were thus the *consequence* of high, and the *cause* of low, investment.

The Hayek process was particularly strong in Austrian industry. Expansion in the tourist industry has up to now continued practically undiminished, so that little malinvestment appeared. The still important artisan sector of the economy remained favoured by the high income elasticity of its products, which are heavily mixed with services, and thus continued to wax opulent. It was industry, which had seized the opportunities of the fifties most quickly, that became relatively depressed, just *because* it had best adapted itself to the boom.

Among industries, malinvestment was, of course, strongest where the specific growth rates had appeared highest, where the income elasticities had seemed particularly favourable, where profits were highest. Everybody remembers the long drawn out crisis of the United States motorcar industry, starting in 1957. A very similar – though weaker – crisis hit the German car industry in 1966–67: a decline in production by about one-sixth, compared with the U.S. decline of about one-third. In Austria the crisis was especially one of the state-owned but privately-managed basic industries, particularly one of steel. After having been highly profitable in the fifties and ploughing back all profits into further investment, their investment declined to very low levels in the sixties. Thus the profit decline followed exactly the Hayekian pattern, being highest in the highest stages of production.

Only in those rare firms which had *refused* to expand heavily was there no marked profit decline, even in the recession of 1967; Mercedes being a famous example. Hayek has, in fact, above all

64 J. R. Meyer and E. Kuh, *The Investment Decision – An Empirical Study*, Cambridge, Mass. 1957, p. 94 ff.

279

raised to the status of a full-scale economic theory the familiar nineteenth-century adage that the astute banker, merchant, or industrialist should not over-expand in a boom!

In contrast to the classical Hayek process, the expansion of the fifties was not fuelled by credit; it was rather fuelled by self-finance. But in the same way as the original Hayek process it had to peter out: this time the lower rate of profit, partly due to malinvestment, caused self-finance to dry up. In Austria this was reinforced by the backwash of the investment-stimulating tax-rebate scheme. Working like an interest-free loan, it had at first increased available self-finance far above profits after tax. Once these loans had to be repaid (from the early sixties onward), self-finance was throttled down to levels much more in line with the now relatively lower profits.

Upon this lower level of available self-finance a type of investment demand is pressing which does not bring about a higher immediate growth rate. Not only had the investment structure been *overextended* in a certain sense, but Hayek's second effect, the simultaneous *lowering* of capital intensity, had to some measure also taken place. Hayek, thinking in this respect of very short-term effects, argued that in rapid development stocks in particular would be overextended. A boom phase as long as the fifties could, on the other hand, not get along without an expansion of both stocks and machines. But it was a boom phase all the same with the accent on investments with a quick return: if possible, there was still a tendency to defer the most durable investments. To a certain extent industrial building, especially building for administrative purposes, was probably deferred. Such building, becoming more and more unavoidable, in the sixties then encroached to a considerable extent on shrinking profits and other means of finance. Still more, in Germany and particularly in Austria infrastructural investments, especially in roads, were deferred. Though government-financed, these too encroach upon industrial investment possibilities: they have to be financed by higher taxes which, to a certain extent, fall upon industry without possibilities of shifting.

It was, however, not only building and infrastructure which was neglected during the fifties. The most 'durable' capital and one whose instalment during crash expansion programs can most easily be postponed, is *research and development*, especially research on basically new processes. As long as demand is buoyant one can expand production of the same old hat and nothing else. Only when demand falters one has to turn to something new: then, however, in order to find that one no longer has the profit margins to sustain a long, but possibly highly rewarding search for major innovations.

Thus, the lower profit margins of the sixties were partly the result of over-investment, particularly in certain directions, and partly due to a neglect of research. The relatively low remaining profits, on the other hand, had to be used to quite a large extent for the completion of long-term 'capital structures' which had been started only in their most urgent aspects in the fifties; and to the payment of a heavier burden of tax. Little profits therefore remained in Austrian industry for starting a new equilibrium expansion. Outside finance, it is true, would have been available. But it was not taken up and this again for a particularly Hayekian reason. Hayek has stressed: 'Most individual acts of investment must be regarded . . . as mere links in a chain which has to be completed if its parts are to serve the functions for which they were intended'.[65] And for the industry of a small country like Austria most links lie abroad: the interdependence is *international*. In the clouded atmosphere of the European trade blocks, the development of which can hardly be foreseen, entrepreneurs may not have perceived the investments to which they could link up; and if they saw them, they might have doubted whether – due to some new quirk in trade policy – they would be allowed to connect up with them.

What is the cure to be recommended for this creeping growth – creeping because it was so high a decade before? For the case of Austria one shrinks from suggesting the classical remedy of Hayek: a higher investment ratio voluntarily achieved. For Austria has raised its investment ratio enormously and is still doing so: The ratio of gross investment on gross national product at current prices was 16·9 per cent in 1950, 23·7 per cent in 1960 (a rate of increase of 3·4 per cent per annum during the fifties) and 26·1 per cent in 1966 (a rate of increase of 1·6 per cent per annum during the sixties). It is probably partly *because* of this rise in investment that the Hayek process turned out as mild as it was. This conclusion is strengthened by comparison with Germany, where investment, though starting from a higher level, rose much less in the fifties and probably not at all in the sixties (ratios of 22·6 per cent in 1950,

65 F. A. von Hayek, 'Investment that Raises the Demand for Capital', *Review of Economics and Statistics*, 19 (1937), p. 174 ff., here p. 174.

26·7 per cent in 1960 and 25·8 per cent in 1966); and consequently the backlash of the fifties in the sixties was stronger.

In fact, the now Minister of Finance, Professor Koren, himself a distinguished economist and Liberal, has made the Hayekian claim that the Austrian recession in 1967 was much weaker than that in Germany (achieving a 3 per cent higher growth rate!) because the government had raised its own investment ratio.[66] This claim points to an interesting possibility of combining Keynesian and Hayekian remedies in fighting a recession by fiscal means: while the government increases effective demand by running a deficit, it should at the same time shift its expenditure from government consumption to investment, particularly to investment compensating for exactly those parts of private investment which are declining most rapidly (in the case of Austria in 1967, building). By such a policy of a simultaneous increase of the public investment ratio a floor is set under total investment. The investment ratio hardly declines in a recession and can thus continue its rise in prosperity. The cumulative adjustment of capital values feared by Hayek is largely prevented.

What is needed in the case of Austria is probably not so much higher savings or investments as a *better saving and investment structure:* savings which are willing to go into long-term private enterprise ventures and into risky ventures; investments which are ploughed into research and development and into the creation of new industries.

VI

After this essay in short-term Hayekian growth economics, let us now turn to long-term growth. Here we have to rely even more specifically upon Hayek's theory of the capital structure.

Where can we nowadays find a system of capital inputs with myopic planning geared to present prices? with an extremely long gestation period in the production of capital goods, so that short-sighted planning is dangerous? with a high degree of irreversibility of the production processes started, i.e. with specific capital goods of long durability? Where can we finally find long-term divergences between cost and demand price, which, due to the difficulties of production, can persist in spite of the fact that they cannot last for

66 *Der Koren Plan*, Vienna 1968, p. 13.

282

ever? The answer to all these questions is simple: in the production of the capital good with the longest gestation period of all goods and with one of the highest degrees of durability and specificity, in the production of *human capital*. Thus Hayek's theory of capital in its most full-scale development finds its most fruitful application today in the *analysis of the problems of qualified labour, of the economics of education.*

In human capital we find all the features of the Hayek process. The 'lengthening of the period of production' is here evident to even the least perspicacious observer. But this lengthening does not proceed at a constant rate. If very profitable opportunities for quick employment at an early age present themselves (e.g. in Germany and Austria in the late forties and early fifties) the average lengthening of the period of production may even be reversed for a short time: 'consumption', so to speak, takes the place of investment. An increase in the length of educational investment is – apart from changes in the state-aid system – probably largely due to changes in the savings of parents. Any speed-up in the accumulation of educational capital will show the opening of the price fan,[67] described by Hayek: 'Capital goods of the highest order', e.g., university professors, will achieve the highest increases in price. We have witnessed this development in the early sixties in Germany and also to hardly a lesser extent in the United States. Before that we have seen it in particular fields of application: rare 'investment goods of a high order', e.g. creative scientists, investment goods which are needed for the 'completion of certain capital structures', will achieve great salary increases.

In spite of the increase in qualified labour long-term divergences between cost and demand price may persist. Already many decades ago, it had been shown that certain types of education 'pay' and certain others do not (rates of return on educational investment are quite different).[68] And it is interesting to note that low returns in one period can very well be followed by high returns in another: they can cause a 'hog cycle'. It will certainly amuse any American reading his figures nowadays that, for the U.S.A. of the thirties, Walsh found doctors *underpaid*;[69] today they certainly are not!

67 See Hayek, *Prices and Production, loc. cit.*, p. 73 ff.
68 J. R. Walsh, 'Capital Concept, Applied to Man', *Quarterly Journal of Economics*, 49 (1935), p. 255 ff.
69 *ibid.*, p. 268 ff.

283

Malinvestments in the field of vocational training are thus very likely; the most glaring example probably being the surfeit of German sociologists who find nothing to do but to revolt.

Just as obvious are Hayek's inverse changes of capital intensities when the period of production lengthens. Crash programs of education will show the same substitution of labour for *material* capital as other crash programs of investment. A good example is the German university expansion in the early sixties. First the number of students increased (higher consumption demand). This was followed by an increase in the number of professors – at rising prices: these were, relative to university education (though not to education in general), the investment goods of the lowest order. (One of those investment goods of lowest order was Professor von Hayek, wafted over to Freiburg in Germany from Chicago, another the author, simultaneously coming from Vienna.) After some time the reservoir of budding teachers in the German system, the number of assistants, was increased too; they are chiefly investment goods of a higher order, but were partly also substitutes for the lower order professors. Finally one found that in the rapid expansion of higher education one had neglected university building: the completion of this costliest part of the 'capital structure' was found to be peculiarly difficult and, in fact, brought about a serious dislocation in 1967. 'Uncompleted structures' in the most literal sense could be seen on most German campuses. The lack of building space and the lack of young teachers and assistants in this disequilibrium expansion process provides one of the reasons for today's revolts in German universities.

But the 'shallowing' of capital in education booms can also appear in the structure of human capital itself. The self-same German boom has brought about the call for a three-year crash program of education for secondary-school teachers, instead of the normal seven years (admittedly too long). More and more teachers with a thin veneer of university education or with no university training at all are made to teach in secondary schools – again at relatively rising prices. Both the lowering of the standard of products which they turn out and their own over-supply in the near future have by now become evident.

What is the cure for these educational difficulties? How can higher levels of education be efficiently achieved? What are the skills and professions whose education we should try to force most?

To these questions very rough-and-ready answers are given nowadays. The most sophisticated answer in 'educational planning' is the application of an input-output analysis of labour qualities needed relative to a given production structure, projected 'appropriately' into the future.[70] But is this analysis not just the misallocation, the creation of malinvestment which Hayek described and feared with a vengeance? Does this not mean making forecasts in terms of present trends in demand – and therefore in terms of present, frequently distorted, prices (in the widest sense)? Does this not mean that the mistake the market tends to make anyhow is raised to the status of an absolute dogma? If we wish to point out educational priorities at all – and not let the market for education settle down in good time and undisturbed in its own equilibrium – should we not at least attempt to use Hayek's idea of the *different* structure of 'production' to be expected when the rapidity of the present increase in the average length of education has slowed down?

70 See e.g. H. R. Widmaier, *Bildung und Wirtschaftswachstum, Eine Modellstudie zur Bildungsplanung (im Auftrag des Kultusministeriums Baden-Württemberg)*, Villingen 1966.

Appendix

A striking verification of Hayek's thesis that, with declining growth, investment switches away from a build-up of stocks to more durable kinds of capital is provided for Western Germany by data of the 'Sachverständigenrat', Jahresgutachten 1968/69 (*Alternativen außenwirtschaftlichen Gleichgewichts*, Stuttgart – Mainz), pp. 121, 128:

Period	Average Growth Rate (%) of Real GNP	Average Shares (%) in Entrepreneurial Investment of		
		Changes in Stocks	Equipment	Buildings
1950–54[1]	9·5[2]	17·8	65·3	16·9
1955–59[1]	6·9	12·9	66·6	20·5
1960–63	5·4	8·8	69·4	21·8
1964–67	4·0	3·2	72·8	24·0

1 Without the Saar and Berlin.   2 1951–55.

285

The New Theory of Corporations
Gordon Tullock

One of the more immutable of the immutable economic laws is that every sentence in the *Wealth of Nations* will eventually become a book. Smith, of course, did not like corporations because he felt that they would be management controlled rather than under the control of the stockholders.

> The trade of a joint stock company is always managed by a court of directors. This court, indeed, is frequently subject in many respects to the control of a general court of proprietors, but the greater part of those proprietors seldom pretend to understand anything of the business of the company and when the spirit of faction happens not to prevail give themselves no trouble about it, but receive contentedly such half yearly or yearly dividends as the directors think proper to make them. . . . The directors of such companies, however, being the managers of other people's money than their own, it cannot well be expected they should watch over it with the same anxious vigilance which partners in a private co-partnery frequently watch over their own. Like the stewards of a rich man they are apt to consider attention to small matters as not for their master's honor and very easily give themselves the dispensation from having it. Negligence and profusion, therefore, must always prevail more or less in the management of the affairs of such a company.[1]

In the nineteenth century a rather badly-articulated theory developed under which a corporation was thought of as a democracy controlled by the stockholders in much the same way that government was controlled by the voters.

The modern orthodoxy returns to Adam Smith and has produced

1 Adam Smith, *The Wealth of Nations*, pp. 699–700.

287

the volumes of books necessary to illustrate the immutable law. A political scientist has made the best statement of the conventional wisdom:

For some time [at least three decades] this (the democratic) theory has been untenable in the light of common knowledge about the realities of corporate life. The now classic work of Berle and Means exploded the idea that ownership meant control in the large corporations of America. Their demonstration of the actual separation of these factors created a sensation, but the demonstration withstood attack and in any event only confirmed what many observers had long sensed. The sheer size of the significant American corporations and the minute fractions of total stockholding that any one owner might possess made obsolete the idea of simple control by ownership [except in a very few corporations, notably the Ford Motor Company]. The development of numerous legal devices and the control of the proxy machine by management made a mockery of any belief that management could readily be challenged by any faction of the corporate citizenry. Proxy fights occurred during the period following World War II in somewhat greater numbers than Berle and Means expected but they remained exceptional.

The question of control once raised proved a Pandora's box.[2]

The theory of management control of corporations, of course, is subject to one very obvious difficulty. It offers no explanation of how managements are changed, and changes of management are an everyday occurrence as any reader of the *Wall Street Journal* can appreciate. It is true that presidents of large corporations frequently stay in office rather longer than the president of the United States, but they don't stay in office as long as congressmen and senators, and we would hardly argue that the long tenure of congressmen and senators indicates that we do not have democracy in the United States. Thus, the current orthodoxy that the management actually runs the corporation cannot explain how the management got there or how the everyday occurrence of a change in management occurs. For some reason, this does not seem to disturb the partisans of the Smith, Berle and Means theory.

2 Grant McConnell, *Private Power in American Democracy*, New York 1967, pp. 130–131.

288

Before attempting to solve this problem, let us turn to another current of recent research which is frequently believed to reinforce the thesis of Smith *et al*. This additional line of reasoning involves pointing out that most human beings are utility maximizers rather than income maximizers and that the managers of a firm presumably have some ends other than maximizing the income of the firm itself. Thus, one would anticipate that they would do certain things which are to their own benefit rather than that of the firm if they were permitted to do so. This line of reasoning which is associated with the name of Armen Alchian is perhaps best expressed in Oliver E. Williamson's *The Economics of Discretionary Behavior? The Managerial Objectives in a Theory of a Firm*.[3]

Williamson first develops a theory of the method in which managers could be anticipated to seek out items which benefit them rather than a corporation, then undertakes some empirical investigations indicating that the phenomenon does in fact exist. This would be evidence that the corporation was under the control of the management rather than the stockholders were it not for certain other research partly done by Williamson and partly by others. This additional research indicates that the degree of management deviation from profit maximizing is higher in regulated utilities than it is in unregulated businesses and higher yet in things like the Savings and Loan Associations,[4] where the ownership is vested in people who are not responsible to stockholders at all. If we assume that the stockholders do have some influence, then this line of regression is understandable. Clearly, they would have no influence on the Savings and Loan, and thus we would expect a great deal of management utility maximizing. In the case of the utilities they have some influence, but in general the utility commissions permit many 'expenses' to be added on to the rate, so stockholders have no great motive for trying to cut costs, although they have some. Last, but by no means least, in unregulated companies they have a positive interest in maximizing profits. Thus, if we assume that stockholders do have some influence, this difference in the amount of management diversion of resources which we observe would be explained.

The second thing which we must note here is that Williamson's figures seem to indicate that only a very tiny amount of the gross

3 Englewood Cliffs, N.J. 1964.
4 Alfred Nicols, 'Stock versus Mutual Savings and Loan Associations: Some Evidence of Differences in Behavior', *American Economic Review*, 57 (1967), pp. 337–46.

income of a company (or indeed of its nett) is characteristically tapped by the management for the purposes of its own utility rather than that of the stockholders. This would be understandable if we assume that the stockholders are in general control of the company, but their supervision is not completely perfect. It is hard to explain, however, on the grounds that the management is actually in control of the company as McConnell argued. Since no human organization controls its subordinate members absolutely perfectly, some slippage, some ability of the managers to obtain things that they want should be anticipated. In many ways what is remarkable about the corporation is how small this amount is. The existence of such a slippage does not necessarily indicate that the Smith, Berle and Means thesis is correct. It could readily be explained as just the nature of any organization. We would have to find out for certain that the management of corporations diverts to its own use a higher percentage of the resources of that corporation than does (let us say) the president's secretary to her own use of the resources which are available to her.[5]

But so far I have merely been pointing out the difficulties in the Smith, Berle and Means thesis. The contrary thesis would appear to be subject to even greater difficulties. This contrary thesis, as I mentioned before, has traditionally not been very well articulated. The proponents of the corporate democracy argument first assume that there is democratic control by the stockholders over the corporation. In view of the rarity of contested elections of management in corporations, this superficially seems a little difficult to accept. Secondly, they normally engage in a great deal of what we may call philosophizing about the corporation [and in recent years the diversified conglomerate corporation] as being a great social invention which has led to much of our present economic progress. In general this discussion has not been, until very recently, either sophisticated or detailed enough so that one can say for certain whether the people who offer these arguments have really thought them through. It is the purpose of this article to argue that the rather badly expressed 'philosophy' is right and that the thesis put forward by Smith, Berle and Means is wrong.[6]

5 Anyone who has had much contact with presidents' secretaries would predict that the contrary would come out of this empirical research, although so far as I know no one has undertaken it.
6 Note that, in general, I will discuss only the situation in the United States. This

290

Before going further, however, I should explain that a very large part of the reasoning which will follow is not original with me. It is to a very considerable extent the work of Professor Henry Manne. Unfortunately, Manne has never produced his *General Theory of Corporations*. In a sense, I have learned of his position from detailed discussions with him and am now producing a summary of a book that has not yet been written.[7] In keeping with the tradition that scholars may not publish anything which is not at least in part original, I will add into the general argument drawn from Professor Manne some points of my own. Generally speaking, however, the remainder of this article will be a presentation of Professor Manne's unpublished work.

If the thesis outlined in this article is correct, then the most widely held modern theory of corporations is wrong and a rather vague argument normally put forward by businessmen rather than economists is correct. Further, the people who advanced this 'democratic' theory in general did not seem to understand it fully before the work of Manne. This raises a problem, and in order to explain how a system which its own proponents did not seem to understand could be correct I should like to begin by referring to Professor Hayek's pamphlet, 'The Confusion of Language in Political Thought'.[8] In this pamphlet it is pointed out that an organization can be something that is designed or it can be something which is formed spontaneously. The Greek word *cosmos* is used for the latter type of order. It is my argument that the present American corporation system is an example of a *cosmos*. Although it is perfectly true that a great many people have made deliberate rational choices in the selection of institutional arrangements or in efforts to operate the institutional arrangements, there is no evidence that they thought of themselves as designing the general system. The general system has come out of a large number of independent decisions.

7 Note that the argument to be outlined below is only a part, and perhaps not by any means the most important part, of Manne's contribution. In particular, I leave out completely all the discussion of the role of information in the operation of a corporation and in the compensation of its managers.

8 Institute of Economic Affairs, Occasional Paper no. 20, London 1968. The particular portion of the paper relevant here is sharpening of reasoning which can be found running through many things done by Hayek in earlier years.

is not because I feel the United States is necessarily a model for all other societies, but simply because I am ignorant of the situation outside of the United States.

291

But the theory that the corporate order in the United States has simply grown and is not the result of design is subject to two immediate objections. The first of these is that all corporations are organized under corporation acts and the legislatures which enacted the corporation acts must necessarily have some idea in mind. Thus, using again Hayek's use of the Greek terms, it could be argued that it is a *taxis* or a designed social organization instead of a *cosmos* or something which just developed. If we look more deeply, however, we discover that in the United States corporations have, on occasion, been organized in states where there was no corporation act. The corporation acts themselves were very generally written by legislatures whose principal objective was to increase the number of corporations registered in their particular state and hence to increase the fees. Thus these acts were, generally speaking, written with the specific objective of giving the organizers of the corporations as much freedom as possible with the idea of attracting them. The aim of the corporation committee of each legislature has not been to design a national corporation system but to attract to that state some of the national corporations. Hence, they were not designing a corporation system. Indeed, it seems likely that the rules requiring certain types of organization before a stock can be listed on the New York Stock Exchange had much more effect on the American corporate structure than the corporation acts. The Stock Exchange is, of course, private.

The second criticism of my statement (that the development of the corporation was an example of *cosmos* rather than *taxis*) is that the corporation law is administered by the courts and they must have some idea in mind. As far as we can find out, however, the courts have gradually over time developed an interesting distinction in corporations which has never been expressed by them at all. In fact, Henry Manne seems to have been the first person to have noted its existence. Corporations that are small enough so that their stock is not readily tradeable are treated by the courts in many ways rather like a partnership with limited liability. The courts permit them to have internal agreements among stockholders which are directly contrary to what the corporation act would appear to require. These have as their normal objective the protection of a minority interest. On the other hand, large corporations where the individual stockholder who feels himself aggrieved by the behavior of his company can readily get rid of his stock are characteristically

292

held to strict observance of majority rule. There is no evidence that the court in developing this distinction (which is in fact more or less the creation of two separate corporation laws) ever gave any general thought to the principle involved. They were simply confronted with a number of practical situations, and in each case reached decisions which seemed to them equitable under the circumstances. The distinction is frequently formalized in European Corporation Law.

Thus, we do have a government body, but it is not a government body which is acting according to plan. The individual judges making individual decisions with respect to specific problems have ended up with what is in fact a fairly rational arrangement. Under present circumstances small corporations are, except that they have limited liability, essentially very much like a partnership in the sense that almost any organizational structure is permissible. Since the people with whom they deal know that they have limited liability and presumably take precautions, this permits the mobilization of small quantities of funds for small operations without imposing upon these small organizations an organizational pattern which is not suitable for them. With large organizations, on the other hand, an almost totally different social structure, the publicly held corporation, exists. The fact that both of these characteristically are registered in the same corporation act and bear the same name should not obscure the fact that we have here two quite radically different types of organization. For the remainder of this article I will discuss the publicly held corporation.

Before discussing how the present corporation works, however, it is necessary to devote a little thought to the details of the Smith, Berle and Means attack on the corporation.[9] Suppose that I have my choice between two types of investment. I can put a certain sum of money into a store which I will then own and manage, or I can buy some stock in a corporation. If I buy the stock in a corporation, I will presumably use the return I obtain on that stock entirely for my own gratification. This gratification might, of course, involve saving some and re-investing it. If, on the other hand, I choose to operate the store itself it is likely that I will not only use the

9 The discussion by Smith is clearly an attack and the Berle and Means discussion of the corporation was also an attack in its first version. Recently, there seems to have been a change here. Berle has been arguing that it has been a good thing that the management controls the corporation rather than the stockholder. Since I do not think that most stockholders would agree with Berle, I will stick to the view that he is engaging in an attack.

monetary returns from the store for my own gratification, but I may also obtain some utility from various things that I do in the management of the store. I may hire a beautiful secretary who is not the best and cheapest typist.

Surely, Smith knew that I could do this in the case of my own property and did not object, but what he objected to in essence was that my hired manager (in the event that I am owner of the stock in a corporation) might maximize his own utility instead of the utility of the ultimate owner. It is by no means obvious that this should in and of itself be regarded as objectionable. Suppose that we have two enterprises. One is a sole proprietorship, and the sole proprietor has hired a relatively inefficient beautiful girl as his secretary. The second is a publicly-held corporation, and the president has hired a beautiful girl who is a relatively incompetent typist as his secretary. I am at a loss to see why, from the standpoint of the community as a whole, we would regard one of these situations as more undesirable than the other. In both cases the monetary profit will be lower than otherwise, and in both cases the management will be receiving some non-monetary return. Indeed, it is likely that sole proprietors spend more of their income in this type of 'utility generation' than do managers of corporations. It is not at all obvious that society has any motive to regard this generation of utility by the manager as in any way inferior to that of the individual owner.

We need here a more subtle distinction than simply between profit maximizing and utility maximizing. After all, the individual owner (or for that matter the stockholder) engages in profit maximizing in order to maximize his utility. If the individual owner chooses to hire a beautiful but incompetent secretary, presumably this is a way of getting on the Pareto frontier. He prefers the presence of the blonde to the monetary saving he could get from a more efficient, if less beautiful, secretary. Further, if we assume that the manager of a corporation has complete control over the corporation, which is more or less what Berle and Means (or at least some of their followers) have assumed, then to all intents and purposes they are in the same position as the stockholder in the traditional theory of the corporation. If they merely pay a certain dividend to the stockholders, as Smith said, then they are the residual owners themselves. There seems no obvious reason why we should object to this.

One might inquire, however, why it is that these managers who arc in complete control of the corporation choose to take out their 'power' in additional consumption of leisure and laziness under the Smith set of criticism or in hiring beautiful secretaries in the way we have described rather than simply increasing their salaries. Clearly, the present managers of United States Steel could, if they are really in control of the corporation, pay themselves perhaps a hundred times their present salary without difficulty. We do not observe this, and I think the explanation is that Smith, Berle and Means really did not mean to imply that the corporate management truly ran the corporation. What they meant to imply was that the actual stockholders are not perfectly efficient in supervising the managers. Being in control of the corporation but not 100 per cent efficient in supervising it, the stockholders are able to prevent the management from increasing its monetary compensation without limit. They are not, however, able to see whether the management spends a little bit too much here and there on its own amenities, or whether the management really works as hard as they would like. Thus, the situation is not necessarily Pareto-optimal. The manager hires a beautiful blonde secretary because he knows he can get away with that, but if he simply pocketed the cost to the corporation of hiring her rather than a more efficient secretary he would probably be in trouble. Nevertheless, cases of this sort are essentially bargaining problems. Further, it would seem a very small matter. Certainly it is not something which we need to regard as a problem of public policy.

To make sense of the Smith, Berle and Means objection to managerial activity of this sort, we must turn from consideration of society in general to examination of the interests of the stockholders. Speaking as a stockholder, I certainly would much prefer that my management worked harder and took less compensation, whether in the form of money or amenities. In practice it might not make much difference. In 'The Influence of Ownership and Control on Profit Rates', D. R. Kamerschen[10] reports an empirical investigation of the profits of American corporations. He found no relationship between the Berle and Means type of 'Management control' and profits. But if we are simply considering the desires of the stockholders, we are hard put to criticize the corporation system. The stockholders have chosen to invest in the corporation because

10 *American Economic Review*, 58 (1968), pp. 432–447.

it improves their utility to a larger extent than does the active management of the business. Indeed, Smith and Berle and Means emphasize this point. They point out that the stockholders reduce the amount of time which they devote to management of these funds to almost zero. Smith, in particular, feels that owners should work hard in detailed management of their investments. But this is inconsistent with Smith's general position. Why not, instead of managing a company directly and getting some utility out of hiring a beautiful secretary, let someone else manage it and get some utility out of the leisure thus obtained?

We can, at this time, point out that the corporate professional management may well be specially trained and more highly talented in management than is the average person who has money to invest. Thus, even if we could somehow prove that the corporate managers were less highly motivated than was the stockholder (and my own impression is that the contrary is true in most modern corporations), superior skill might still be a more important consideration. There is, of course, the further asset of the possibility of mobilizing the capital in a corporation, but here we are going off into what one might refer to as the traditional explanation of corporations. The real question is one of efficiency.

Here we may, again, turn to Professor Hayek's paper cited above. In his terminology, the corporate system would be a *cosmos*, and the individual corporations (since they are consciously set up) would be a *taxis*. On page fifteen of his pamphlet he discusses the need for using general rules in a *taxis* and says:

> The reason why an organization must to some extent rely on rules and not be directed by particular commands only also explains why a spontaneous order can achieve results which organizations cannot. By restricting actions of individuals only by general rules they can use information which the authority does not possess. Agencies to which the head of an organization delegates functions can adapt to changing circumstances known only to them and therefore the commands of the authority will generally take the form of general instructions rather than a specific order.

Clearly if we could establish the single general rule: 'make as much money as you can', then the stockholders could maximize the return on their investment and also get the additional advantage of leisure.

296

They could, also, avert some risk to their investment by spreading it over a number of different investments instead of one without having this result in the management being relatively inexpert in each individual field. As a stockholder, I can have a number of experts work for me.

I think the substance of the Smith, Berle and Means objection to the corporation is simply that this general rule (make as much money as you can) is not entirely adhered to by the managements, but this (even if true) is by no means a conclusive argument. I might well prefer to invest in a corporation even though I knew that the management was less efficient than my own direct management would be because of the advantages which the corporate form brings to me. Under these circumstances the cost of the use of the corporate form would include a certain amount of inefficiency. I would take these costs into account and would thus end up with the type of investment which seemed to me best. It might, or might not, lead to the choice of a corporation, just as the choice of a machine does not normally turn on whether the machine is perfect. We are interested in comparative efficiency, not in attempting to obtain a utopian perfection.

The real problem, then, raised by the critics of the corporation is simply that the stockholders are not obtaining theoretically perfect performance from their managers. This has been exaggerated into alleging that the stockholders get nothing out of the managers, but it is very hard to explain such things as dividends (or, for that matter, stock appreciation) under this approach.

Let us, then, turn to the remedies which are available to the stockholder if he becomes dissatisfied with the corporation. Firstly, of course, there is the derivative suit. Let us suppose that the Board of Directors of United States Steel decided to pass the dividend in order to devote the entire profits to building themselves a set of private yachts, homes in Brazil, and Swiss bank accounts. This would be a clear and easy case for a suit by some stockholders representing the whole against the Board of Directors, and there is no doubt that they would collect.

Secondly, and in my opinion more importantly, there is the proxy fight. Since the proxy fight is relatively rare in the modern world, its importance is (I think) frequently overlooked. Again suppose the Board of Directors did something which would reduce the profits to the stockholder, but which might nevertheless be looked upon with

297

some approval by the court system. As an example, let us suppose they decided to devote regularly half their profits to the Poverty Program. I take it that they would be removed with great speed by the stockholders. Stockholder proxy fights are rare to a considerable extent because the threat of them is so omnipresent that an open disregard of the stockholder is almost never seen. The management of a corporation must (and it has considerable facilities for this) keep the fact secret that it is not solely engaged in maximizing the well-being of the stockholder. The moment that it begins to permit the stockholders to realize that there is some deviation of their resources into the pockets of the management,[11] the management is in danger. In considering these two methods of dealing with management which does not have the interest of the stockholders whole-heartedly in mind, we are immediately reminded of the problem of the public good. Any individual stockholder is unlikely to take action because the return to him is proportional to his stock while the return to the entire community of stockholders is vastly greater.[12] As Paul Samuelson has taught us, in those cases where there is a public good we cannot expect private persons to invest very many resources in producing the good. Thus, one would anticipate there would be a comparative under-investment of resources in finding out what the management is doing and then taking action against it.

This under-investment may well be what the critics of the corporation have in mind. If this is so, however, it should be noted that exactly the same effect applies to political democracy. Indeed, the average stockholder of United States Steel probably has a stronger motive for becoming informed about the behavior of United States Steel than he does as a voter for the American government.

Thus the traditional 'corporate democracy' model is in this case closely approximated. It might be nice if we could attain a mechanism under which supervision was free of the problem of the public good. I think most people would agree, however, that it would be more desirable to obtain this for the government than to obtain it for the individual corporation. The restriction on the efficiency of the stockholder for voter supervision raised by the problem of the public

11 Beyond the compensation necessary to hire management of equivalent quality.
12 Those lawyers who specialize in derivative suits, of course, have very strong reason for entering into such situations.

298

good does mean that the management will not be overwhelmingly efficient. Clearly, it could, for example, not work very hard, run up the costs around its headquarters by improving office conditions, hiring friends as sub-managers, etc. Indeed, the empirical evidence indicates that managers do just this to some extent.

If, however, we observe the behavior of corporations we quite frequently find that there are changes in the personnel of the Board of Directors or of the higher management which do not seem to be the result of any direct proxy fight. To a considerable extent these changes, insofar as they are not routine retirements, can be explained in terms of the dissatisfaction with the performance of the company by either the stockholders or by certain fiduciaries. Let us suppose a corporation which has several large stockholders (each one holding, let us say, five or six million dollars worth of stock) and the rest of the stock dispersed in small amounts throughout the community. If these large stockholders all became dissatisfied with the management, it would be fairly obvious to the other stockholders that this dissatisfaction was justified.

The small stockholders would realize that they do not know very much about the corporation, but that the big stockholders in general have the same interest as the small stockholders and considerable additional information. Thus, the small stockholders would be readily motivated to vote with the large stockholders if the large stockholders *as a block* became dissatisfied with the management. Note that this does not require the large stockholders to hold any particular percentage of the total stock outstanding. All that is required is that they be united and that their individual stockholdings be large enough so that the smaller stockholders could safely assume that the larger stockholders were (a) well informed about the corporation and (b) primarily interested in increasing its value.

In general, a proxy fight by the united large stockholders would be fairly simple and straightforward. It would only be if the management also had some large stockholders on its side, some people who could say with equal plausability, 'We are worried about our investment, and don't want the new management in,' that the large collection of small stockholders might split. Under these circumstances control of the proxy mechanism might be of great importance. As a consequence, if one looks at corporations, one normally finds that the larger stockholders are either directly represented on the Board of Directors, or at least are listened to with great attention by the Board of Directors. If they become unhappy, they can change the Board of Directors and the management quite readily. Since they have strong motives to keep the corporation functioning relatively efficiently, one can anticipate that they will take advantage of this opportunity. Once again the problem of the public good would indicate that the resource they would invest in supervising this company would be less than if they owned all the stock. Still, they will invest enough resources so that the management cannot engage in more than minimal diversion of resources from the stockholders to its own utility.

Under present circumstances, of course, the existence of a certain number of large individual stockholders is greatly re-enforced by the existence of a very large number of fiduciary stockholders. There are many institutions in our society (banks, investment trusts, pension funds, etc.) which have large holdings of common stock. The directors of these agencies are normally not very much interested in the management of any given corporation, but they are interested in maximizing returns on their investment. They are apt to be critical judges of management performance and to feel that 'shake-ups' of relatively unsuccessful managements are desirable. Note that both of the factors we have been discussing so far mean that managements are in danger if their profits are less than expected. This would be so even if their poor return is just bad luck.

Managements worry a great deal about the present price of their stock, and maximizing present value is the obvious objective of the shareholders. We shall shortly indicate that there is another reason (an even stronger reason) why they should worry about this, but so far it should be noted that even using a model which only deals with existing stockholders the management is well advised to make as much money as it can. Naturally, I am not alleging that managements are solely and entirely devoted to making the highest possible profit for the stockholders. I am simply pointing out that they are under considerable pressure to increase profits. Further, the more money it can make the safer the management is. The less money it makes, the more likely it is to be thrown out.

We may here temporarily pause to consider two possible reasons why management might not be doing as well as the stockholders would wish. The first of these reasons would be that the management is diverting to increasing its own utility resources which could be devoted to the firm's profit. It is to be assumed that at least a small amount of this goes on in all large organizations, and one of the objectives of the corporate organization is simply to keep this factor minor. The second reason why the profits might be low is that the management is genuinely inefficient in the sense that it lacks the necessary talents to take advantage of profit opportunities, cut costs, etc. The second can be dealt with only by removing the present management and putting a new one in. But the stock-holders need not concern themselves greatly with which of these two reasons is the cause of a poor performance of their company. Firing the present management will cure either of them. If the poor performance of the company is a matter of bad luck, on the other hand, firing will do no good; but there is no obvious reason to believe it will do much harm. Thus, 'shaking up' the management whenever the profits are a little lower than anticipated is probably a good and simple rule.

But so far we have been talking about methods by which the existing stockholders can change the management of companies. This is, in a way, the *ultima ratio regum* of the corporation, but it should be realized that more often than not changes in corporation management take another route. There are people and organiza-tions in the world today who are (at least in part) in the business of making money by obtaining control of poorly-managed corporations and converting the management to a more profit-oriented approach. This raises the capital value of the corporation and, hence, the stock purchased to obtain control. As an example, we may note what happened to American Motors a year or so ago. The management was apparently thought by certain outsiders (notably Mr. Chapin) to be inefficient and the stock was certainly selling well below its high. Mr. Chapin and some of his friends proceeded to buy a quite large block of stock.

Note when I say 'quite' large I do not mean that they bought 51 per cent or even 5 per cent. They simply bought enough stock so that improved management of the company would redound to their benefit. They also, of course, called the attention of various fiduciary stockholders to their view that the management was inefficient. As a result the corporation was re-organized and Mr. Chapin became president. In this particular case he has been unable to work a miracle, but this may simply indicate that he was wrong in believing that the corporation was badly managed. It may have been the natural state of the market that forced the corporation value down. At any event, the previous corporation management was displaced because its profits were low.

This type of activity is quite widespread in the United States. There are individuals like Mr. Wolfson, families like the Rockefellers, and indeed corporations that are engaged in this particular activity. If one can find a corporation, the management of which is diverting any significant part of the returns of the corporation to maximizing its own utility rather than to increasing the value of the stock, then very large profits can be made from displacing that management. Since the managements know this, this particular problem is unlikely to arise. It is, however, true that frequently the problem is not that the management is diverting money but is simply inefficient. In this case, again, very large profits can be made by eliminating the incompetents and putting in more skilled operators. Both types of activity occur.

As another technique which is rather more common in England than in the United States, there is the take-over bid. Some individual or corporation offers to the stockholders of a corporation a price, normally above the current market value of their stock, provided only that a fixed percentage (almost uniformly more than 51 per cent) of the stock is tendered to the purchaser before some particular date. Once again, this technique presents a real hazard to managements which are either inefficient or are diverting the resources of the corporation from the stockholders. The last, however, and certainly the most common of all of these techniques, is the merger of the inefficient company with a more efficient management unit, frequently but not always a conglomerate. In this case the inefficient management usually has some elements of control over whether or not the merger goes through. As a result it is normally paid off by the new management in the sense that the members of the to-be-displaced management are guaranteed sinecures after the merger. It should be noted, however, that the degree to which the existing management can keep a new management from merging into the corporation is greatly limited by the availability of the techniques for seizing control which we have described before.

But let us pause and sum up what we have said so far about the control of the stockholders over their management. Note that I have not argued that the stockholders engage in any detailed supervision of the company. In general, there will be stockholders who are motivated to obtain detailed information on the company, or there will be certain outsiders who are motivated to obtain information on many corporations with the idea of becoming major stockholders in those cases where the present management is not coming fairly close to maximizing the value of the stock. In general, due to problems of the public good, the resources they are willing to invest in this activity are not as great as those which would be invested by the stockholders acting as a block. Nevertheless, the management is confronted with a risk schedule.

In general, the higher the profit it can make, the less likely it is that it will suddenly find itself displaced. On the other hand, as profits go down the chance of being displaced increases. Further, high profits at any given time are apt to get capitalized into the value of the stock so that it is necessary for the management that wishes to be really safe to improve continuously its profit returns. Litton Industries recently suffered what almost all of the commentators referred to as a stockmarket disaster, not because the management produced losses or because it did not make a good profit, but simply because in one six-month period (for the first time in the history of the company) the profit was no larger than it had been in the previous six-month period.

But this structure, in which risks of replacement of management are fairly low if the profits are high and rising, and quite high if they are low or declining, does not completely control management. It simply puts a premium on efficiency which varies inversely with the profit. Thus, we would anticipate that we would find more of the 'gravy' in very profitable corporations than in less profitable corporations. Examination of the data seems to indicate that we do.[13] Further, one would anticipate that whenever a corporation finds itself in difficulties, i.e. its profits begin to go down, higher management would put the 'squeeze' on those activities which may reduce the profits of the stockholders. Once again, we find that this is so. In general, however, we can feel confident that the total amount that is diverted from benefiting the stockholder to benefiting the management must always be quite small. The reason for this is simply that the management risk is proportional to the percentage of the total income which is so diverted.

Still, it is fairly clear that the individual corporation management

13 Williamson, *op. cit.*

303

does have some possibility of reducing the return of the shareholders in order to improve its own utility,[14] just as lower level officials can, to some extent, avoid strict compliance with the orders of their superiors. But recent organizational developments in the American corporate system are probably sharply reducing even this amount of discretion on the part of the management. It is by no means obvious that this is the reason which has led to these developments, but once again a *cosmos* may change in a way which leads to ends which are no person's intention. The first of these new developments has been the steady and continuous development of more and more investment trusts, together with the fact that the investment trusts have in recent years become extremely competitive. Each investment trust now is pressed by the so-called 'go-go' funds to make a really good return. Further, newspapers publish statements as to what the returns of various funds are. Under these circumstances, the managements of these funds are impelled (in order to make their own profits)[15] to back any proposal to improve the efficiency of any corporation in which they have large amounts of stock.

Secondly, if they observe a situation in which improvements could be made, they may buy stock for the purpose of making improvements. I must say, however, that in both of these fields, as far as I can see, the investment trusts have not played a very active role. Normally, they have waited for other people to observe the desirability of changing mangement and then have simply followed the specialized entrepreneurs. The investment trusts apparently regard their primary expertise as predicting future behavior on the market rather than as improving corporate managements. They are willing to give their full co-operation to anyone who wished to improve the management, but they don't do it themselves. This may change in the future. Still, the existence of these very large holders of corporate securities who are interested in getting the last penny out of their stock does mean that the managers of the operating corporations are subject to considerable pressures for efficiency. It is not necessary for anyone to obtain anything near control of a

14 Once again, this is above and beyond the amount of utility that is necessary to attract a suitably competent management.
15 Due to the peculiarities of an act passed by Congress in 1940, the managements of the investment funds are very complex and the profits drawn by the entrepreneurs of these funds are drawn in peculiar ways. Nevertheless, it is still true that their profits are very largely affected by the amount of money they can attract from the market.

corporation in order to displace the present management if he can convince a limited number of investment trust managers that the present management is inefficient.

The second major improvement in the efficiency of corporate systems is the conglomerate. Like the investment trusts, conglomerates have been around for a long time. There have been, for many years, corporations engaged in many lines of business. The so-called agency companies that were such an important part of the economy of the British Empire are examples, as were such Zaibutsu as the House of Mitsui. They have perhaps been less common in the United States than in the less developed parts of the world, but they were not unknown. Their recent expansion has not been the development of a brand new structure, but growth of an existing institution.

I do not argue that the principal motive which has led to the establishment of the conglomerate is an effort on the part of the stockholders to reduce the ability of their management to divert funds from the stockholders' benefit to utility maximizing. Nevertheless, it has its effect. Let us suppose, for example, a hundred small companies. Each one of them is relatively small and inconspicuous and can anticipate that most of its stockholders will only rarely know what it is doing. Further, a company in some particular line of business may well find that its profits for a year are down or up for reasons that have nothing whatsoever to do with the efficiency of the management. The market for coal may be off, the cost of the raw material may be up, somebody may have invented a competing product, etc. It would be irrational for the stockholders to depend simply on the profit return of the company as their sole data in determining whether or not it is well managed. Thus, the management of this small company is able to divert some of the stockholders' resources to maximizing its own utility. As we have pointed out, the amount that it can divert is probably small, but it is not zero.

Now let us suppose that the small company is purchased by a conglomerate. Immediately, it finds itself in quite a different position. In the first place it is subject to close supervision from the central organization.[16] The central organization will probably not

16 The parent company also provides a wide variety of management services to the small company. These services are valuable but have been discussed so much elsewhere that I will not discuss them here.

305

wish to devote all of its time to this one corporation; it may own a hundred others, but it will devote enough time to this corporation so that its central management can be fairly confident that the small unit cannot divert many resources from profit maximization.[17] Thus, we would anticipate the individual small corporation in such conglomerates closely to approximate profit maximization.

Needless to add, this says nothing at all about the funds which can be transferred to the use of themselves rather than the well-being of the stockholders by the central management of the conglomerate, but we should note here that the central management of the conglomerate will normally be very much smaller than the sum total of the managements of the corporations which it has acquired. Thus, if we assume that they are able to make exactly the same diversion per man they will be able to make less. In fact, however, they probably can make much smaller diversion per man. In the first place, the conglomerate is much more conspicuous. Instead of being a corporation with a capital of (let us say) fifty million dealing in the West Virginia coal mines, it is a corporation with a capital of one billion five hundred million dollars with operations all over the world. The doings of its directors are news. The office of its president may be frequently entered by reporters who are interested in producing articles for the financial press. Altogether it is harder to divert funds inconspicuously.

Secondly, and even more importantly, the conglomerate cannot 'explain' the failures of its profit in terms of special business conditions in any line of business. It exists for the sole purpose of making profits for its stockholders in whatever line of business is profitable. If I buy stock in a coal-mining company, I am presumably aware of the fact that the returns will depend on business in the coal-mining industry; if I buy stock in Litton Industries and it then proceeds to buy coal mines which five years later turn out to be unprofitable because of some disaster in the coal trade, I can reasonably take the view that the management of Litton's should be fired – not because of the disaster in the coal trade, but because they should not have bought the mines. They are hired to invest their stockholders' money in good entrepreneurial opportunities. If they fail in this, they can hardly offer as an excuse that a particular

17 In this connection see my *The Politics of Bureaucracy*, Washington, D.C. 1965, ch. 16.

line of business is having a bad year. This simply raises the question of why they are in that line of business.

Thus, it is much easier for the stockholder to tell whether the management of a conglomerate is doing a good job or a bad job than it is for him to tell whether the management of an individual company in an individual industry is doing well. Here, simply following the rule of firing the management whenever the profits fall may well be an optimal technique for operating the company. Granted that much of its stock will be held by the investment trusts and that the operation is sufficiently conspicuous so that it will attract entrepreneurs who might be interested in changing the management, the management of such a large conglomerate is subject to a very great pressure to turn its principal attention to the benefit of the stockholders and divert money to its own utility only to a modest degree.

What, then, is the end of our investigation? In the first place, it should be noted that we do not deny (and I don't think anyone can deny) that on occasion corporate managements may be able to perform in a way which is not perfectly adjusted to the desires of their stockholders to make more money. The question is whether this is a large factor or a small one, and I have argued that the corporate organization is such that it is probably a very small factor. The second point to be noted is simply that even if the management does behave in this way, there is no reason to regard this as a defect in the corporate system. It would mean that potential investors when making the choice between the purchase of stock or starting a company of their own would have to take this factor into account. But I would like to emphasize that there is nothing in this paper or in the new view of the corporations which should be taken as indicating that we are necessarily living in the best of all possible worlds. What has been demonstrated is simply that a great many of the criticisms of the corporations are false; it does not follow from this that we cannot make improvements. I, myself, have no improvements to offer, but I see no reason to believe *per se* that there are none. In order to improve on the present corporate organization, it is necessary first to understand it; and the recent work disposing of the Smith, Berle and Means theory of corporate control has contributed greatly to that end.

Bibliography of the Writings of Friedrich A. von Hayek

Books

Geldtheorie und Konjunkturtheorie, Vienna and Leipzig 1929 (England 1933, Japan 1935, Spain 1936)

Prices and Production, London 1931 (Austria 1931, Japan 1934)

Monetary Nationalism and International Stability, Geneva 1937

Profits, Interest and Investment, London 1939

The Pure Theory of Capital, London 1941 (Spain 1946, Japan 1952)

The Road to Serfdom, London and Chicago 1944 (Australia 1944, Sweden 1944, France and Germany 1945, Denmark, Portugal and Spain 1946, Netherlands 1948, Norway 1949, Japan 1954, China 1956)

Individualism and Economic Order, London and Chicago 1948 (Germany 1952)

John Stuart Mill and Harriet Taylor, London and Chicago 1951

The Counter-Revolution of Science, Glencoe Ill. 1952 (Germany 1959, France excerpts 1953)

The Sensory Order, London and Chicago 1952

The Political Ideal of the Rule of Law, Cairo 1955

The Constitution of Liberty, London and Chicago 1960

Studies in Philosophy, Politics and Economics. London and Chicago 1967

Freiburger Studien. Gesammelte Aufsätze, Tübingen 1969

Pamphlets

'*Das Mieterschutzproblem, Nationalökonomische Betrachtungen*', Vienna 1928

'*Freedom and the Economic System*', Chicago 1939

'*The Case of the Tyrol*', London 1944

'*Reports on the Changes in the Cost of Living in Gibraltar 1939–1944 and on Wages and Salaries*', Gibraltar, no date (1945)

'*Individualism? True and False*', Dublin 1946

'*Wirtschaft, Wissenschaft und Politik*', Freiburg 1963

'*Was der Goldwährung geschehen ist. Ein Bericht aus dem Jahre 1932 mit zwei Ergänzungen*'. (Walter Eucken Institut: Vorträge und Aufsätze, 12), Tübingen 1965

'*The Confusion of Language in Political Thought, With Some Suggestions for Remedying It*' (Institute of Economic Affairs, Occasional Paper 20), London 1968

Books edited by F. A. von Hayek or containing contributions by him

Gossen, H. H., *Entwicklung der Gesetze des menschlichen Verkehrs*, 3rd ed., Berlin 1927. Introduction by F.A.H.

Wieser, Friedrich Freiherr von, *Gesammelte Abhandlungen*, Tübingen 1929. Introduction by F.A.H.

Cantillon, Richard, *Abhandlung über die Natur des Handels im Allgemeinen* (translated by Hella von Hayek), Jena 1931. Introduction and annotations by F.A.H.

Beiträge zur Geldtheorie (by Marco Fanno, Marius W. Holtrop, Johan G. Koopmans, Gunnar Myrdal, Knut Wicksell). Vienna 1931. Preface by F.A.H.

Collectivist Economic Planning, London 1935. Introduction and Conclusion by F.A.H. (France 1939, Italy 1946)

Brutzkus, Boris, *Economic Planning in Soviet Russia*, London 1935. (Together with the volume above edited and prefaced by F.A.H.)

The Collected Works of Carl Menger, 4 vols., London 1934–1936. Introduction by F.A.H. – 2nd ed.: Carl Menger, *Gesammelte Werke*, Tübingen 1968 *et seq.* Edited and introduced by F.A.H.

Thornton, Henry, *An Enquiry into the Nature and Effects of the Paper Credit of Great Britain (1802)*, London 1939. Introduction by F.A.H.

John Stuart Mill, *The Spirit of the Age*. Chicago 1942. Introduction by F.A.H.

Capitalism and the Historians, London and Chicago 1954. Introduction by F.A.H.

Articles in scientific periodicals or collections of essays

'Das Stabilisierungsproblem in Goldwährungsländern', *Zeitschrift für Volkswirtschaft und Sozialpolitik*, N.S. 4 (1924)

'Die Währungspolitik der Vereinigten Staaten seit der Überwindung der Krise von 1920', *Zeitschrift für Volkswirtschaft und Sozialpolitik*, N.S. 5 (1925)

'Bemerkungen zum Zurechnungsproblem', *Jahrbücher für Nationalökonomie und Statistik*, 124 (1926)

'Wieser, Friedrich Freiherr von', *Jahrbücher für Nationalökonomie und Statistik*, 125 (1926)

'Zur Problemstellung der Zinstheorie', *Archiv für Sozialwissenschaften und Sozialpolitik*, 58 (1927)

310

'Das intertemporale Gleichgewichtssystem der Preise und die Bewegungen des Geldwertes', *Weltwirtschaftliches Archiv*, 28 (1928)

'Einige Bemerkungen über das Verhältnis der Geldtheorie zur Konjunkturtheorie', *Schriften des Vereins für Socialpolitik*, 173/2 (1928); also discussion, *loc. cit.*, 175 (1928)

'Theorie der Preistaxen' (in Hungarian; reprint in German), *Häzgasdasagi Enciclopedia*, Budapest 1929

'Gibt es einen Widersinn des Sparens?', *Zeitschrift für Nationalökonomie*, 1 (1929) – English: 'The paradox of saving', *Economica*, 11 (1931)

'Reflections on the Pure Theory of Money of Mr. J. M. Keynes', *Economica*, 11 (1931) and 12 (1932)

'The Pure Theory of Money: A Rejoinder to Mr. Keynes', *Economica*, 11 (1931)

'Money and Capital: A Reply to Mr. Sraffa', *Economic Journal*, 42 (1932)

'Kapitalaufzehrung', *Weltwirtschaftliches Archiv*, 36 (1932/II)

'A Note on the Development of the Doctrine of "Forced Saving"', *Quarterly Journal of Economics*, 47 (1932)

'Hermann Heinrich Gossen', *Encyclopaedia of the Social Sciences*, vol. VI, New York 1932

'Henry D. Macleod', *Encyclopaedia of the Social Sciences*, vol. X, New York 1933

'George W. Norman', *Encyclopaedia of the Social Sciences*, vol. XI, New York 1933

'Eugen von Philippovich', *Encyclopaedia of the Social Sciences*, vol. XII, New York 1934

'Saving', *Encyclopaedia of the Social Sciences*, vol. XIII, New York 1934

'The Trend of Economic Thinking', *Economica*, 13 (1933)

Contribution to: *Der Stand und die nächste Zukunft der Konjunkturforschung. Festschrift für Arthur Spiethoff*, Munich 1933

'Über "Neutrales Geld"', *Zeitschrift für Nationalökonomie*, 4 (1933)

'Capital and Industrial Fluctuations', *Econometrica*, 2 (1934)

'On the Relationship between Investment and Output', *Economic Journal*, 44 (1934)

'Carl Menger', *Economica*, N.S. 1 (1934)

'Preiserwartungen, Monetäre Störungen und Fehlinvestitionen', *Nationalökonomisk Tidskrift*, 73 (1935)

'The Maintenance of Capital', *Economica*, N.S. 2 (1935)

'Spor miedzy szkola "Currency" i szkola "Banking"', *Ekonomista* (Warsaw), 55 (1935)

'Edwin Cannan' (obituary), *Zeitschrift für Nationalökonomie*, 6 (1935)

'Technischer Fortschritt und Überkapazität', *Österreichische Zeitschrift für Bankwesen*, 1 (1936)

'The Mythology of Capital', *Quarterly Journal of Economics*, 50 (1936)

'Utility Analysis and Interest', *Economic Journal*, 46 (1936)

'La situation monétaire internationale', *Bulletin Périodique de la Société Belge d'Etudes et d'Expansion*, (1936)

'Economics and Knowledge', *Economica*, N.S. 4 (1937)

'Einleitung zu einer Kapitaltheorie', *Zeitschrift für Nationalökonomie*, 8 (1937)

'Das Goldproblem', *Österreichische Zeitschrift für Bankwesen*, 2 (1937)

'Investment that Raises the Demand for Capital', *Review of Economic Statistics*, 19 (1937)

'Economic Conditions of Inter-State Federation', *New Commonwealth Quarterly* (London), 5 (1939)

'Pricing versus Rationing', *The Banker* (London), 51 (1939)

'The Economy of Capital', *The Banker* (London), 52 (1939)

'Socialist Calculation: The Competitive "Solution" ', *Economica*, N.S. 7 (1940)

'The Counter-Revolution of Science', pts. I–III, *Economica*, N.S. 8 (1941)

'Maintaining Capital Intact: A Reply to Professor Pigou', *Economica*, N.S. 8 (1941)

'Planning, Science and Freedom', *Nature*, 148 (1941)

'The Ricardo Effect', *Economica*, N.S. 9 (1942)

'Scientism and the Study of Society', part I: *Economica*, N.S. 9 (1942), part II: *ibid.* 10 (1943), part III: *ibid.* 11 (1944)

'A Comment on an Article by Mr. Kaldor: "Professor Hayek and the Concertina Effect",' *Economica*, N.S. 9 (1942)

'A Commodity Reserve Currency', *Economic Journal*, 53 (1943)

'The Facts of the Social Sciences', *Ethics*, 54 (1943)

'The Geometrical Representation of Complementarity', *Review of Economic Studies*, 10 (1943)

'Gospodarka planowa a idea planowania prawa', *Economista Polski* (London), (1943)

Edited: 'John Rae and John Stuart Mill: A Correspondence', *Economica*, N.S. 10 (1943)

'The Economic Position of South Tyrol' in: *Justice for South Tyrol*, London 1943

'Richard von Strigl' (obituary), *Economic Journal*, 54 (1944)

'The Use of Knowledge in Society', *American Economic Review*, 35 (1945)

'Time-Preference and Productivity: A Reconsideration', *Economica*, N.S. 12 (1945)

Edited: ' "Notes on N. W. Senior's Political Economy" by John Stuart Mill', *Economica*, N.S. 12 (1945)

'Nationalities and States in Central Europe', *Central European Trade Review* (London), 3 (1945)

312

'Fuld Beskaeftigelse', *Nationalökonomisk Tidskrift*, 84 (1946)

'The London School of Economics 1895–1945', *Economica*, N.S. 13 (1946)

'Probleme und Schwierigkeiten der englischen Wirtschaft', *Schweizer Monatshefte*, 27 (1947)

'Le plein emploi', *Economie Appliquée*, 1 (1948)

'Der Mensch in der Planwirtschaft' in Simon Moser (ed.), *Weltbild und Menschenbild*, (Innsbruck and Vienna 1948)

'Wesley Clair Mitchell 1874–1948' (obituary), *Journal of the Royal Statistical Society*, 111 (1948)

'The Intellectuals and Socialism', *The University of Chicago Law Review*, 16 (1949)

'Economics', *Chambers's Encyclopaedia*, vol. IV, Oxford 1950

'David Ricardo', *Chambers's Encyclopaedia*, vol. XI, Oxford 1950

'Full Employment, Planning and Inflation', *Institute of Public Affairs Review* (Melbourne, Australia), 4 (1950)

'Capitalism and the Proletariat', *Farmand* (Oslo), Feb. 17, 1951

'Comte and Hegel' *Measure* (Chicago), 2 (1951)

'Comments on "The Economics and Politics of the Modern Corporation",' *The University of Chicago Law School, Conference Series* no. 8, Dec. 7, 1951

'Die Überlieferung der Ideale der Wirtschaftsfreiheit', *Schweizer Monatshefte*, 32 (1952)

'Die Ungerechtigkeit der Steuerprogression', *Schweizer Monatshefte*, 32 (1952)

'Entstehung und Verfall des Rechtsstaatsideales' in *Wirtschaft ohne Wunder* (Albert Hunold, ed., Volkswirtschaftliche Studien für das Schweizerische Institut für Auslandforschung), Zürich 1953

'Marktwirtschaft und Wirtschaftspolitik', *Ordo*, 6 (1954)

'Degrees of Explanation', *The British Journal for the Philosophy of Science*, 6 (1955)

'Towards a Theory of Economic Growth, Discussion of Simon Kuznets' Paper' in: *National Policy for Economic Welfare at Home and Abroad.* Columbia University Bicentennial Conference, New York 1955

'Comments' in: Congress for Cultural Freedom (ed.), *Science and Freedom*, London 1955 (Proceedings of the Hamburg Conference of the Congress for Cultural Freedom. Also in German)

'Reconsideration of Progressive Taxation', in Mary Sennholz (ed.), *On Freedom and Free Enterprise. Essays in Honour of Ludwig von Mises.* Princeton 1956

'The Dilemma of Specialization' in Leonard D. White (ed.), *The State of the Social Sciences*, Chicago 1956

'Über den "Sinn" sozialer Institutionen', *Schweizer Monatshefte*, 36 (1956)

313

'Was ist und was heißt "sozial"?' in Albert Hunold (ed.), *Masse und Demokratie*, Zürich 1957

'Grundtatsachen des Fortschritts', *Ordo*, 9 (1957)

'Inflation Resulting from the Downward Inflexibility of Wages' in Committee for Economic Development (ed.), *Problems of United States Economic Development*, vol. I, New York 1958

'La Libertad, La Economia Planificada Y El Derecho', *Temas Contemporaneos*, 3 (1958)

'The Creative Powers of a Free Civilization' in F. Morley (ed.), *Essays in Individuality*, Philadelphia 1958

'Freedom, Reason, and Tradition', *Ethics*, 68 (1958)

'Gleichheit, Wert und Verdienst', *Ordo*, 10 (1958)

'Liberalismus (1) Politischer Liberalismus', *Handwörterbuch der Sozialwissenschaften*, vol. IV, Stuttgart-Tübingen-Göttingen 1959

'Bernard Mandeville', *Handwörterbuch der Sozialwissenschaften*, vol. VII, Stuttgart-Tübingen-Göttingen 1959

'Unions, Inflation and Profits' in Philip D. Bradley (ed.), *The Public Stake in Union Power*, Charlottesville, Va. 1959

'Freiheit und Unabhängigkeit', *Schweizer Monatshefte*, 39 (1959)

'Verantwortlichkeit und Freiheit', in Albert Hunold (ed.), *Erziehung zur Freiheit*, Erlenbach − Zürich 1959

'Marktwirtschaft und Strukturpolitik', *Die Aussprache*, 9 (1959)

'An Roepke', in Wilhelm Röpke, *Gegen die Brandung*, Zürich 1959

'The Free Market Economy: The Most Efficient Way of Solving Economic Problems', *Human Events*, 16 (1959)

'The Social Environment' in B. H. Bagdikian (ed.), *Man's Contracting World in an Expanding Universe*, Providence Rh. I. 1960

'The Corporation in a Democratic Society: In Whose Interest Ought It and Will It Be Run?' in M. Anshen and G. L. Bach (eds.), *Management and Corporations 1958*, New York 1960

'The Non Sequitur of the "Dependence Effect",' *The Southern Economic Journal*, 27 (1961)

'Die Ursachen der ständigen Gefährdung der Freiheit', *Ordo*, 12 (1961)

'The Moral Element in Free Enterprise' in National Association of Manufacturers (ed.), *The Spiritual and Moral Element in Free Enterprise*, New York 1962

'Rules, Perception and Intelligibility', *Proceedings of the British Academy*, 48 (1962)

'Wiener Schule', *Handwörterbuch der Sozialwissenschaften*, vol. XII, Stuttgart-Tübingen-Göttingen 1962

'Alte Wahrheiten und neue Irrtümer' in *Das Sparwesen der Welt* (Proceedings of the 7th International Conference of Savings Banks), Amsterdam 1963

'Arten der Ordnung', *Ordo*, 14 (1963)

'Recht, Gesetz und Wirtschaftsfreiheit' in *Hundert Jahre Industrie- und Handelskammer zu Dortmund 1863–1963*, Dortmund 1963

Introduction to 'The Earlier Letters of John Stuart Mill', *Collected Works of John Stuart Mill*, vol. XII, Toronto and London 1963

'The Legal and Political Philosophy of David Hume', *Il Politico*, 28 (1963)

'The Theory of Complex Phenomena' in Mario Bunge (ed.), *The Critical Approach to Science and Philosophy. In Honor of Karl R. Popper*, Glencoe Ill. 1964

Parts of 'Commerce, History of', *Encyclopaedia Britannica*, vol. VI, Chicago 1964

'Die Anschauungen der Mehrheit und die zeitgenössische Demokratie', *Ordo*, 15/16 (1965)

'Kinds of Rationalism', *The Economic Studies Quarterly* (Tokyo), 15 (1965)

'Personal Recollections of Keynes and the "Keynesian Revolution"', *The Oriental Economist*, 34 (1966)

'The Misconception of Human Rights as Positive Claims', *Farmand*, Anniversary Issue 1966

'The Principles of a Liberal Social Order', *Il Politico*, 31 (1966). German reprint in *Ordo*, 18 (1967)

'Dr. Bernard Mandeville', *Proceedings of the British Academy*, 52 (1966)

'L'Etalon d'Or—Son Evolution', *Revue d'Economie Politique*, 76 (1966)

'The Results of Human Action but not of Human Design' in *Les Fondements Philosophiques des Systèmes Economiques*. Textes de Jacques Rueff et essais rédigés en son honneur. Paris 1967 (in French)

Remarks on 'Ernst Mach und das sozialwissenschaftliche Denken in Wien' in Ernst Mach Institut (ed.), *Symposium aus Anlass des 50. Todestages von Ernst Mach*, Freiburg/B. 1967

'Rechtsordnung und Handelnsordnung' in Erich Streissler (ed.), *Zur Einheit der Rechts- und Staatswissenschaften*, Karlsruhe 1967

'The Constitution of a Liberal State', *Il Politico*, 32 (1967). German reprint in *Ordo*, 19 (1968)

'Bruno Leoni, the Scholar', *Il Politico*, 33 (1968)

'A Self-Generating Order for Society' in John Nef (ed.), *Towards World Community*, The Hague 1968

'Economic Thought, VI: Austrian School', *International Encyclopaedia of the Social Sciences*, vol. IV, New York 1968

'Carl Menger', *International Encyclopaedia of the Social Sciences*, vol. X, New York 1968

'Scientismus' in W. Bernsdorf (ed.), *Wörterbuch der Soziologie* 2nd ed. Stuttgart 1969

'Three Elucidations of the "Ricardo-Effect"', *Journal of Political Economy*, 77 (1969)